Developed Socialism in the Soviet Bloc

Westview Special Studies on the Soviet Union and Eastern Europe

Developed Socialism in the Soviet Bloc: Political Theory and Political Reality
edited by Jim Seroka and Maurice D. Simon

This book traces the evolution of Soviet and East European responses to the multifaceted pressures of a rapidly changing world and looks at the implications of ideological developments in the Soviet bloc for economic reforms, general policymaking, and political and social change. The authors discuss the concept of developed socialism and its essential components as seen in communist societies; analyze current policy and likely future policy directions in the Soviet Union, Czechoslovakia, Hungary, Romania, Poland, and Yugoslavia in light of the concept; and assess the impact that ideological trends have had, and are likely to have, on the Soviet Union and Eastern Europe in general.

Jim Seroka is assistant professor of political science at Southern Illinois University specializing in Eastern European political systems. Maurice D. Simon is assistant professor of political science at the University of North Carolina. He is coeditor of *Background to Crisis: Policy and Politics in Gierek's Poland* (Westview).

Developed Socialism in the Soviet Bloc: Political Theory and Political Reality

edited by Jim Seroka and
Maurice D. Simon

Routledge
Taylor & Francis Group
LONDON AND NEW YORK

This book is dedicated to

John M. Echols III

First published 1982 by Westview Press, Inc.

Published 2018 by Routledge
52 Vanderbilt Avenue, New York, NY 10017
2 Park Square, Milton Park, Abingdon, Oxon OX14 4RN

Routledge is an imprint of the Taylor & Francis Group, an informa business

Library of Congress Catalog Card Number 82-50727
ISBN 13: 978-0-367-01927-3 (hbk)

Contents

List of Tables and Figures vi
Preface, Jim Seroka and Maurice D. Simon viii

PART 1 NATIONAL PERSPECTIVES

1 DEVELOPED SOCIALISM: A POLITICAL FORMULA FOR THE BREZHNEV ERA, Donald R. Kelley 3

2 IS DEVELOPED SOCIALISM A SOVIET VERSION OF CONVERGENCE? Jeffrey W. Hahn 21

3 HUNGARY AND CZECHOSLOVAKIA: RATIONALIZING THE PREVAILING POLICIES, David W. Paul 37

4 DEVELOPING SOCIALISM AND WORKER-PARTY CONFLICT, Daniel N. Nelson 61

5 DEVELOPED SOCIALISM IN YUGOSLAVIA: SOCIALIST SELF-MANAGED PLURALIST DEMOCRACY, Jim Seroka 79

6 DEVELOPED SOCIALISM AND THE POLISH CRISIS, Maurice D. Simon 99

PART 2 CROSS-NATIONAL PERSPECTIVES

7 PARTY LEADERSHIP AND MASS PARTICIPATION IN DEVELOPED SOCIALISM, Jack Bielasiak 121

8 DEVELOPED SOCIALISM AND CONSUMPTION POLICIES IN THE SOVIET BLOC: AN EMPIRICAL EVALUATION, Cal Clark and John M. Echols III 155

Index 189
List of Contributors 196
Other Titles of Interest from Westview Press 198

Tables and Figures

Tables

3.1 Per Capita Gross National Product, 1960-1979 40
3.2 Personal Consumption: Selected Foods and Durable Goods. 41
3.3 Health Care: Medical Doctors and Hospital Facilities 43
3.4 Enrollments in Institutions of Higher Education, 1978-79. 43
4.1 Romanian Socioeconomic Change in Comparative Perspective. 66
4.2 Demographic/Social Indicators. 67
4.3 Economic Indicators. 68
7.1 Communist Party Memberships: Total (in thousands) and as % of Population 130
7.2 Communist Party Memberships: Average Annual Rates of Growth (%). 131
7.3 Social Composition of the Communist Parties (%). 134
7.4 Participation in Factory Meetings by Workers 142
7.5 Workers' Opinions on Factory Relationships in Hungary. 143
7.6 Soviet Workers' Attitudes Toward Work (%). 145
7.7 Representation Coefficients by Political Affiliation and Occupation in Soviet Factories 147
8.1 Growth of Real Per Capita Disposable Income in the Soviet Union 159
8.2 Annual Growth Rate in Real Wages Per Capita of State Employees. 160
8.3 Annual Growth Rate in Real Income Per Capita 161
8.4 Annual Growth Rates of Per Capita Personal Consumption. 165
8.5 Bloc Rankings on Consumption and Development Level 168
8.6 Comparative East European Consumption. 169
8.7 Growth Rates for Per Capita Food Outputs 171
8.8 Shares of Capital Investment in the National Economy . . . 172
8.9 Ratio of Growth Rates of Consumer to Producer Goods for Gross Industrial Production. 173

8.10 Soviet Welfare Expenditures 175
8.11 Soviet Annual Growth Rates of Personal and Social Consumption. 176
8.12 Policy Impact of Regime Successions 178
8.13 Indicators of Housing Conditions. 180
8.14 Public Expenditures as a Percentage of Factor Price GNP 181

Figures

5.1 Typology of Modern Social Systems According to Conflict Between Economic Growth and Political Participation 85
5.2 Typology of Modern Social Systems According to Conflict Between Equality and Freedom 86

Preface

Fifteen years have passed since Leonid Brezhnev endorsed the theoretical doctrine of "Developed Socialism." For many observers, this doctrine signified a new commitment to economic and political pragmatism and flexibility in the Soviet Union and socialist Eastern Europe. The grim realities of the martial law declared in Poland on December 13, 1981, present a stark contrast to the optimistic themes of the "Developed Socialism" doctrine. The maintenance of political control through the exercise of military power is a far cry from the internal reforms and changes implied by developed socialism. This collection of essays examines the varied meanings and preliminary applications of developed socialism taking care to distinguish between doctrine and practice.

In DEVELOPED SOCIALISM we explore how the doctrine established an introductory procedural framework for legitimized change and reform of the socialist system throughout the Soviet Union and Eastern Europe. We also examine how differing Soviet and East European interpretations of the doctrine have affected processes and prospects for meaningful internal reform and, in particular, how the specific states have coped with various pressures associated with industrialization and development. Finally, the essays consider why the process of reform implied by the doctrine of developed socialism has been limited in its scope and impact, and thus is unlikely to herald a departure from authoritarian patterns of governance.

DEVELOPED SOCIALISM is divided into two sections. The first part contains a series of essays dealing with specific countries, including contributions by Donald Kelley and Jeffrey Hahn on the Soviet Union, David Paul on Czechoslovakia and Hungary, Daniel Nelson on Romania, Jim Seroka on Yugoslavia, and Maurice Simon on Poland. The essays in this section demonstrate how social pressures for material welfare and political participation have affected the ideological and political systems of specific socialist states. In short, the first section of DEVELOPED SOCIALISM analyzes how this doctrine, while originating from a common source, has generated divergent political discussions and policy impacts in European socialist societies.

Donald Kelley, in his selection on the impact of developed socialism in the Soviet Union, analyzes the standard formulation of the doctrine. He investigates how the doctrine envisions the role of the party and its potential effects upon the operation of the Soviet bureaucracy, the system of management, and the party apparatus. Kelley's description of the new party role as a coordinating unit within a complex, interest-based milieu is of great significance, for it suggests that it may thereby become an effective agency for broad-based societal reform.

Jeffrey Hahn examines whether the doctrine of developed socialism is a Soviet version of convergence theory. He specifically compares the main premises of the Soviet interpretation of developed socialism and Western treatments of convergence theory, suggesting that although the forces which generated these discussions are very similar, their theoretical and practical applications have not been satisfactorily explored.

David Paul's comparison of Czechoslovakian and Hungarian treatments of developed socialism vividly illustrates the variability of interpretations of the doctrine, as well as the difficulties involved in its empirical measurement in terms of policy outputs. Paul's essay delineates the divergent policy choices made by Czech and Hungarian authorities in the past fifteen years and explains how the malleability of the developed socialism doctrine has served to legitimate these decisions. In short, Paul argues that the very ambiguity of the doctrine of developed socialism has been manipulated in a way which provides flexibility for policy-makers operating in very different national environments.

The Romanian approach to developed socialism is analyzed by Daniel Nelson, who identifies certain forces which have necessitated its formulation: namely, the need for participation in political life and the need to redistribute economic resources. These forces, he claims, operate in all European socialist societies to provide the dynamic basis for change. Nelson notes how the Romanian version of developed socialism, while still stated in a rather preliminary form and limited in its application, suggests a sensitivity toward the presence of future sources of instability within the Romanian state.

The case of Yugoslavia also emphasizes the doctrinal cross-national commonality of developed socialism. Jim Seroka reemphasizes the need for societal reform, revitalization of the party, and reinvolvement of the masses in basic decision-making. Yugoslavia's parallels with the political debates in Eastern Europe and the Soviet Union are even more striking when Yugoslavia's doctrinal independence from the Soviet bloc is acknowledged. This particular case may indicate that the need for reform and democratization of political processes in Marxist-Leninist states is universal and genuinely felt.

Maurice Simon's contribution on Poland closes the circle on the variability of the developed socialism doctrine across nations. Simon notes how a reformist interpretation of the doctrine emerged during the 1970s in a political context that facilitated change. The reformist version of developed socialism advocated by some leading party figures and activist intellectuals called for the recognition of social pluralism through administrative decentralization and the provision of institutional mechanisms for greater citizen participation. The existence of such proposals furthered opportunities for cooperation between disaffected workers and intellectuals during the

Polish "renewal" of 1980-1981, presenting the party with a united front that was difficult to resist. The developed socialism discussion was, in part, a precursor of the ill-fated Polish reform movement.

The second part of the book is broadly comparative in approach. The contributors examine the major thematic policy issues of developed socialism and compare how they were dealt with in the various European socialist states. Jack Bielasiak, for example, analyzes how the doctrine of developed socialism affected the party's political role. Specifically, how would the party foster socialist democracy while still retaining the party's leading role? Bielasiak finds that the party's role was generally consistent: the intensification of socialist democracy was interpreted and implemented by expanding the functions of party organizations and increasing the responsibilities of activists and cadres. Democracy in terms of increased citizen participation and influence was given low priority.

The concluding essay by Cal Clark and the late John Echols investigates the link between developed socialism and the communist consumer revolution. Their extensive empirical investigation indicates that there is no common policy impact of developed socialism in terms of increased citizen benefits. Developed socialism, in brief, can be considered a political rather than an economic program for action.

Together, both sections of DEVELOPED SOCIALISM trace the involvement of policy-makers in the evolution and application of the doctrine. The essays give the reader a basis for the evaluation of the present and future performance of these states. The essays indicate that attention to policy output alone affords only a fragmentary basis for judging the doctrine's effectiveness. For comparative purposes, the real significance of the developed socialism doctrine stems from its emphasis upon citizen participation in policy formulation and implementation, and it implies the deepening legitimation of these states through both economic development and intensified citizen participation.

Jim Seroka
Maurice D. Simon

Part 1

National Perspectives

1 Developed Socialism: A Political Formula for the Brezhnev Era

Donald R. Kelley

Whatever other functions an ideology may perform, it is also commonplace for it to embody implicitly or even openly what may be termed the "political formula" of an era. Certainly, traditional Marxism interprets all previous ideologies in this fashion, seeing them as a mixture of intellectual frames of reference, as explanations and rationalizations of the social and political order, and as explications, however tenuous, of an image of the future. The history of Soviet Russia from 1917 onward supports the notion that each phase of development will possess both its own dialectically legitimate formula and political arrangements, sometimes expressed through the evolutionary development of a succession of more "mature" constitutions and sometimes embodied more subtly in interpretations and convoluted recastings of the party program. This formula both sets the tone and parameters of political life and defines the nature of the current tasks confronting party and state.

Viewed as such a formula, the doctrine of developed socialism--or "mature socialism," as it is also known--clearly expresses the political realities, the victories, losses and stalemates of elite conflict, and the aspirations of the current regime. It is therefore no simple body of thought; its initial message that in the 1960s Soviet society entered a more "mature" phase of its development within which the groundwork would be laid for the transition to communism rapidly fractures into a discussion of multiple and differently paced trends of economic, social, cultural, and political development. What is clear is that society is now envisioned as more complex, as responsive to more sophisticated economic and political-administrative levers, and is increasingly in need of the guiding and coordinating role of the communist party to assure stability and continued evolutionary development.[1]

The seeming contradiction between stability and evolutionary development lies at the heart of the complex nature of developed socialism. For political reasons dating from the coup against Khrushchev in 1964 and sustained by the continuing dominance of an aging elite, developed socialism as a political formula clearly bears a conservative imprint. One need only recall that Khrushchev's principal offense against the forces that eventually overthrew him was his incessant "hare-brained" scheming to reorganize and reform both party and state--that is, his efforts to up-grade and modernize the party apparatus and the state bureaucracy through compelling existing elites to learn more sophisticated techniques or through promoting younger, better trained personnel as rapidly as possible. Both policies were inherently threatening to less reform-minded elements, and this, coupled with the First Secretary's repeated attempts to escape the boundaries of collective leadership, finally produced the critical mass of opposition to his programmatic reforms and personal style that came together in October, 1964.

The political situation after the October coup dictated a more conservative approach both to intra-elite affairs and to the further evolution of the Soviet system. In the former instance, the tone of the new regime quickly came to be expressed in the term "trust in cadres," which signaled reassuringly to those upper- and middle-level party and state officials, who were the intended victims of Khrushchev's reforms, that their positions were reasonably secure (although the new regime would apply increasing pressures for improved performance) and that their views would be taken into account. For the first half decade of its existence, the Brezhnev regime walked a political tightrope, performing a delicate balancing act that ended only with the General Secretary's rise to preeminence in the late 1960s and early 1970s and with the recognition that certain deeply rooted economic and administrative problems could not be dealt with if the overly cautious "trust in cadres" approach remained completely dominant.[2]

The question of the direction and pace of further social evolution also initially received a conservative treatment from the new regime. Khrushchev's optimistic views, expressed in the 1961 party program which envisioned the beginning of the transformation into a communist state by the 1980s, were quietly shelved, and conspicious silence rather than outright repudiation greeted innovations such as the all-people's state and the enhanced role of public organizations. Again for the first half-decade of the Brezhnev era, it seemed as if Khrushchev's irrepressible drive to move society forward had given way to a sort of don't-rock-the-boat <u>immobilisme</u>, or at least to a greater level of pragmatism in day-to-day affairs that seemed unconcerned both with the larger theoretical significance of policy decisions and with a coherent plan for further development.

By the end of the first half-decade of Brezhnev's rule, the regime found itself still confronted with many of the same economic and administrative problems and dilemmas that had bedeviled its predecessors, and it was anxious to articulate a more forceful style of leadership. Increasingly the often repeated paean concerning "trust in cadres" was coupled with clear statements that a certain "exactingness" and competence were required of even the most loyal party and state officials. Viewing the sagging growth rate of their economy and its seeming inability to speed necessary technological modernization, Soviet leaders attached principal blame to the poor and overly cautious performance of both economic officials and their party superiors. The themes of "trust" and "exactingness"--that is, the reassurance that capricious sanctions would not be forthcoming but that high quality performance was expected--were inexorably linked from the late 1960s onward. Although the regime promised such discipline "would not be built on fear or on methods of ruthless administrative fiat," it also pointed to the need for greater "responsibility" and warned that "executive posts are not reserved for anyone forever."[3]

Realizing that their cautious personnel policies and unwillingness to exert pressure on inept cadres had contributed to the growing economic malaise, Soviet leaders set about the task of defining a new approach to planning and administrative tasks and identifying new levers and incentives to elicit desired behavior. It is in this vein that the notion of developed socialism first acquired its reformist imperative. Previously, the emphasis had fallen on the celebration of the system's maturity, the assertion that the USSR had "made it" as an advanced industrial power, and the reassurance that future transformations would be gradual and untraumatic. Now, the emphasis shifted to the "imperatives" of the "scientific and technological revolution," which required the studied modernization of political and social as well as economic life, and the assertion that aggressive reforms were needed in virtually all spheres of social, economic, and political affairs. While these reforms were always represented as mere fine-tuning of the mechanisms of party and state to cope with an increasingly sophisticated economic and social order and to set the stage for further evolutionary development, it was readily apparent to those involved--and especially to those cadres whose performance was under review--that the demands for improved performance, for more "scientific" planning, and for better coordination and a centralized "systems" perspective carried a clear political threat to the ossified bureaucracy that had initially interpreted the "trust in cadres" approach both as a victory over the upstart Khrushchev and as a pledge by his successors not to rock the boat.[4]

The new reformist bent of the Brezhnev regime hardly signaled a direct onslaught on resistant cadres reminiscent of Khrushchev's incautious style. To the contrary, pressures were gradually applied on several fronts. The notion of developed socialism itself became one of the subtle weapons in top leaders' hands through the shift to stressing its reformist and transformationist implications. The doctrine was now read as suggesting both the mechanisms by which the future would be built--the scientific and technological revolution; the "further perfection" of the state machinery, meaning both improved output and better management; and an enhanced and more "scientific" role for the party--and as demanding that meaningful reforms be undertaken <u>now</u> in order to keep the further development of Soviet society on track.

But on other fronts, the regime balked at applying hard sanctions to force its will on recalcitrant middle- and lower-level cadres. To be sure, there were occasional dismissals at the highest levels of party and state, and some were clearly linked either to policy failures or to the vagaries of factional politics. For the most part, however, no extensive personnel changes were undertaken, or even threatened, to bring younger and presumably more forward-looking leaders to the fore. In the absence of the credible threat that top leaders would apply the ultimate sanction of dismissal, deeply rooted and inherently skeptical party and state officials simply dug their heels in and either blocked reform efforts outright or successfully emasculated new programs at the implementation stage.

This is not to say that an identifiable and coherent reformist group did not emerge within the Politburo and like-minded party and state bodies; such a nucleus was clearly there from the late 1960s onward. It linked top leaders like Brezhnev and Kosygin, who were concerned with implementing systems-like centralizing reforms to make the bureaucracy more responsive to Moscow's control, and other elements concerned with high-technology industries or the growth of neglected sectors of the economy such as consumer goods. Nevertheless, this group was never able to impose its will completely either on other top-level skeptics or on subordinate party and state agencies. Never willing--and perhaps simply not able--to bite the political bullet and accept the notion that the "trust in cadres" approach would have to be ended if meaningful reforms were to be forced upon reluctant middle-level and senior officials, the reformist elements found themselves both frustrated by the *de facto* nullification of their efforts and left with only the weakest of levers and incentives with which to work their will. Thus top-level reformers alternatively blustered and cajoled, demanded and plaintively entreatied their counterparts and subordinates to accept the notion that the forward-looking reforms which they sought did not necessarily embody any lasting political threat either to the stability of the system or the fate of reasonable and equally forward-looking party and state officials.

In this setting, the notion of developed socialism itself became an important element of the continuing debate. Its conservative and reformist interpretations reflect the fears or aspirations of those who understood the political overtones of the dialogue.

DEVELOPED SOCIALISM: A CONSERVATIVE OR REFORMIST DOCTRINE?

Inevitably, the product of the conflicting political pressures which surrounded its birth, the doctrine of developed socialism is itself a combination of conservative and reformist themes. Thus, the political formula that it articulates has consequently embodied both the compromises and the inherent tensions and frustrations that have characterized Soviet politics from the early 1970s onward. The official line has always held--at least for the sake of public pronouncements--that the conservative and reformist tendencies are compatible within the framework of controlled and gradual evolution toward even higher dialectical stages.[5] However, a close reading of the literature reveals divergent schools of thought. Different sources evidence a reformist or conservative bias; still others differ over the policy implications of a particular facet of the theory or whether yet another transitional stage lies ahead (perhaps "more developed socialism?").[6] Nevertheless, on the whole, both the theoretical discussion and the practical political considerations that surround developed socialism have been at a point of stalemate since the mid-1970s. If one assumes, however, that the stalemate may well be broken with the eventual political demise of Brezhnev, one can then read the doctrine as constituting a virtual Pandora's box of political, economic, and social issues which will confront the new regime and possibly serve as viable issues for conflicting factions. To be sure, the whole notion of developed socialism may be laid to rest as a vestige of the Brezhnev era, just as Khrushchev's theoretical innovations were temporarily shelved by his successors. But the issues with which the theory deals--economic growth, political change, and the growing complexity of society--and the tacit political battles between reformers and conservatives which the doctrine uneasily bridges are far less likely to disappear. What follows in this essay, then, is an exercise of extrapolation and conjecture--extrapolation of the possible development of the conservative and reformist elements of developed socialism and admittedly modest conjecture on implications for Soviet politics should either school clearly prevail.

DEVELOPED SOCIALISM: A POLITICAL DEFINITION

The discussion of the meaning of developed socialism and of its programmatic implications has, at least in part, entered into the realm of what Myron Rush has termed the esoteric language of Soviet politics.[7] The shadings of opinion on the immediate impact on social and governmental institutions and the pace of the inevitable process of further maturation clearly speak to political as well as to theoretical issues. Although the discussion has been muted by present political realities and by the obvious caution of conservatives and reformers alike, the issues being raised by either school are at the very center of the political arena.

The conservative aspects of the doctrine are most easily seen in the treatment of the nature of contemporary institutional forms such as the state and in the limitations and safeguards which surround interest aggregation and articulation. In the first instance, the doctrine of developed socialism seems firmly rooted in the dual principles that (1) present institutional forms will dominate in the early phases of developed socialism, giving way to higher forms only through the "gradual perfection" of existing bodies, and (2) the process of change throughout the period will be both gradual and untraumatic. While no specific timetable is set forward by official commentaries or even suggested by the myriad of serious scholarly interpretations which have come forth in the last decade, it is asserted that "developed socialist society ... constitutes a relatively long period of development on the path from capitalism to communism."[8]

The dominant theme running throughout the descriptions of the institutional features of the developed socialist era is the maintenance of the role of the state in future socio-political evolution. Even though Khrushchev's successors have resurrected his notion of the "all-people's state," they have invested it with a more cautious content, stripping it of its previous implications that the state would rapidly be transformed through an intensified role for public organizations. Under the present doctrine, the role of the state is to grow gradually during the period of developed socialism because it is to be the "main element" in the construction of the material and social basis of communism. And while it is to undergo a process of "further perfection" as society matures toward even higher forms of socialism, such "perfection" is described more in terms of its increasing technical and managerial competence to administer an advanced economy and coordinate an increasingly complex social order than in terms of any fundamental transformation of the nature of the institutions themselves.[9] Indeed, considerable care is exercised to point out that only embryonic and nascent beginnings of the future institutional order will emerge within the developed socialist era; any rapid evolution toward more advanced institutional forms is specifically rejected. Speaking at the time of adoption of the new 1977 constitution which affirms the continued role of the state organism, Brezhnev specifically criticized unnamed theorists who had apparently requested that the new document provide for the creation of transitional institutions for "putting the cart before the horse."[10]

The new orientation toward the role of mass organizations also marks a more conservative interpretation of one of Khrushchev's more adventuresome initiatives. Such institutions are now labeled as "supplemental" to the functions of the state, although it is suggested that their scope of activities and depth of penetration into the society will increase with the maturation of developed socialism. The further developement of public organizations is itself dependent upon both the "further perfection" of the state machinery--i.e., its more efficient operation through much-touted systems and planning reforms and its increasing ability to accept and productively employ public organizations as client groups and pseudo-administrative extensions of the bureaucracy itself--and the increasing maturity and sophistication of the general public, which will gradually become involved in quasi-governmental tasks through the public organizations. There is clearly no sense that public organizations will take the lead in fostering such change; rather they will be the inevitable beneficiaries of the growing maturation of the bureaucracy and the public.[11]

The role of the party and its eventual transition into an "all people's party" have also received more cautious treatment in the explication of developed socialism. The central message of the doctrine is unambiguous: the party will remain the centerpiece of Soviet political life through its now constitutionally strengthened role as the central core of all organized social, economic, and political life and its penetration of society through the _nomenklatura_ system. The 1977 constitution codifies the _de facto_ role of the party by writing its mandate to rule directly into the document, a step which both enhances the party's legitimacy and even further strengthens its coordinating role. Even if Robert Sharlet is accurate in pointing out that the new, constitutionally mandated role also implicitly suggests the possibility of future limitations on the party through the requirement that "the decisions of the party must be carried out through Soviet organs within the framework of the Soviet constitution," in the short run the party emerges with no immediate strictures on its guiding role.[12]

The party will come to play an even more crucial role in the developed socialist phase because it alone is capable of providing the integrative leadership needed by an increasingly complex and differentiated society. While the implications of this new role are at the core of the long-term reformist dimensions of developed socialism (see below), the short-term impact has been to reassert the party's traditional dominance over socio-political life. Party leaders have intensified their demands on party cadres for better performance; at virtually all levels of the apparatus, party officials have been called upon to adopt more advanced managerial techniques and to function as the catalysts of reform. But the paradox noted earlier remains. While the party is explicitly guaranteed its dominant role within the system, the successful performance of that role is seen as increasingly dependent on it getting its own house in better managerial order to cope with the ever rising demands of the economy and society. That, in turn, requires hard and politically distasteful decisions. It is precisely these sorts of decisions that top leaders have avoided, preferring instead to apply only limited pressure and to eschew the ultimate sanction of dismissal in all but a few blatant exceptions. Thus, the conservative aspects of developed socialism are rooted more firmly in these political realities than inherently present in the doctrine _per se_. Whether one reads that political reality as a masterful accomplishment in which skillful and moderate leaders have avoided the worst excesses of intra-party conflict or, alternatively, as an unintended stalemate which has produced _de facto immobilisme_, one must still deal with the possibility that the present regime's successors may well choose to break the tacit peace.

The doctrine also implicitly contains both theoretical and institutionalized mechanisms which attempt to limit the aggregation and articulation of economic and societal demands outside of narrowly defined approved structures. In theoretical terms, the enunciation of the strengthened role for party and state mechanisms and the diminished prerogatives of public organizations can be read as constraints on the potential sources of policy initiative. Even though the 1977 constitution contains some provisions that would seemingly permit greater latitude in using the courts to raise political issues and policy-related demands--especially if the still vague "right to complaint" provisions of Article 58 are liberally interpreted--it also blantantly acknowledges the dominant role of the party and imposes a greater array of civic duties and responsibilities on the average citizen.[13]

Perhaps more importantly, the administrative reforms which have become the day-to-day policy imperatives of the Brezhnev regime have acted--or, more correctly, have been intended to act--as _de facto_ restraints on one of the most divergent and combative source of demands: the major bureaucratic and regional interests whose conflicts are endemic to any highly politicized bureaucracy. Whatever the rhetoric, and whatever the hopes reform-minded Soviet leaders may have had in terms of the emergence of substantively better policy from the wide-ranging systems and planning reforms, it is also clear that these reforms were intended to provide for a greater measure of centralized authority and to reduce the latitude within which even the most aggressive and enterprising ministry or regional coalition could hope to influence policy.[14] That Soviet politics since Stalin's time has been characterized by the interplay of intensely competitive bureaucratic and regional interests is hardly a new revelation, nor is the regime's attempt to control the pulling and tugging of disparate interests a unique phenomenon. But the Brezhnev approach is markedly different from that of his predecessor. While Khrushchev sought to manage such conflicts through a combination of joining in as an arbiter and occasional combatant or through unpredictable dismissals and reorganizations to throw the bureaucracy off balance, the Brezhnev regime has attempted to rely on the more orderly (and less successful) process of regularizing decision-making channels and imposing a more hierarchical planning system.[15]

In the long run, these reforms hold forth the potential for substantial changes that would actually broaden participation in the political process. But in the short run, they have acted to restrict the conventional give and take of policy making by re-emphasizing the "rational" and "scientific" nature of the planning process at the expense of the *de facto* process of bargaining and adjustment that occurred *sub rosa*. The limited success of these reforms, especially in the economy, testifies to the real importance and tenacious hold of the *sub rosa* processes that, in fact, had produced the informal adjustments and implicit deals that had permitted the mission-oriented or regional coalitions to reconcile their own immediate interests with the larger definition of national priorities.[16]

THE REFORMIST IMPLICATIONS

As a future-oriented doctrine, developed socialism simultaneously addresses the problems facing top Soviet leaders in a pragmatic fashion and sets forth those economic, technological, and social trends which are seen as shaping the next several decades. It is in the latter realm that the reformist implications are most apparent, for they articulate not only the current tasks of the present regime—tasks which that regime has consistently since the early 1970s interpreted in terms of far-reaching economic and administrative reforms--but also set at work and legitimate an array of scientific, economic, and social forces which carry long-term reformist implications.

In the short run, the reformist imperatives of developed socialism are most clearly embodied in (1) the emphasis now placed on the qualitative improvement of policy outputs in the economy and in other spheres, and (2) the impact of the scientific and technological revolution, which is seen as providing the key to the socialist equivalent of what Western theorists have termed the "second industrial revolution."[17] In the context of qualitative improvements, the regime's short-run priorities have focused principally on the question of improving economic performance and on the related issue of administrative reform. Emphasis has been placed both on the "balanced" or "proportional" growth of the economy--that is, the mutually dependent expansion or improvement in agriculture, consumer goods, and heavy industry, although the marginal priorities still are a source of conflict--and on the shift from "extensive" to "intensive" economic growth. The latter discussion provides the conceptual bridge to the second issue of the impact of the scientific and technological revolution, which has preoccupied Soviet theorists for the last decade. Cast in terms of their analysis of the evolution of contemporary Soviet society, the shift from "extensive" to "intensive" growth signals that the simplistic past formula that the economy grew simply with ever greater inputs of manpower, capital, and material is now no longer relevant. Rather future growth and the up-grading of existing industrial stock is seen as animated by the increasing reliance on advances in science and technology, on higher productivity per worker or per unit of investment, and on more sophisticated information systems. As a consequence, the tasks of managerial and administrative reform necessarily entail not only pressures on current party and economic leaders for improved performance in the short run, but also involve the creation of the groundwork for a substantially improved system of management that differs strikingly, at least in terms of work style if not in terms of institutional configuration, from the present system of "muddling through."[18] As Donald Barry has noted, over the last decade Soviet thinking has shifted from the static "administrative law" approach to the more dynamic conception of "administrative science," and this transformation has entailed a serious reinterpretation of the functioning of administrative bodies and the course of their evolution during the developed socialist phase.[19] Under current projections, administrative bodies will become increasingly dependent on the quality and quantity of data provided by ever more sophisticated information systems and come to function more as coordinating or "matrix" agencies, especially in the more complex areas of socio-economic planning involving issues of intersectoral linkages, than as straight-line branch ministries.[20]

Viewed in terms of immediate policy implications, both the upgrading of policy outputs and the shift to "scientific" management have translated into strong pressure on party and state cadres not only for better goods and services but also for a change in the day-to-day functioning of the cumbersome Soviet bureaucracy. As I have suggested above, the track record has been mixed. While the regime has had respectable success in placing its imprint on policy outputs and articulated national priorities, it has paradoxically had less influence in its attempts to transform the internal work styles of the bureaucracies themselves. Yet it is principally upon this issue--that is, in the creation of new forms of "scientific" management and planning--that the regime has pegged its hopes for future reforms.[21]

The long-term reform implications of the doctrine of developed socialism are even more far reaching. The entire doctrinal edifice may suffer the same fate as many of Khrushchev's innovations. However, another scenario is equally possible. It is possible that the doctrine and its practical ramifications could become the theoretical legitimation and action program of a reformist coalition bridging across the reform-minded members of the current regime and lower-ranking party and state officials. Given a prolonged succession battle after Brezhnev's demise and/or a substantial escalation of economic and social problems, the emergence of a reform-oriented coalition is certainly tactically feasible within the parameters of Soviet political behavior. In fact, such a coalition would have much to build upon--the demonstrable existence of intensifying economic and social problems that must be confronted (unless, of course, the Brezhnev regime itself, and therefore implicitly its doctrinal innovations, are made the scapegoat for these problems) and the inevitable upward mobility of younger, better trained cadres who at least have the potential to be more understanding and tolerant of the implications of the "scientific management of society" approach associated with developed socialism. Any student of Soviet politics could quickly point out, of course, there is no guarantee that such a coalition would form, much less win, or that the next generation of Soviet leaders would be any more "scientific" and less political than the last. Jerry Hough has offered us a timely warning in reminding us that in each succession period since Lenin conventional wisdom has always argued that the next regime would be "more of the same"--and that conventional wisdom was always wrong.[22] Yet the East European experience does suggest that the doctrine may become the cutting edge for reform efforts that apparently reach far beyond the intentions of present leaders who copied the Soviet developed socialism model in their own nations. As several of the studies in this volume clearly demonstrate, reformers advocating controversial issues such as greater decentralization or devolution of power, greater mass participation, and the rationalization of state and planning agencies have turned to developed socialism as a protective theoretical umbrella.

The long-term implications of developed socialism hold forth the possibility of significant changes not only in the nature and functioning of the major political institutions but also in the larger question of the interface of the regime and society. Perhaps the potentially most important theoretical implication is the assertion that developed socialism evolves according to its own laws of dialectical evolution, not all of which are currently known or fully understood by contemporary theorists.[23] Brezhnev himself has referred to it as "the stage of the perfection of socialism *on its own basis*," and more scholarly commentators have pointed out that more complete explications of the nature of the growth process and the successive stages inherent in the "further perfection of socialism" are a subject of continuing conjecture.[24] Such caution about asserting the nuts and bolts dimensions of the transition process may simply be a part of the generally cautious bent of the present regime. But on the other hand, such reticence and indecision about the laws of development which govern the further evolution of developed socialism have also provided an open ground for a debate among Soviet scholars filled with important implications for the future reformist or conservative nature of the doctrine. To the extent that developed socialism remains synonymous with the scientific and technological revolution, and with attempts to reform economic and administrative agencies, and to the extent it remains sufficiently flexible to respond to the latest definitions of the reformist imperatives, the doctrine may continue to play a long-range legitimating role for future would-be reformers.

A second reform-oriented implication also emerges from the fact that the laws of developed socialism are regarded as at least partially *sui generis*. Both the literature on the development of the administrative sciences and the larger body of empirical sociological theory imply that many of the new laws of development particular to the developed socialist phase can be identified only through empirical organizational or sociological research. Important advocates of "the scientific management of society" such as V. G. Afanasev suggest that much of the fine tuning of future economic and social mechanisms will be heavily dependent on the newly emerging social sciences, which--

working within a proper Marxist framework, of course--will discover middle-level theory linking the prescribed dialectical trends with concrete economic and social manifestations. Much of this operational middle-level theory is regarded as sui generis within the developed socialist phase, and even though theorists predictably shy away from suggesting that it is antithetical to Marxist conventional wisdom about the role of various institutions and socio-economic forces, they do clearly imply that it will function with a high degree of independence in defining the day-to-day functioning of contemporary Soviet society.[25] While the manipulatory potential of these new laws may bear an ominous and even Orwellian tone suggestive of what Allen Kassof has termed an "administered society," it nonetheless remains true that such improved techniques of social engineering are also consistent with the reformist imperatives of developed socialism, especially to the extent that they lend impetus to an acknowledgment of the growing complexity and multifaceted nature of society and to an improvement in the day-to-day functioning of party and state mechanisms.[26]

Further strengthening the stress placed on sui generis patterns of development and the growing significance of the social and administrative sciences is the emphasis now given to the "subjective factor" in future social evolution. In this context, the subjective factor simply refers to the increasing need for conscious, sophisticated planning of all aspects of economic and social life. Soviet theorists now acknowledge that future development is no longer dependent upon the more primitive "objective" laws governing socialist accumulation and the earlier stages of a socialist society; in a developed socialist society, the critical decisions that pave the way toward even higher socialist and communist forms are seen as consciously controlled by party and state planners, whose understanding of the world around them and administrative skills must rise to ever higher levels to meet the demands of a mature socialist system. In simple terms, the present leadership and its successors must bear greater responsibility for the further development of the system.[27]

The evolving role of the party during the developed socialist era also holds forth at least some prospects that the reformist tendencies of the doctrine will be strengthened. Speaking to the twenty-fifth party congress, Brezhnev stressed the themes of change and the increasingly "scientific" nature of party work:

> Of course, there is nothing immutable about either the party itself or the nature of its activity. At every stage, the party's work is filled with new content. Therefore, it is natural that the new tasks the 25th congress will pose will continue to require that the forms and methods of party work be improved on a scientific basis.[28]

In the short run, the ramifications of the statement are hardly revolutionary; the reformist themes stressing change within the party and improvement in its relationship with society have been commonplace for the last decade. But in the long run, the new tasks the party must face and the nature of the response it is being asked to make suggest the possibility of deep reaching transformations. Even discounting for a moment the generational changes in top- and middle-level cadres which will occur over the next decade, it is still possible to conjecture that the present challenge to master the scientific and technological revolution and to function in a coordinating and integrative role will change both its workstyle and interface with other socio-economic institutions. In the first instance, the mastery of new techniques of economic and social management is meant simultaneously to alter the workstyle of the party itself and to improve party capability to deal with the increasingly demanding tasks confronting it. Simply put, these tasks are now seen as more complex than ever before. In response, the party is expected to modernize its own internal work style in terms of managerial reforms.

In the second instance, the party is expected to assume both a more aggressive initiating role in fostering further reforms and a more sophisticated coordinating role in terms of integrating an increasingly complex economic and social order. While the first role includes much of the traditional sense of the party's "guiding and directing" functions, it goes beyond conventional definitions to include a clear mandate to serve as the cutting edge in the development and direction of those forces which will ultimately convert a developed socialist society into communism. Implicit in the literature is the suggestion that present leaders are deeply concerned with an absence of positive leadership and with a sense of malaise within the party and wish to summon it once again to the barricades--be they now scientific and administrative barricades--for the sake of building the new order.[29]

The new emphasis placed on the party's role as a coordinator also goes far beyond traditional definitions in which it articulated overall national priorities and functioned as an _ad hoc_ coordinating agency whose mandate and intra-organizational ties cut across conventional bureaucratic and/or regional divisions. While that element certainly remains present, the party has also been given a new mandate to function as what Western students of public administration have termed a "matrix organization," i.e., a fluid administrative network which is charged with the task of overseeing complex multifaceted or intersectoral tasks that involve groundbreaking and previously unstructured projects in the areas of technological development or complex socio-economic change. What is significant is that the time-honored mandate to cut across departmental barriers (without, of course, engaging in "petty tutelage") is now elevated to a new area of administrative science and a realm in which the mastery of these new skills is seen as the key to the successful management of the ever more complex problems of a developed socialist society.[30]

The doctrine of developed socialism also implicitly opens the door to a proliferation of the nature and sources of demands on the institutions of party and state. Three aspects of the theory are potentially significant. First, Soviet theorists now acknowledge the existence of legitimate "interests" within their society; while such interests are held to be non-antagonistic--that is, to possess no true class relevance--they are reflective of long-term social and institutionalized forces within the Soviet Union and thusly must be reckoned with by policy makers. The recognition of such interests explicitly opens the door to and further legitimates the de facto reality of an interest-based political process within which issue generation and advocacy are increasingly vested in various regional or functional interests. This is not to suggest, of course, that the party has inadvertently created the theoretical basis for the elimination of its own unique role; but it is to suggest that the party is now willing to acknowledge the complex interest-based milieu within which it must operate.[31]

Second, social differentiation and the complexity of the social structure are seen as intensifying during the developed socialist era. In the long run, of course, social structure will ultimately simplify under communism. But in the short run, the rapid growth of the intelligentsia and the proliferation of highly skilled professional and occupational groups, and the relatively slower convergence of physical and intellectual labor, and the nature of urban and rural life create a society where factors such as occupation, standard of living, and location of residence give rise to significant social differences and discernible "interests."[32]

Finally, the further professionalization of managerial tasks as a consequence of the scientific and technological revolution itself creates new strata and presumably new demands both in terms of policy content and in terms of legitimate claims for participation in the policy-making process. Implicit in the discussion of the "scientific management of society" is the assumption that the new methods of social management will both better interpret and channel existing demands and generate their own dynamics in terms of requiring the efficient management of the affairs of party and state.[33] Thus both the style of managerial work and the internal dynamics of an increasingly fractionalized professional workforce are seen as having long-term effects on the nature of the political process. In the longer perspective, the success or failure of the theory in the post-Brezhnev period may well turn upon how well it provides the theoretical rationale for offering controlled access to the decision-making process writ large to new social and professional elements, for in an era in which much of the aging top- and middle-level elite will inevitably yield to the next generation, this issue raises the central question of any political system: who rules?

THE PRESENT STATE OF DEVELOPED SOCIALISM

In the latter phase of the Brezhnev regime, which we may realistically assume extends from the late 1970s into the 1980s, there has been little effort to expand the concept of developed socialism beyond the theoretical explication and practical political significance that gave structure and meaning to the theory in the mid-1970s. This is not to say, of course, that Soviet theorists are now backing away either from the detailed description of the future contained within the doctrine or, more importantly, from the practical reform agenda suggested by the day-to-day implications of the theory. Rather the substance and tone of recent comments imply merely that the notion of the essential validity of developed socialism is now taken as a fait accompli, as a theoretical centerpiece of the Brezhnev regime which now draws little attention either from top leaders themselves who have become preoccupied with the increasingly accute problems of managing the economy or from those sub rosa political forces that will take the field after the General Secretary's demise. As a theory--that is, as an intellectual description and rationalization of an age--the notion of developed socialism has become a singular success; there is virtually no serious challenge to the present assertion that it constitutes the proper Marxist interpretation of an advance socialist industrial order.

Yet in the same vein, the theory of developed socialism also continues to function both as an increasingly frustrated reform agenda and as an indictment of the present ills of Soviet society. The treatment of the doctrine at the twenty-sixth party congress, held in 1981, reveals two at least partially contradictory conclusions concerning the further maturation of Soviet society. On the one hand, Brezhnev's comments clearly represented the attainment of the stage of developed socialism as a fait accompli; gone were the brave-new-world descriptions of the nature of a developed socialist society and the self-congratulatory celebration that the Soviet Union had entered into this new and important phase. For the first time at a major party congress, the attainment of developed socialism was treated as a routine affair, to be noted in the description of the present state of Soviet reality, but not to be regarded as a recently attained stage of development. Thus the specific references to "developed" or "mature" socialism were largely pro forma, with the only explicit theoretical exception coming in a reminder that this would be an "historically long period" in the life of Soviet society which might call for the preparation of a new party program replacing the until-now ignored 1961 Khrushchev version.[34]

In another sense, the practical descriptions of the problems facing a developed socialist society clearly resulted in a sense of deja vu. Despite the seeming acceptance that developed socialism is an accomplished theoretical fact, there was no diminution in the insistance that the reform agenda imbodied within the doctrine be carried forth as party policy. The catalog of complaints and shortcomings that had emerged in the early and mid-1970s as the standard and oft-repeated litany of "immature" features of a mature socialist society remained virtually the same, and the tone of evident frustration on the part of top Soviet leaders confirmed that they are now as greatly, if not more, concerned that forward motion toward a more mature social order has been retarded by the intentional resistance and natural bureaucratic lethargy of the Soviet establishment. If Brezhnev's comments to the twenty-sixth congress are any indication of that frustration, then many of the same issues on the reform agenda formulated in the early 1970s clearly remained as items of concern. Brezhnev once again, in even stronger terms, lamented the "inertia" on the part of senior party and state officials that retarded reform efforts and called for party officials to impose "stiffened demands" on their colleagues and counterparts in the state bureaucracy. As before, party bodies were called upon to "show even greater initiative" in their supervision of state agencies and in their efforts to improve the selection of technically competent cadres for party and state work. In the long range, the ritual commentary that the concept of developed socialism had witnessed productive "elaboration" over the last decade was joined with the call for ever more pragmatic and useful development of social and econometric theories whose current manifestations were labelled as unnecessarily "pedantic."[35]

On the whole, the record of the twenty-sixth congress represents a decidedly mixed picture. On the one hand, the comments of virtually all major party figures seemed to indicate that--at least for the remainder of the Brezhnev period--the overarching characterization of the epoch as "developed socialism" will remain unchallenged. Whether this represents a uniform consensus about the true nature of the era or a mere tactical concession by either conservative or liberal forces is still open to question. What is apparent is that no real or potential protagonist wishes to attack developed socialism _as a political formula_ at this time. Judging from the actual substance both of Brezhnev's commentary and the subsequent comments by others, however, the specific economic, political, and social issues that comprise the notion of developed socialism _in toto_ are individually open to exceptionally critical commentary, whether from Brezhnev and others who wish to blame the shortcomings of the system on the "inertia" of others or potential critics who implicitly attempt to suggest that the problems and dilemmas are attributable, in one way or another, to the nature of the present leadership.[36]

DEVELOPED SOCIALISM AFTER BREZHNEV

Whether the conservative or reformist implications of developed socialism dominate the thinking of Soviet theorists under the next generation of Kremlin leaders, and perhaps whether the doctrine survives at all, will ultimately depend, of course, on the nature of the now-unknown regime that will replace not only the current General Secretary but also the vast majority of an aging party elite. Although considerable speculation has surrounded this question over the last half-decade, no one knows with certainty whether all of the appropriate scenarios have been devised, much less which of them accurately sketches even the barest outlines of future events. Certainly the most complete examination of the possible outcomes has been presented by George Breslauer in his _Five Images of the Soviet Future_, which assembles and comments critically on the most common scenarios suggested by American, European, or emigre thinkers.[37] While it is beyond the scope of this essay to explore all of the possible theoretical implications of each scenario, it is possible to assess which would likely provide a favorable milieu for the continued development of the reformist elements of the doctrine and which would likely reverse that trend or abrogate the tacit understandings that have elevated the scientific and technological revolution and its ramifications on the economy and society to a dominant national priority under the current regime.

What is initially most striking is that some prospects for the survival of developed socialism as a pragmatic, reformist doctrine exist under all but one of the possible scenarios. The only pattern which explicitly _excludes_ developed socialism as it is presently understood is a "Russite-fundamentalist reaction," which bears a distinctly regressive stamp and is led by conservative and presumably chauvanistic Russite elements such as the military and police, local party secretaries, and officials in culture and indoctrination. Most importantly, it is characterized both by a sense of anti-intellectualism and a resuscitation of traditional Russian values (including a possible arrangement with the Russian Orthodox Church) and by a persistent deterioration of the economy and the stability of the society. The only other possible pattern which is potentially antithetical to developed socialism is a variation within Breslauer's "instability" scenario described as "separatism." Suggested most prominently by the writings of Andrei Amalrik, this option provides for the growing dominance of ethnic concerns and the creation of a "Russite military dictatorship;" implicit within this configuration is the same sort of anti-intellectualism and economic stagnation described above, compounded by growing salience of ethnic hostilities and the repressiveness of the regime.

More sanguine prospects for the survival of developed socialism are found under the three left-to-center options: "Socialist democracy," which will be led by the party intelligentsia, finds its social base among the critical intelligentsia, youth, and advanced workers, and encourages open political discussion and mass participation. It is inspired by the spirit of the scientific and technological revolution; "Elitist liberalism," which will be directed by an increasingly hereditary "aristocratizing elite" of technocrats. It enjoys the support of intellectuals, elite service personnel, and skilled workers, and combines the themes of economic efficiency and hereditary privilege; and "welfare state authoritarianism," in which the leading functional elites will secure the support of sub-elites and the masses through a combination of an ever-improving standard of living and reliance on a growing sense of Soviet nationalism.

While each of these possible scenarios stresses somewhat different features of the doctrine, all place emphasis on the improved performance of party and state agencies in up-grading the activities of the elite itself and/or in improving the standard of living. Perhaps understandably, these left-to-center options focus on efforts to win support from both an increasingly differentiated (although perhaps "hereditary") elite and an ever more demanding general public. Thus appeals are made to the elite which involve either the recognition of the relevance and increasing professionalization of these strata--a position entirely consistent with the reformist implications of developed socialism--or a tacit acceptance of its desire to perpetuate its ruling status through preferential treatment for its offspring and further consolidation of its influence vis-a-vis the more liberal threat of democratic socialism or the right-wing danger of "Russite fundamentalism." In either instance, both the elite's interest in improving its ability to deal with an increasingly complex society, to say nothing of its own desire for a materially more rewarding life, and its need to reward legitimate public demands (or simply to buy off potential opposition) create conditions in which the instrumental reformist implications of developed socialism are sustained. At the worst, the elite's concern with its continued dominance, or its fear of a more fundamentalist reaction, would suggest the sort of cautious and politically tempered reformism that is the present political formula of the Brezhnev regime.

NOTES

1. For a history of the development of the doctrine, see Alfred B. Evans, Jr. "Developed Socialism in Soviet Ideology," Soviet Studies, 29, July 1977, pp. 409-428.

2. See my discussion in "The Communist Party," in Donald R. Kelley, ed., Soviet Politics in the Brezhnev Era, New York: Praeger, 1980, pp. 29-35.

3. L. I. Brezhnev, comments to the 24th Party Congress, Pravda, March 31, 1971.

4. Kelley, op. cit.

5. Iu. A. Tikhomirov, "Gosudarstvo v razvitom sotsialisticheskom obshchestve," Kommunist, no. 10, 1979, pp. 10-11.

6. A. M. Kovalev, "Razvitoe sotsialisticheskoe obshchestvo -- zakonomernyi etap kommunisticheskoi formatsii," Kommunist, no. 6, 1979, pp. 48-49.

7. Myron Rush, The Rise of Khrushchev, Washington, D.C.: Public Affairs Press, 1958, pp. 3-9.

8. L. I. Brezhnev, comments on the 1977 constitution, Pravda, October 5, 1977.

9. V. I. Lesnyi and N. N. Chernogolovkin, Politicheskaia organizatsiia razvitogo sotsialisticheskogo obshchestva: struktura i funktsii, Moscow: Izdatelstvo Moskovskogo universiteta, 1976, pp. 36-54; E. M. Chekharin, Sovetskaia politicheskaia sistema v usloviiakh razvitogo sotsializma, Moscow: Mysl, 1977, translated as The Soviet Political System Under Developed Socialism, Moscow: Progress, 1977; and G. E. Glezerman, ed., Razvitoe sotsialisticheskoe obshchestvo: sushchnost, kriterii zrelosti, kritika revizionistskikh kontseptsii, second edition, Moscow: Mysl, 1975, p. 154.

10. Brezhnev, Pravda, October 5, 1977.

11. Lesnyi and Chernogolovkin, op. cit., pp. 93-104; Chekharin, op. cit., pp. 220-229; and Dobrovolnye obshchestva pri sotsializme, Moscow: Nauka, 1976.

12. Robert Sharlet, "Constitutional Implementation and the Juridicization of the Soviet System," in Kelley, Soviet Politics, p. 206.

13. Ibid., pp. 222-28.

14. Kelley, "Communist Party."

15. Paul Cocks, "The Policy Process and Bureaucratic Politics," in Paul Cocks, Robert V. Daniels, and Nancy Whittier Heer, eds., The Dynamics of Soviet Politics, Cambridge: Harvard University Press, 1976, pp. 156-178.

16. Kelley, "Communist Party," pp. 41-42.

17. V. V. Kosolapov, Cheloveschestvo na rubezhe XXI veka, Moscow: Molodaia gvardiia, 1973, translated as Mankind in the Year 2000, Moscow: Progress, 1976; E. D. Mordzhinskii and Ts. A. Stepanian, Budushchee chelovecheskogo obshchestva, Moscow: Mysl, 1971; and V. G. Afanasev, The Scientific and Technological Revolution: Its Impact on Management and Education, Moscow: Progress, 1975.

18. I. I. Kuzminov et al., *Ekonomicheskie problemy razvitogo sotsializma i ego pererastaniia v kommunizm*, Moscow: Mysl, 1977, pp. 82-96: L. S. Bliakhman and O. I. Shkaratan, *Man at Work: The Scientific and Technological Revolution, the Soviet Working Class, and the Intelligentsia*, Moscow: Progress, 1977; L. M. Gatovskii et al., *Materialnotekhnicheskaia baza kommunizma*, vol. 2, Moscow: Mysl, 1977, pp. 287-283.

19. Donald D. Barry, "From Administrative Law to Administrative Science: Lawyers and the Development of a New Discipline," paper presented at the Conference on Soviet and East European Law and the Scientific and Technological Revolution, Rutgers University, Camden, New Jersey, February 29 to March 2, 1980.

20. Paul Cocks, "Rethinking the Organizational Weapon: The Soviet System in a Systems Age," *World Politics*, 32, 3, January, 1980, pp. 235-239.

21. Kelley, "Communist Party," pp. 41-42.

22. Jerry F. Hough, "The Generation Gap and the Brezhnev Succession," *Problems of Communism*, 28, July-August, 1979, p. 1.

23. Tikhomirov, *op. cit.*, p. 6; V. I. Kasianenko, *KPSS: Organizator stroitelstva razvitogo sotsializma*, Moscow: Politizdat, 1974, pp. 14-15; and Glezerman, *op. cit.*, p. 19.

24. Brezhnev, *Pravda*, October 5, 1977.

25. Tikhomirov, *op. cit.*

26. Allen Kassof, "The Administered Society: Totalitarianism Without Terror," *World Politics*, 16, 4, July, 1964, pp. 558-575.

27. V. Sikorskii, *KPSS na etape razvitogo sotsializma*, Minsk: Izdatelstvo Belorusskogo universiteta, 1975, pp. 130-133: and Kasianenko, *op. cit.*, pp. 175-177.

28. L. I. Brezhnev, comments on the 25th Party Congress, *Pravda*, February 25, 1976.

29. For an example, note the tone of the November, 1978 Central Committee plenum, reported in *Pravda*, November 28, 1978.

30. A. Egorov, "Kommunisticheskaia partiia v usloviiakh razvitogo sotsializma," *Kommunist*, no. 1, October, 1976, pp. 56-57; Sikorskii, *op. cit.*, pp. 39-47, 72-78; Glezerman, *op. cit.*, pp. 268-77; and V. S. Shevtsov, *KPSS i gosudarstvo v razvitom sotsialisticheskom obshchestve*, Moscow: Politizdat, 1974, pp. 53-60.

31. Bliakhman and Shkaratan, *op. cit.*, p. 149.

32. G. I. Pivtsaikin, *Obshchestvennye otnosheniia razvitogo sotsializma*, Minsk: Nauka i tekhnika, 1973; Kasianenko, *op. cit.*, pp. 181-94; and Bliakhman and Shkaratan, *op. cit.*, p. 149.

33. D. M. Gvishiani et al., *The Scientific Intelligentisia in the USSR*, Moscow: Progress, 1976; and *Partiia i intelligentsiia v usloviiakh razvitogo sotsializma*, Moscow: Mysl, 1977.

34. *Pravda*, February 24, 1981.

35. *Ibid.*

36. *Ibid.*

37. George W. Breslauer, *Five Images of the Soviet Future: A Critical Review and Synthesis*, Berkeley, California: Institute of International Studies, University of California, 1978.

2
Is Developed Socialism a Soviet Version of Convergence?

Jeffrey W. Hahn

On the face of it, the Soviet concept of developed socialism would seem to bear a strong resemblance to Western theories of "convergence" which flourished in the nineteen-sixties and early seventies. Both views share a fundamental starting point in contending that societal change is essentially a function of economic development. Thus, Western convergence theorists argue that the social and political consequences of industrial development are more or less universal and that mature industrial societies therefore become increasingly alike in many ways over time. Ideological and national differences, according to this view, are diminished in importance by neutral technology, the engine of modern industrial society, and all industrial societies, whether communist or capitalist, will advance steadily into a brave, new, post-industrial world. Soviet theorists of developed socialism also maintain that there are universal societal consequences which flow from what they call the "scientific-technological revolution" (STR). What they vigorously reject, however, is the suggestion that capitalist and socialist societies will lose their class character and become alike.

The following discussion presents first a comparison of the industrial society model accepted by most Western convergence theorists with the Soviet model of developed socialism. Attention is focused on those economic, social, and political changes which appear to be common to both theories. Secondly, the principal criticisms of convergence theory by both Soviet and Western analysts will be summarized. Those rejecting the convergence thesis in both East and West are seen as doing so out of ideological considerations rather than scientific ones. None of the critiques offers a truly scientific evaluation of the convergence concept. This would require the establishment of operational criteria which could be measured empirically and then tested with data.[1] The concluding section suggests that the dismissal of convergence theory by both Soviet and Western critics, for reasons that are essentially ideological, is both hasty and un unwarranted. The concept of developed socialism may serve, however unintentionally, to renew interest in the question of what kinds of societal changes the Soviets share with other mature industrial societies as a result of their commitment to growth through technology.

Convergence Theory

While there are several varieties of "convergence" theory,[2] it is the view of industrial development which emerged in the late nineteen-fifties and the nineteen-sixties which received the most attention. In retrospect, it probably should come as no surprise that this view was generally benign and optimistic.[3] The fifties had provided a period of relatively steady economic growth in the West and a relative absence of conflict in international affairs. New technology was widely believed to be the key to even greater increases in productivity in the developed societies, while the emergent "Third World" would benefit through technology transfers which would enable them also to embark on the "stages of economic growth" leading to industrialization.[4] The absence of class conflict in the developed industrial societies and the rise in the standard of living across classes suggested the emergence of a homogenous middle-class society in which questions of ideology had lost their relevance.[5]

An optimistic view of the future which had been expressed by Pitirim Sorokin twenty years earlier now seemed reasonable. If war could be avoided, he has written, the Soviet Union and the United States would converge into an "integrated type" which would fuse the best features of communism and capitalism. In the West, the government would assume an ever larger role in the management of the economy, while the Soviet Union, freed from the crisis economy of the Stalinist years, would become more flexible, less controlled.[6]

Sorokin's vision found ready echos in the "new industrial state" of John Kenneth Galbraith[7] and the "post-industrial society" of Daniel Bell.[8] In an interview with Anthony Lewis of the New York Times in 1966, Galbraith expressed perhaps most clearly the spirit of optimism and the faith in reason and progress which so infused convergence thinking.

> The nature of technology, the nature of the large organization that sustains technology, and the nature of planning that technology requires, has an imperative of its own, and this is causing a greater convergence in all industrial societies. In the East European societies it is leading to a decentralization of power from the state to the firm; in the West European societies, it is leading to a kind of ad hoc planning. In fewer years than we can imagine, this will produce a rather indistinguishable melange of planning and market influences.... The requirements of deep scientific perception and deep technical specialization cannot be reconciled with intellectual regimentation. They inevitably lead to intellectual curiosity and to a measure of intellectual liberalism.[9]

The confidence that advanced industrial society would necessarily be accompanied by affluence, world peace, and "intellectual liberalism" was quickly challenged. Critics from both the left and the right argued that industrial society was more to be feared than hoped for. Charles Reich rejected the values of industrial society as dehumanizing and antithetical to personal growth. He called for a new "consciousness" which judged people by "what they were," rather than by what they consumed or by what positions they had achieved.[10] Theodore Roszak described a generational reaction against the justification of the economic status quo implicit in the advanced industrial society model, calling this movement the "counterculture."[11] Finally, the Club of Rome's study on "The Limits of Growth" concluded that exponential population growth combined with rapidly shrinking finite resources would bring lower, not higher levels of consumption, and that technology was not the panacea predicted by the industrial society model.[12] The stagnation of economic growth in the Western industrial economies, combined with higher inflation and unemployment rates, seemed to confirm this pessimistic assessment. The hopes for improved East-West relations with which the decade began, had been replaced by 1980 with a return to the antagonistic postures of the Cold War.

The optimism of the convergence theories of the nineteen-sixties was almost certainly misplaced. However, it would be a mistake to dismiss the explanation of social change offered by the industrial society model which lies at the heart of these theories. Industrialization does induce changes in society, for better or worse. Technological advances do influence behavior and affect values. This much is shared by the theory of developed socialism which will be discussed below. For the sake of comparison, let us synthesize the major societal changes which are thought to accompany industrialization.[13] These may be thought of as a series of hypotheses with industrialization as the independent variable in each.

Economically, as societies industrialize:

1. the proportion of the population engaged in agriculture decreases; the industrial portion increases.
2. technology becomes an increasingly important source of growth in productivity.
3. there is an increasingly complex division of labor; occupational mobility increases rapidly, and is based on achievement rather than ascription.
4. there is a high degree of structural differentiation; planning becomes more long-range, and management is conducted according to the principles of modern bureaucracy emphasizing hierarchical relationships.
5. manual and unskilled labor is needed less as jobs requiring such labor are automated; the proportion of the population working in white collar and professional occupations increases.

Socially, as societies industrialize:

1. there is a controlled rate of population growth; the small nuclear family replaces the extended family; women are freed from child-rearing roles to enter the workplace.
2. the great inequalities of wealth and class characteristic of traditional societies give way to a middle

class society ushered in by the spread of universal literacy and education; there is progressive absence of class distinction based on property.
3. urbanization leads to greater anonymity and autonomy in interpersonal relationships.
4. communication becomes more technologically conditioned as we learn about others through the media rather than face to face; single-stranded relationships replace multi-stranded ones.
5. culturally, there is an increasing secularization of values; belief in metaphysical explanations is replaced with a faith in rationality, hard work, technology, science and progress; a new "industrial culture" emerges.

Politically, as societies industrialize:

1. there is a demand for greater popular participation in politics as a result of universal education.
2. there is a diffusion of political power as decision-making elites must increasingly rely on the expertise of technical specialists.
3. the state plays an increasingly larger role in economic planning and the management of technology.
4. the application of law becomes "universalistic" rather than "particularistic;" positive law replaces custom and tradition.

The industrial society model does not portend the complete identity of any two societies. However, it does contend that the similarities between advanced industrial societies are more significant than the differences, especially when compared with non-industrial societies. In this context, the improvements in the standard of living and the de-Stalinization which accompanied Khrushchev's ascendence to power in 1956 seemed to confirm that the Soviets were beginning to behave as one would expect of an advanced industrial society. By the late nineteen-sixties, however, the Soviets were developing their own theories about "mature" or "developed" socialism. It is to the similarities and differences of the Soviet theory that we must now turn our attention.

Developed Socialism

When Khrushchev proclaimed in the 1961 Party Program that the phase of building socialism had been completed in the USSR and that Communism would be built by 1980, he left to his successors the knotty ideological dilemma of explaining what he really meant. It has been Party Chairman Brezhnev's singular contribution to the development of Soviet Marxist thought that what The Program really meant was that a distinct, advanced stage of socialism would be achieved which was itself the first stage of full communism.[14] This stage, which is called the period of "developed" or "mature" socialism, would last for an historically long period and gradually, almost imperceptably, evolve into communism. While the boundary between "developed socialism" and communism is blurred, the transition from the socialist phase of development to developed socialism is marked by a qualitatively new basis of production--the scientific-technological revolution, or STR. The STR involves the application of science to the task of increasing production. In this "revolution," technology progressively replaces manual labor in the production process thereby changing fundamentally not only the nature of labor, but many other aspects of life as well.[15] Developed socialism is defined, in the Soviet view, as the combination of the STR, which has a universal character, with the benefits of socialism.

There is no need here to trace the evolution of the concept or its implications for Soviet policy, foreign and domestic. This ground has been covered very well by others.[16] The most important point to be made for purposes of this discussion is the Soviet argument that this new stage of economic development will inevitably result in changes "in the economic, social, political, and cultural spheres of life" as well.[17] Probably the best official summary of the Soviet view of what these changes will be appears in a work published in 1979 by the Party Central Committee's late ideological guardian, Mikhail Suslov. According to Suslov, the movement into the phases of developed socialism will be accompanied by ten basic changes. These include:

1. a guarantee of a high level of development of productive forces on the basis of applying the new discoveries of the scientific--technological revolution;
2. the further development of socialist property in both its basic forms--state and collective--and their gradual coming together;
3. the steady growth of the people's well being, which is the main goal of the socialist national economy;
4. the continuation for a long period of the completely socialist principle of distribution according to work as the basic method of distribution;
5. progressive changes in the social structure: the growth of the leading role of the working class and the strengthening of its union with other strata, the reinforcement of the unity of society and its movement towards social homogeniety, the ever greater ideological and political coming together (sblizhenie) of all nations and nationalities of the USSR on the basis of equality and the com community of communist ideals;
6. the transformation of the dictatorship of the proletariat into a socialist state of all the people, including the deepening and many-sided development of socialist democracy;
7. a further rise in the level of education and culture, the growth of political consciousness, ideological maturity and a scientific Marxist-Leninist world-view among the broad masses;
8. the strengthening of cooperation with fraternal socialist countries;

9. foreign policies designed to guarantee more favorable international conditions for the development of socialism and communism;
10. an increase in the leading role of communist and workers' parties in all spheres of human life as the main condition for the victory of socialism and communism.[18]

Suslov's formulation is cited here because it is the standard one, and because, as dogma, it is the most cautious presentation and also the most widely accepted. Beyond this general formulation, however, one can identify more specific changes being discussed by Soviet specialists in various fields. For the sake of convenience and comparison, we will summarize them in the same categories used earlier in the discussion of the industrial society model.[19] In the Soviet view, then, developed socialism will be accompanied by the following changes.

Economic Changes

At the time of his death in 1953, Stalin left to his successors an economy which was industrialized, but which contained serious structural defects. Since the preponderance of Soviet investment during the Stalin period had been in the heavy industrial sector, agriculture remained essentially underdeveloped. Consumer goods were also in short supply and of poor quality. Moreover, the five-year plans were based on essentially quantitative indices of growth. These may show high rates of growth during a period of crude capital formation, but they are inherently inefficient and will not sustain economic growth once the industrial base is in place. In many respects, the STR can be seen as the Soviet reaction to these structural defects. Another contributing factor was the impending manpower shortage which was predicted as a result of a rapidly declining rate of population growth already visible in the early nineteen sixties. Increased labor productivity was needed to compensate for the loss of manpower.

As stated earlier, the essence of the STR is the application of science to the tasks of production. In doing so, there will be a shift from "extensive" to "intensive" development, meaning the more widespread use of mechanization and automation to improve labor productivity.[20] Increased labor productivity is seen as the key to increased production in both agriculture and light industry, the areas most related to raising the Soviet standard of living. Ridding themselves of the Stalinist obsession with heavy industrial production, balanced and "proportional" development will be characteristic of developed socialism.

The successful harnessing of the STR to the tasks of increasing productivity depends principally on the growth of two other sectors of the economy: the high technology industries and the scientific research community. As Kelley has stated, the Soviet belief that science and technology are central to economic growth differs little, if at all, from Daniel Bell's assertion that post-industrial society is distinguished by the "centrality of theoretical knowledge."[21] According to the Soviets, however, what remains "socialist" about developed socialism is first, that the principle of distribution is according to work rather than need as will be the case under communism and second, that the form of property ownership found on the collective farms will not have given way to a completely state-owned system although the economy will move in this direction.

Social Changes

Soviet theorists urge that a number of changes in the social structure will accompany developed socialism. Significantly, they do not speak of a class structure, since there is no property basis for antagonistic classes. They do acknowledge two "non-antagonistic classes," the collective farmers and the workers; and a "social stratum," the intelligentsia. In the middle and late nineteen sixties, however, Soviet sociologists offered a more complex picture of the social structure. Specifically, they pointed to the growth of "intra-class" distinctions reflecting essentially differing skill levels, educational levels, and remuneration. Moreover, the growth of these within-class differences was attributed to industrial development.[22] While developed socialism will bring with it the progressive narrowing of interclass differences, intra-class distinctions will actually increase because of the increased importance of skills and because distribution will still be "according to work."[23] Only in full communism will these distinctions disappear. With respect to the gap between the working class and the intelligentsia, an ever more highly educated and skilled working class will eventually merge with it, although this will take longer. The disappearance of the differences between manual and mental labor will take the longest of all.[24] Finally, developed socialism will also see the abolition of political and economic differences among the nationalities, although secondary cultural differences will remain. "Homogeneity" and "integration" are the words most frequently used to describe the evolution of the social structure under developed socialism.

A comparison with the industrial society model is possible on a number of points. First, this model also projects the disappearance of class distinctions based on the ownership of property, and the creation of an essentially single class. Second, industrial society retains status distinctions based on having education and skills recognized as vital to the functioning of industrial society. Third, the new dominant elite, according to Bell, will be a "knowledge class," a group corresponding in STR to the scientists and technicians who create the new technology and to the managers who apply it. Finally, the erosion of nationality differences will also accompany modernization. Traditional patterns of behavior will become increasingly irrelevant in both developed socialist society and in industrial society. Thus, for example, demographic patterns involving family size, the role of women, regional shifts of population, and the birthrate are essentially similar. Many Soviet specialists now recognize these social changes as the more or less universal consequences of industrialization.[25]

Political Change

The industrial society model argued that modern industrial development would lead to a greater role for the state in managing society, the rise of the technocrat, increased political participation, the establishment of universalistic legal norms, and, in the most optimistic theories, a measure of world peace. The political changes that are to accompany developed socialism bear a marked resemblance to them. With respect to the role of the state, the dictatorship of the proletariat will give way to a "state of all the people."[26] In part, what this means is that the state as an instrument of coercion will gradually disappear, as Lenin and Engels had predicted. What will replace it is an enhanced legal consciousness combined with greater mass political participation through the organs of local government--the soviets, and through public organizations. At the same time, the managerial and administrative role of the state will actually grow due to the need for experts to guide the STR. That is, the planning function of the state will increase in importance, not only in the economic field, but in all other areas of society as well. As society becomes more complex, the role of the technical expert in the making of decisions becomes correspondingly greater. In all industrial societies, such expertise usually finds its way into the bureaucracy.

The role of the Party is also scheduled to increase in the period of developed socialism. If the Party can be seen as a giant broker of competing demands coming from various groups in Soviet society, then indeed the Party's role will have to expand since there is likely to be more competition as these various constituencies proliferate. This, in turn, will require not merely political skills, but technical ones as well. If this is so, one might hope that the next generation of Soviet leaders may be less threatened by suggestions for reform. At the least, one can expect that those who have risen in the ranks since 1953 to look at the world differently than the present leadership whose cautiousness reflects the socialization of those who came to power under Stalin.

Finally, in the area of international relations, Soviet writings suggest that during the period of developed socialism, the "world correlation of forces" will shift decisively in favor of world socialism. This is seen as a progressive and inevitable world-historical process which, unless interrupted by nuclear war, will result in world peace. Indeed, the only version of "convergence" which the Soviets accept is a sort of *pax sovietica* in which the world conforms to the Soviet vision of Marxism. That such a world-view naively underestimates the diversity which characterizes socialism in the world today is to suggest that the Soviets are as ideocentric as those proponents of the industrial society model who saw world peace as proportionate to the number of countries embracing the American prototype of democracy.

Soviet Criticism

Despite the obvious parallels between the Soviet theory of developed socialism and Western theories of industrial society, the

Soviets consider any suggestions of "convergence" between the two systems as anathema. While the Soviet criticism is voluminous and vociferous, and comes in a wide variety of shapes and sizes, depending on the intended audience, the basis of this criticism comes down to one point: they are a socialist society and the United States is not. It will be useful to expand on this explanation.

The Soviet argument against any kind of convergence between capitalist and socialist societies into a single industrial type is rooted in the different property relations found in the two societies. The continued existence of the private ownership of the means of production in capitalist systems inevitably will produce antagonistic class relationships between owners and producers. Society will be governed in the interest only of the owning class. In abolishing the institution of the private ownership of the means of production, socialism destroys the basis for class conflict. Only in such a society is governance in the interests of all possible. Since industrial society preserves the property relations of capitalism, the benefits of economic development in the period of advanced industrialism will continue to be enjoyed only by the few. This, in turn, can lead only to an increase in class antagonisms, not to their amelioration. In the Soviet view, growing dissimilarity, not convergence, will characterize the development of the two societies. Convergence theory is dismissed as an attempt by bourgeois apologists to provide a theoretical justification for preserving a status quo beneficial only to the interests of monopoly capital. It is therefore an instrument of anticommunism.

A good expression of this viewpoint is found in the Soviet discussion of the role of the state in modern industrial society. Soviet authors agree that the role of the state in economic development increases. However, in place of the passive role assigned to the state under laissez-faire capitalism, under state-monopoly capitalism the state is seen as an ever more active partner in the exp exploitation of the working class. One fairly standard presentation in this thesis is that of Professor G. Chernikov writing in Pravda. Citing Rostow and Galbraith in particular, he writes:

> The thesis itself of the proponents of convergence concerning the increasing role played by the state in the economy of capitalist countries arouses no objections. But bourgeois ideologists steer clear of the decisive question: what is the social nature of the state and in whose interest does it participate in the reproductive process, regulating and programming the economy? The facts show that the system of state-monopoly capitalism operates in the interests of the upper crust. The consolidation of state-monopoly capitalism results in that the financial oligarchy extends its oppression to the entire life of the nation.[27]

Soviet theorists do not deny that there are common features which are a consequence of industrial development. They argue, however, that the similarity is in form rather than content. The technical process of manufacturing steel in Novosibirsk and in Gary, Indiana may be the same, as Galbraith had argued, but these processes cannot be separated from the larger society which will determine the uses to which they are put. The major advantage of the socialist system, in addition to the distribution of benefits, is its ability to control, plan, and manage. Expressing this in the context of the environmental costs of industrialization, Professor D. M. Gvishiani writes:

> At the level of an individual enterprise, both in socialist and capitalist society, there is a certain similarity in how technical and organizational tasks are solved; but when we speak of the whole of society, the fundamental differences between socialism and capitalism become apparent. The unquestionable advantage of the socialist system in organizing and managing social production are particularly conspicuous today when involving processes engendered by the scientific and technological revolution....
>
> The contemporary rates and methods of capitalist production accelerate processes whereby natural resources become exhausted, ecological equilibrium is disrupted, and the biosphere polluted, creating a real threat to mankind. This danger can be averted only by some reasonable organization of all economic activity and purposeful guidance of social development.[28]

In short, the Soviets reject all arguments of a growing similarity between social systems, and specifically, the argument that capitalism can evolve into socialism without nationalizing the means of production. While the processes associated with STR may be universal, their consequences cannot be. Under capitalism, science and technology serve a particular and private good, not a public one. By nature then, their application is ad hoc and random, resulting in problems like pollution, urban decay, unemployment and so forth. Only under socialism can adequate planning be instituted to solve these problems, and only under socialism will the increase in productivity resulting from the STR be made available for society as a whole. It is in this sense that the Soviet criticism of convergence theory is essentially ideological in nature.

Western Criticisms

Like a mirror image, much of the criticism of convergence theory found in the Western literature shares the ideological character of Soviet writings on the subject. There is a similar emphasis on uniqueness; no matter how much the Soviets industrialize and modernize they will remain totalitarian and undemocratic. Often this uniqueness is attributed to cultural influences which have their genesis in history and tradition, and which transcend the industrial experience. The Russians cannot become like us, the argument seems to run, because they are, after all, Russians. The essential difference, however, is that they are communist and we are not, the assumption being that political democracy and a socialist economy are incompatible. One of the most vigorous convergence critics, Bertram Wolfe, attacked Galbraith along these lines. Asserting that "there is mischief as well as error in convergence theory" he went on to write that:

> It is terribly easy to forget that technology is neutral as regards freedom, that it may be used either to liberate or enslave, to inform or to brainwash.... Harvard Professor Galbraith could not be a professor in a Soviet university; A.D.A. leader Galbraith could not be a political leader; author Galbraith could not get a book published if it maintained that the two systems are getting to be indistinguishable....
>
> To sum up: the convergence theory will not stand up to examination in the light of history, nor to an actual examination of the two countries that are supposed to be converging. The likelihood is that each will continue to move towards its own future under the influence of its own heritage, its traditions, and its institutions, which will be both conserved and altered more by the actions of men than by the weight of things.[29]

While Professor Wolfe finds convergence theory positively pernicious for failing to emphasize that we are free and they are not, the book, Political Power: USA/USSR by Brzezinski and Huntington, though less polemical, is equally critical of convergence theory. The authors set out explicitly to examine the similarities and differences between the two countries, and thereby test the convergence theory. After a lengthy analysis, the authors make four basic points regarding convergence. First, economic development does not lead necessarily to the creation of a common industrial culture, especially in the area of political culture. The authors use the example of "archaic society" to show that "not every common economic pattern dictates a common political structure" and they use Nazi Germany to demonstrate that technological achievement does not lead to democracy. Second, they argue that since economic development was forced in the USSR, but more or less spontaneous in the West, the relationship between politics and society in the two countries is fundamentally different. Third, while the Soviet Union will gradually evolve into a relatively "affluent society," it will be an "affluent collectivism" which will present no impediment to continued political control from above. In fact, it may remove a source of internal tension. Finally, they reject the argument that industrial society convergence will bring a more peaceful international order. The final conclusion, much like Wolfe's, is that the Soviet Union will remain an exception because it will remain unfree and totalitarian.

> What distinguishes this general trend (to technocracy in the West J.W.H.) from the Soviet version is that in the advanced countries it is accompanied by the maintenance of civil liberties and individual rights and above all by the political system's acceptance of pluralism in popular outlook and expression.... The further modernization of the Soviet Union is likely to be accompanied by efforts to maintain both the political and ideological

> monopoly of the Party bureaucracy and the interdiction of any politically significant social or ideological pluralism.[30]

Conclusions

Both Soviet and Western rejections of convergence theory reflect essentially ideological preoccupations rather than an empirical evaluation of whatever merits the industrial society model might have in explaining social change. From the Soviet point of view, the main stumbling block to the convergence of social systems is economic. The US cannot become like the USSR because the US is capitalistic. The only version of convergence accepted as theoretically possible in official Soviet thinking presupposes the disintegration of capitalism in the West and the ultimate merger of all societies into one communist system. In short, we must conform to their vision of the future. The Soviets do not expect this to happen soon. In the West, on the other hand, the objections to convergence are more political. The Soviet system cannot become like ours, the argument runs, because it cannot tolerate political pluralism; because it is communist and, perforce, totalitarian. In this perspective, in order for the Soviet system to bear any similarity to ours, they would have to adopt the principles and practices of Western style democracy. This, critics insist, cannot happen as long as the Soviets remain communist.

In pursuing these lines of argument, the opponents of convergence, intentionally or otherwise, avoid the central issue. The issue which convergence theory raises is not whether the US is becoming more socialistic or whether the Soviets can become more democratic, but whether both systems are changing in similar ways in response to certain imperatives implicit in modern industrial development. To dismiss convergence theory on the grounds that the private ownership of the means of production will perpetuate class conflict and that therefore capitalist and socialist societies cannot have much in common, as the Soviets do, simply derails an empirical consideration of the relationship between industrialization and social change by introducing a value judgement about the "best" society.

A similar problem exists with the Brezezinski-Huntington argument that the criteria for any degree of similitude between the two systems is whether the Soviets can become democratic.[31] Since the Soviets also claim to be "democratic," the semantic differentiation is again reduced ultimately to a question of values (i.e., whose definition of the term is right). Recent discussions of political participation in the USSR, surely essential to any concept of democratization, reveal the dilemma one encounters when trying to operationalize the concept without introducing value judgements. Discussions of what constitutes "genuine" participation raises the question of what standards of measurement are used. In the light of empirical research on political participation in the US, why is participation by Soviet citizens less "meaningful" than that of Americans?[32] Moreover, convergence theory pessimists point out that any technocratic society is essentially anti-democratic even though it may preserve democratic forms.[33] In any case, the criticism of convergence theory on these grounds becomes an argument about values.

Meanwhile, empirical evidence exists to suggest that both societies have exhibited similar kinds of social, economic, and political changes as a function of their modern industrial development.

In conclusion, a more objective appraisal of convergence theory would probably indicate that its explanatory value is greater in some areas than others, and that is more useful in interpreting general trends than specific ones. Doubtless, there are important respects in which the convergence thesis is inadequate. It is less sensitive to cultural and historical differences; and the version discussed earlier was probably both ethnocentric and overly optimistic in its forecasts of growing peace and democracy. Nevertheless, the rejection of this theory on ideological grounds alone also seems unwarranted. The concept of developed socialism, despite Soviet disclaimers, and despite the efforts of Soviet officialdom to use the concept for legitimizing its own power position, may serve to open a wider debate about the nature of change in modern societies.

NOTES

1. This point is also made by Alfred G. Meyer in his excellent review, "Theories of Convergence," in Chalmers Johnson (ed.) Change in Communist Systems (1970), see esp. pp. 338, 341.

2. Ibid., see p. 337 for a summary of four approaches.

3. In addition to those listed in the immediately following footnotes, those adhering to one or another variety of convergence include Clark Kerr, et al., Industrialism and Industrial Man (London: Heinemann, 1962) and to a lesser extent, Maurice Duverger in Introduction a la Politique (Paris: 1964). Meyer lists Isaac Deutscher, probably for The Unfinished Revolution, as well as his trilogy on Trotsky. However, Deutscher, a Marxist, never sees convergence as mutual. Gabriel Almond and James Coleman should probably be included for their model of political systems based on economic development, in The Politics of Developing Areas (Princeton: 1961), although neither author forecasts convergence. Alfred Meyer's view of the USSR as a corporate structure "writ large," represents a sort of convergence as he himself notes in "Theories of Convergence," op. cit. See also, The Soviet Political System (New York: Knopf, 1965).

4. W. W. Rostow, The Stages of Economic Growth (London: Cambridge University Press, 1960).

5. Daniel Bell, The End of Ideology (New York: Collier Books, 1961).

6. Sorokin expressed his belief in convergence as early as the nineteen-forties, in Pitrim Sorokin, Russia and the United States (New York: Dutton, 1944). See also his article "The Mutual Convergence of the United States and the USSR," International Journal of Comparative Sociology I (September, 1960). Reprinted in Sorokin, The Basic Trends of Our Times (New Haven: University Press, 1964).

7. John Kenneth Galbraith, The New Industrial State (Boston: Houghton Mifflin, 1967), and The Affluent Society (New York: New American Library, 1958).

8. Daniel Bell, The Coming of Post-Industrial Society (New York: Basic Books, 1973).

9. John Kenneth Galbraith, interview, "The World Through Galbraith's Eyes," New York Times Magazine (December 18, 1966), p. 92.

10. Charles Reich, The Greening of America (New York: Random House, 1969).

11. Theodore Roszak, The Making of a Counter Culture (Garden City: Doubleday, 1970).

12. The Club of Rome, The Limits of Growth (New York: Universe Books, 1972).

13. These hypotheses are embedded in the literature on industrial society reviewed in the preceding sections, esp. Clark Kerr, et al., op. cit. It also makes use of a similar list compiled by David Lane in Politics and Society in the USSR, 2nd ed. (New York: New York University Press, 1978), pp. 186-188. The present list is by no means exclusive, nor would every item be accepted by each of those sponsoring some version of convergence theory.

14. Indeed, Brezhnev apparently intends to rewrite the Program to reflect his views. See his speech to the 26th Congress (1981) in the Current Digest of the Soviet Press, Vol., 30, No. 9, p. 14.

15. For two good reviews of the STR, see P. N. Fedoseev, "Social Significance of the Scientific and Technological Revolution," in Rolf Dahrendorf, et al., Scientific-Technological Revolution: Social Aspects (London: Sage, 1977) and Erik Hoffman, "Contemporary Theories of Scientific, Technological and Social Change," in Soviet Studies of Science, No. 9 (February, 1979), p. 110. See also, Frederic Fleron, Technology and Communist Culture (New York: Praeger, 1977).

16. See especially Alfred Evans, "Developed Socialism in Soviet Ideology," Soviet Studies, Vol. 29 (July, 1977), Donald Kelley (ed.), Ch. 8, Soviet Politics in the Brezhnev Era (New York: Praeger, 1980) and Robin Laird and Erik Hoffman, "The Scientific-Technological Revolution, Developed Socialism, and Soviet International Behavior," in Hoffman and Fleron (eds.). The Conduct of Soviet Foreign Policy, 2nd ed. (New York: Aldine, 1980). On the concept of developed socialism in East Europe, see Maurice Simon, "Developed Socialism, Reformist Policies, and Participation in Poland," (a paper presented at the Mid West Slavic Conference held at the University of Illinois, April 11, 1981) and Daniel Nelson, "Worker-Party Conflict in Rumania," in Problems of Communism (September-October, 1981).

17. V. X. Semenov, "V. I. Lenin o dialektike razvitiia sotsia sotsialisma," Voprosy filosofii, No. 4 (1980), p. 52.

18. M. A. Suslov, Marsizm-Leninizm i sovremennaya epokha (Moscow: 1979), pp. 10-11.

19. An excellent summary of the economic, social and political changes accompanying developed socialism based on a more extensive review of the Soviet literature than has been attempted here may be found in the article by Professor Kelley cited earlier. More recently, the same author has made a comparison of the economic, social, and political changes attending post-industrial society as envisioned by Bell with the changes seen by Soviet denial, "the concepts of post-industrial society and developed socialism are cut from the same theoretical cloth." See Donald Kelley, "Developed Socialism as Post-Industrial Society," (paper delivered at the APSA annual meeting in New York on September 5, 1981), p. 3. Both efforts have proven very helpful to the present author.

20. V. S. Semenov, "Ucheniye o razvitom sotsializme i evo pererastanii v kommunizm," (The Theory of Developed Socialism and its Transition Into Communism), Voprosy filosofii (No. 7, 1980).

21. Donald Kelley, "Developed Socialism as Post-Industrial Society," op. cit., p. 3.

22. See discussion by Jeffrey W. Hahn, "The Role of Soviet Sociologists in the Making of Social Policy," in R. Remnek (ed.) Social Scientists and Policy-Making in the USSR (New York: Praeger, 1977), pp. 48, 49.

23. V. Pechenev, "The Concept of Developed Socialism in the CPSU's Strategy and Tactics," Pravda (May 8, 1981). (CDSP: Vol. 33, No. 19, p. 7).

24. M. N. Rutkevich, "The Social Structure of Developed Socialist Society," Pravda (July 4, 1975). Translated in Reprints from the Soviet Press, Vol. 21, No. 5 (September, 1975).

25. See esp. A. G. Vishnevskii, Demograficheskaya revolutsiia (The Demographic Revolution) (Moscow: Statistika, 1976), p. 236.

26. Much of the following discussion is based on Iu. A. Tikhamirov, "Gosudarstvo v razvitom sotsialisticheskom obshestve," (The State in Developed Socialism), Voprosy filosofii (1979), No. 10. The 1977 Soviet Constitution is seen as reflecting these political changes. This view is expounded more fully in L. I. Brezhnev, "An Historic Stage on the Road to Communism," World Marxist Review (1977), No. 12.

27. Professor G. Chernikov, "The Convergence Theory as an Instrument of Anti-Communism," Pravda (September 16, 1969). Translated in Reprints from the Soviet Press, Vol. IX, No. 9 (October 31, 1969). The thrust of Soviet criticism has changed remarkably little over the past decade. For a more contemporary formulation which is interesting for its rejection of "social progress pessimists" as well as convergence theory, see E. V. Demenchonok and Iu. N. Semenov, "A Critique of Contemporary Bourgeois Concepts of Social Progress," Voprosy filosofii (1979), No. 12, translated in Soviet Studies in Philosophy, Vol. XIX, No. 2 (Fall, 1980).

28. D. M. Gvishiani, "Nauchna-tekhnicheskaya revolutsiya i sotsialny progress," (The STR and Social Progress), Voprosy filosofii (1974), No. 4.

29. Bertram D. Wolfe, "Russia and the U.S.--A Challenge to Convergence Theory," The Humanist (September/October, 1968), p. 8. A similar position is taken by Ian Weinberg, "The Problem of Convergence of Industrial Societies," Comparative Studies of Society and History (January, 1969).

30. Zbighiew Brezezinski and Samuel Huntington, Political Power: USA/USSR (New York: Viking Press, 1964), p. 434, see also pp. 419-436.

31. Ibid., pp. 429-436.

32. Two articles which raise the problem of comparing political participation in the US and USSR are D. Richard Little, "Mass Political Participation in the USA and USSR," Comparative Political Studies, Vol. 8, No. 4 (January, 1976), and Jerry Hough, "Political Participation in the USSR," Soviet Studies, Vol. XXVIII, No. 1 (January, 1976). For a response and criticism invoking the need to make "qualitative" distinctions, see T. H. Rigby, "Hough on Political

Participation in the USSR," Soviet Studies, XXVIII, No. 2 (April, 1976); John Barry, "A Criticism of Hough's Views," in S. Hendel (ed.), The Soviet Crucible, 5th ed. (North Scituate, Mass.: Duxbury Press, 1980); and D. Richard Little's review, "Political Participation and the Soviet System" in Problems of Communism, Vol. XXIX, No. 4 (July-August, 1980).

33. See Alfred Meyer's discussion of this point of view in "Theories of Convergence," op. cit.

3
Hungary and Czechoslovakia: Rationalizing the Prevailing Policies

David W. Paul

Major theoretical innovations emanating from the Soviet Union are regarded throughout Warsaw-Pact officialdom as universally valid, so when Secretary Brezhnev introduced the notion of developed socialism, it was inevitable that the leaders of Czechoslovakia and Hungary would pursue the implications for their own societies. They too must pass through the stage of developed socialism enroute to communism, and although their passage will occur sometime later than that of the USSR, it will be characterized by the same general conditions, problems, and tasks. Moreover, Soviet theorists presume that in the period of developed socialism, the general features of all societies will become more and more uniform, and the transition to communism (farther down the road) will occur among countries that resemble each other in many fundamental respects.[1]

Brezhnev's discovery in 1967 that the Soviet Union had entered the new stage a few years earlier was reminiscent of Molière's bourgeois gentilhomme, who was surprised to discover that he had been speaking prose all along. Brezhnev's East European allies were even slower to realize the implications of the new stage, but by and by, "developed socialism" entered their vocabularies, too. In the early 1970s, discussions of the new doctrine began to appear in the theoretical journals of the Hungarian Socialist Workers' Party (HSWP) and the Communist Party of Czechoslovakia (CPC). By the time of the Eleventh Congress of the HSWP in 1975 and the Fifteenth Congress of the CPC in 1976, the party leaders were attempting to define their policies in terms of developed socialism. Interestingly, however, their policies in the 1970s suggested quite different interpretations of the theory, and the two divergent visions of developed socialism emerging in Prague and Budapest would appear to challenge the Soviets' confident prediction of increasing uniformity.

Like all doctrines of Marxism-Leninism, developed socialism is meant to serve both as a description of reality in some aspect of being or becoming and as a general guide to political action. The Soviet model of a developed socialist society is presumed to serve as an example to be emulated elsewhere, allowing for some relatively minor variations in the specific patterns of evolution from country to country. Descriptions of the USSR as a society already having entered the new stage, however, are in many respects vague and contradictory. Empirical indicators of developed socialism are ambiguous, because some of the defining features of the new stage appear to prevail more in countries other than the Soviet Union. East Germany, for example, is comparatively more highly industrialized than the USSR, and both the GDR and Czechoslovakia have a generally higher standard of living; even Hungary's standard of living is equal to, or higher than, the USSR's. The student of comparative communism, therefore, finds it difficult to recognize the point of transition to the new stage.

The first question that must be faced when examining the implications of developed socialism for Eastern Europe is, what exactly does the concept mean? More specifically, if the USSR has already entered this new stage of history and its smaller allies have not, then what are the critical characteristics of the Soviet model that define developed socialism as a reality, and in what respects does that reality differ from the situation in other socialist countries such as Czechoslovakia and Hungary?

The theory foretells an increasingly stronger economy and a higher standard of living, continued progress in the elimination of class distinctions, more advanced forms of management and administration, and an ever-broadening base of popular participation in the governing of society. These features serve to define the evolving reality of developed socialism, however loosely, but they are open to different interpretation in their concrete realization. Obviously, there are policy implications for the communist regimes, so a second question becomes pertinent: does the concept of developed socialism translate into any clear guidelines for the policy makers in Prague, Budapest, and elsewhere as they seek to move their societies farther along the path of socialism?

The validity of major communist doctrines can be demonstrated only in a comparative context. For our purposes, the usefulness of Brezhnev's theory as an analytical concept depends on its capacity to enlighten us about the future of those societies that are supposedly less advanced than the Soviet Union. If developed socialism has a real meaning, then we should be able to project a roughly similar future for Czechoslovakia and Hungary. The evidence to be presented in this chapter suggests numerous ambiguities in the two countries' evolving realities and, at least in the opinion of this author, raises doubts about the degree to which developed socialism as a concept enlightens Czechoslovak and Hungarian domestic policies.

DEVELOPMENTAL INDICATORS

Let us first assume that developed socialism offers us a description of society in a particular stage of passage. What does the doctrine tell us about developmental patterns, and can we deduce from it any empirical benchmarks against which a given society's progress can be measured? More concretely, what is it about the Soviet Union, already a developed socialist society, that distinguishes it from Czechoslovakia and Hungary, two socialist countries that have not yet entered the new, higher stage?

First and foremost among the variables determining the nature of developed socialism is a cluster of economic factors. According to the Soviet definition, a society has reached the stage of developed socialism when its productive forces have matured to a high degree and its standard of labor productivity is generally high; when production relations are characterized, in the words of a Soviet theorist, by a predominance of "large state or cooperative enterprises with an up-to-date technico-scientific foundation"; when management methods are highly refined and maximally effective; and when the economy is sufficiently balanced to provide not only a continuous pattern of growth and a secure military defense, but also a comfortable standard of living for every citizen.[2]

Closely linked to these economic factors are conditions in the social fabric. A rising standard of living is not to be taken as a goal in itself; one finds in the theorists' discussions many warnings to the effect that Western-style consumerism must be avoided, along with its urge to individual materialism, status consciousness, and wastefulness. Care must be taken to provide a just distribution of material goods in the interest of a well-rounded social welfare.[3] Along with this, further progress is foreseen toward the elimination of class distinctions, as well as the removal of inequalities arising from nationality. Ending these distortions in society will allow individuals to become fully integrated and socially conscious, as well as to develop their spiritual qualities and creative potential to the fullest.[4]

In the political superstructure, developed socialism implies efforts to perfect the institutions of socialist democracy and draw all workers into a participatory role. Especially important is an increased level of participation in the decision-making processes of the workplace, but some attention is also given to political institutions, especially on the local level. In countries of mixed ethnic composition, effective institutions are to be developed for affording cultural equality while at the same time serving to draw all citizens together in a spirit of unity that transcends nationalism.

In their effort to spell out the characteristics of developed socialism, the theorists have left many details vague. The Soviet Union has already crossed the threshold into the new stage, but it is not clear how to recognize the threshold when it is being crossed. The theorists seem to believe that quantitative indices of economic and social development are unreliable markers in themselves, and what really counts is an inadequately described qualitative condition that serves to manifest an easily recognizable social maturity. Like speaking prose, one can recognize the condition only after having arrived there.

Economic Benchmarks

The importance of qualitative conditions notwithstanding, the theory implies that certain quantitative indices might be useful as benchmarks of maturing socialist societies.[5] The theorists agree unanimously that the first criterion of developed socialism is an advanced economy capable of supporting a high and ever-improving standard of living. In this instance, however, the criterion would not appear to be very meaningful, for the Soviet Union holds no clearcut lead over Czechoslovakia and Hungary.

The Gross National Product (GNP) per capita immediately comes to mind as a possible measure of comparative development. The USSR appears to have surpassed Czechoslovakia in per capita GNP during the 1970s, but Czechoslovakia was in the lead at the time the Soviet Union reportedly entered the stage of developed socialism. Hungary, the least industrialized of the three countries, has narrowed the gap slightly vis à vis Czechoslovakia but is not catching up with the USSR. (See Table 3.1.)

TABLE 3.1
Per Capita Gross National Product, 1960-1979

	1960	1965	1970	1975	1979
USSR	$2,748	$3,350	$4,072	$4,821	$5,219
Index (USSR=100)	100	100	100	100	100
Czechoslovakia	$3,336	$3,582	$4,175	$4,764	$5,039
Index (USSR=100)	121	107	103	99	97
Hungary	$1,990	$2,324	$2,670	$3,076	$3,336
Index (USSR=100)	72	69	66	64	64

Source: Author's calculations based on CIA estimates of total GNP, from U.S. Central Intelligence Agency, Handbook of Economic Statistics, 1980 (Washington, D.C.). The estimates of GNP are based on average purchasing price or estimated prices of goods and services, in constant (1979) U.S. dollars.

Despite GNP statistics that favor the Soviet Union, both the Czechoslovak and the Hungarian economies afford their workers a more comfortable standard of living than that enjoyed by Soviet workers. Official data show that Czechoslovakia leads in private ownership of most durable consumer goods generally associated with the material standard of living -- including television sets and refrigerators -- and would appear to lead in private automobiles as well, although lack of comparable Soviet data in this case makes judgment speculative. Statistics on food consumption show that the average Soviet diet, comparatively speaking, falls short of the Czechoslovak and Hungarian standards in that most sensitive culinary category, meat (Table 3.2). Comparable data on housing are not published, but there is no reason to infer from the fragmentary information available that the comparison would be greatly different from that of other consumer goods.

TABLE 3.2
Personal Consumption: Selected Foods and Durable Goods

	USSR	Czechoslovakia	Hungary
(A) Food: Annual Per Capita Consumption (kg.) in 1977			
Meat and Poultry	56.0	81.4	68.9
Vegetables	88.0	75.3	86.0
Fruits	41.0	48.8	78.0
Sugar	42.4	35.6	34.9
(B) Ownership of Durable Goods: Number of Items Per 100 Households in 1978			
Private Automobiles	*	38.0	22.3
Washing Machines	70.0	120.0**	80.4
Refrigerators	78.0	88.0	75.0
Television Sets	82.0	100.0	69.9

* Data not available.
** Datum includes both washing machines and clothes dryers and, therefore, is not comparable.

Sources: Narodnoe Khoziaĭstvo SSSR v 1978 g. (Moscow, 1979); Statistická ročenka ČSSR 1979 (Prague, 1980); Statisztikai évkönyv 1978 (Budapest, 1979).

A Western economist has judged that Soviet per capita consumption as of the early 1970s was substantially lower than that of Czechoslovakia and roughly equal to that of Hungary.[6] By the late seventies Hungarian consumption had forged ahead of the USSR's in most measurable categories. Gains in Hungarian agricultural production plus an ever-increasing volume of Western consumer goods imports have produced a continuing improvement in the Hungarian standard of living. The Soviet Union comes out rather poorly in these comparisons, then, particularly when we recall that the USSR is said to have entered the "developed" phase in the early 1960s.

It can be argued that the Soviets must divert a large proportion of their national resources to the production of military hardware at the expense of the Soviet consumer, while the two smaller allies are spared the massive investment of resources in strategic weapons and delivery systems. Nevertheless, the doctrine holds that the economy of a developed socialist state can provide ample supplies of both guns and butter, and the Soviet performance has thus far fallen short of the mark. We are therefore to understand that neither the overall level of economic development nor the standard of living is in itself a definitive criterion for distinguishing between developed and not-yet-developed socialist societies.

Soviet theorists might argue at this point that the satisfaction of public needs is a more appropriate measure of socialist development than the satisfaction of private material wants. Social consumption, therefore, might be a better key to comparative development than personal consumption. Here again, however, it is hard to argue that the Soviet Union is substantially out in front. Both the Hungarian and the Czechoslovak regimes have provided well for their societies such public facilities as roads, schools, hospitals, and sanitation services, as well as cradle-to-grave welfare programs. For what it is worth, Tables 3.3 and 3.4 display three types of data comparing aspects of social consumption in the three countries: per capita number of medical doctors, hospital beds, and students enrolled in higher education. The USSR does indeed look better according to these statistics, but the data are inconclusive if we allow for a time lag. By 1965, the Soviet Union had supposedly entered the more advanced stage, so the Soviet data from that year should compare favorably with the Czechoslovak and Hungarian data from the late 1970s if the empirical indicators are meaningful. This is not manifestly the case, and we are left with more ambiguity. Reliable benchmarks must be sought elsewhere.

One very significant factor in socialist development is the degree to which the economic basis has been socialized. Soviet theorists argue that developed socialism is characterized by the completion of the transition to socialist ownership, something that has been accomplished in the Soviet Union.[7] Here is an area where the Soviets can be said to have outdistanced Hungary, but not Czechoslovakia.

Capitalism, that is, the private ownership of industry, has of course been abolished in Hungary and Czechoslovakia. However, the two countries' progress toward the ideal of total socialist ownership varies. In Czechoslovakia, only 0.3 percent of the population are engaged in (nonagricultural) independent professions and private crafts, and slightly over two percent in private farming; the latter group is made up entirely of small landholders in the mountains of Slovakia, where the practicality of organizing collectives is dubious but where a semivoluntary collective movement is being cautiously pursued.[8] In contrast, approximately five percent of Hungary's work force, producing about two percent of the national income, comprises the private sector (agricultural and nonagricultural).[9] Interestingly, while further agricultural cooperativism is being promoted gradually on a voluntary basis, the opposite is being followed -- cautiously, to be sure -- with respect to private, nonagricultural enterprises. The Hungarian leadership has made a virtue of the country's growing private sector, arguing that it is needed to produce certain goods and services that state-owned and cooperative enterprises cannot or do not produce as efficiently, and, within the limits of the legal restrictions, the state encourages the functioning of small producers, private shopkeepers, and craftsmen. (Hungarians themselves sometimes refer to these people, not disparagingly, as the "new bourgeoisie.")

TABLE 3.3
Health Care: Medical Doctors and Hospital Facilities

	USSR	Czechoslovakia	Hungary
(A) Number of Practicing Medical Doctors (in all specializations) Per 10,000 Inhabitants in			
1965	23.9	20.5	19.2
1970	27.4	23.1	22.7
1978	35.4	30.2	27.3
(B) Number of Hospital Beds Per 1,000 Inhabitants in			
1965	9.6	7.9	7.7
1970	10.9	8.0	8.2
1977	12.2	7.7	8.7

Sources: Same as for Table 3.2 (various years). Author has calculated Hungarian data in part B from total number of hospital beds.

TABLE 3.4
Enrollments in Institutions of Higher Education, 1978-79

	USSR	Czechoslovakia	Hungary
Total Number of Students	5,109,800	183,632	105,926
Number of Students Per 10,000 Citizens	194.7	121.0	99.4

Sources: Same as for Table 3.2.

Social Differentiation

In theory, the social structure of developed socialism is not yet classless, although it is, like that of the earlier socialist phase, devoid of exploiting classes. Soviet society today has two classes, the proletariat and the peasantry. The former is acknowledged to contain two strata, intellectual (or, roughly, white-collar) workers and manual laborers. According to the theory, the two classes will merge as society approaches communism, but because that threshold is still a long time in the future, the two classes have not yet become one, and significant distinctions continue to exist between the two strata of the proletariat as well.

There appears to be some disagreement among Soviet sociologists and theoreticians about the degree of social differentiation that still exists, as well as the question of whether society is becoming more or less differentiated in the current phase. Ideology generally predicts a gradual breaking down of social differentiation as all groups undergo a developmental process that emphasizes and strengthens their common features.[10] On the other hand, there is plenty of evidence that interstrata differentiation is increasing rather than decreasing, particularly as the complex tasks of the modern economy require many types and degrees of specialized training. Soviet policy makers are torn between their desire to promote social equality and the temptation to maximize efficiency by rewarding the highly skilled for their expertise. In educational policy, attempts to democratize access to higher learning have had mixed results, and the educated elites tend to pass their social status on to their own children.[11]

The question of social differentiation and stratification is a very murky and ideologically troublesome one for communists. The more pragmatic Hungarians admit that their country is "socially heterogeneous," and while the party officialdom most often projects the Soviet picture of a three-tiered stratification, unofficial versions popular among sociologists describe as many as five distinct strata.[12] A similar, although apparently more rigid, dichotomy of views exists in Czechoslovakia. The official view divides society into mental workers, manual workers, and what is now called the class of collective farmers (rather than "peasantry"). Unofficially, a few scholars have argued that the proletariat alone contains as many as five strata and that the intelligentsia can be broken down into even more numerous substrata.[13]

Despite official views, the best evidence from each country suggests that social stratification is by no means diminishing and may in fact be growing more rigid. Citizens tend to be very conscious of status and prestige, and they are well aware of differences in economic and political privilege. Moreover, the regimes may one day find themselves openly faced with a question that raises an ideologically explosive issue: is it even possible for an advanced society to strive for social equality when the demands of the technological world seem ineluctably to erect barriers of educational achievement, specialization, and therefore differing world views between the social groups? In Czechoslovakia, the primacy of political objectives since 1969 has favored the children of the proletariat in education and professional advancement, but the economy has suffered. In Hungary, an uneasy balance between political and economic objectives in the regime's policies has seemingly produced substantial, though not unmixed, economic advancement; the Kádár approach has been to overlook inequalities in order to encourage productivity -- even to the point of allowing many cases of individual enrichment.[14]

Thus the economic goal of a bountiful and well-balanced production system developed by means of the most advanced modern technology might be incompatible with the political objective of greater social equality. In any event, it is hard to measure social equalization comparatively for the three countries in question, and therefore it would appear fruitless to judge the progress of Czechoslovakia and Hungary toward developed socialism by measuring their social equality against that of the Soviet Union.

A special problem of social integration and equalization is presented by differences among nationalities. This is a matter of great sensitivity to the Soviets, who rarely approach the subject with complete candor. Nearly a decade ago, Brezhnev confidently proclaimed that the national question in the USSR "has been resolved completely, definitively, and irrevocably."[15] On the other hand there have been growing reports in recent years of nationalist unrest in the Baltic republics, the Ukraine, and Georgia, and among the Muslims of Soviet Central Asia, who, it is said, have not been unaffected by the Islamic rebellions in Iran and Afghanistan. Western analysts differ on the significance of nationalism within the Soviet Union, as well as the degree to which the Soviet nationalities are or are not being assimilated.[16] It is well known, however, that levels of economic development, standards of living, and education vary substantially from republic to republic, and these variations tend to reinforce cultural differentiation among the nationalities.

The nationality question is of no significance to the integration of the Hungarian state. There are lingering resentments over the territories lost in 1919 with their large numbers of Hungarian co-nationals, but within the current boundaries the existing ethnic minorities are small, amounting to less than 6 percent of the total population.

Czechoslovakia, of course, is an entirely different story. With a legacy of conflicts among Czechs, Germans, Slovaks, and Hungarians, Czechoslovakia has always had to grapple with a complicated and persistently vexing nationality problem. The expulsion of Germans from Czechoslovakia after 1945 eradicated one source of the problem, but the other aspects did not go away. Federalization, enacted in 1968 and put into effect in 1969, has been combined with determined efforts to bring the economy of Slovakia up to the level of the Czech lands. Administrative recentralization during the 1970s diminished the political importance of federalism, but the division of the country into two national republics has had a lasting symbolic importance. Policies of economic equalization have had spectacular success; to be sure, there remain many rural pockets of poverty and backwardness in Slovakia, but gross production statistics show that the republic as a whole has virtually caught up with the Czech republic.[17] Still, there remain difficulties; while many Czechs are reportedly envious of Slovak advances, officials admit lingering tendencies to Slovak nationalism among some segments of the population.[18] Equally troublesome is the question of the Hungarian minority. Efforts are made to involve Hungarians in planning related to language training and cultural development, but yet the Hungarians are not being effectively integrated, and disaffection among them is widespread. The federal system, therefore, has proven to be a less-than-perfect solution to the Czech-Slovak conflict, and no appropriate institutional solution at all has been found for the problem of the Hungarian minority.[19]

Attitudinal Divergences

Another sticky problem in Czechoslovakia's advancement toward developed socialism -- and, perhaps to a lesser degree, Hungary's as well -- is the strength of socialist attitudes among the citizenry. As society moves toward communism, citizens' attitudes should undergo a gradual transition toward the ultimate ideal of the so-called socialist man. Here again the Soviet Union is presumed to hold a substantial lead over the other socialist countries. Soviet spokesmen are willing to admit that "negative phenomena" still exist in this respect, but they are not prepared to believe that any politically significant, large-scale opposition is to be found in their society. As for the dissident groups whose activities are followed closely by the Western press (but whose overall political significance, objectively speaking, is debatable), the Soviets are quick to write them off as exceptional or deviant. According to the official image, major social contradictions have been eradicated, along with the "objective roots" of bourgeois, antisocialist, revisionist, and pluralist ideologies.[20] Certainly, there has been no hard evidence in recent years to suggest the contrary.

This is not so true of Hungary and Czechoslovakia, and both countries' leaders are willing to admit the existence of problems. The conflicts of 1956 and 1968 reflected deep political cleavages, and the scars from those conflicts have not yet disappeared. In Hungary's case, the conflict took place an entire generation ago, and the pain is no longer so acute. The communists' policies in the sixties and seventies have succeeded to a great degree in stabilizing their rule and undercutting the appeal of dissent. Dissident voices are nonetheless still heard from time to time -- as in the celebrated cases in the 1970s of critical Marxists associated with the so-called Budapest School -- but whatever dissent may exist more widely in society is sporadic and restrained. In Czechoslovakia, the memories of 1968 are fresher, and the government's efficacy in overcoming the residual bitterness has been minimal. Charter 77, though itself small and greatly persecuted, is only the most visible manifestation of a disillusionment that, in fact, runs very deeply through society.[21]

Indeed, workers' morale is the most serious problem faced by the current leadership in Prague. Despite their public utterances, the leaders are aware that the events of 1968 were not merely the product of a few counterrevolutionaries, that Charter 77 bespoke the political aspirations of a population much larger than the several hundred who signed it, and that the rising standard of living in the early seventies -- which has since leveled off and gotten caught on periodic shortages -- has not won over the hearts and minds of the workers. To this day, the party chiefs complain that the destabilizing events of 1968-69 set back socialist development substantially.[22] Thus the official explanation of Czechoslovakia's position along the road to developed socialism is that there was some backsliding in the 1960s, and the policies since 1969 have had to make up for lost ground. As for political nonconformists, therefore, the regime considers itself justified in its efforts to suppress them, for these troublemakers have upset the society's historical momentum and disoriented large numbers of citizens. The logical response, in the party's eyes, is to suppress and harass the remaining activists from 1968 and 1977, at the same time allowing (or pressuring) some to emigrate from time to time in the hope that the opposition, thereby atomized, will eventually die. In the meantime, the regime holds society in a vicelike grip, perhaps less brutal than that of the Stalin era but in many respects reminiscent of that period in its impact upon public morale and political behavior patterns.

In contrast to the political tension running through Czechoslovak society, the atmosphere in Hungary is one of controlled tolerance. Kádár's now-famous slogan, "He who is not against us is with us," familiar almost to the point of being a cliché, is nonetheless an appropriate description of the party's attitude toward society. The dissenters who were the object of punitive actions in the late 1970s -- sociologists György Konrád, András Hegedűs, and Iván Szelényi, philosophers Ágnes Heller, Ferenc Fehér, and others of the Budapest School -- evidently crossed the line that separates those the party considers loyal critics from those deemed to be hostile. Far more numerous are those who, according to official interpretations, do not yet fully identify with the communist cause but who nevertheless restrain their criticisms and participate in the building of socialism. It was noted at the Eleventh Party Congress (1975) that "bourgeois and petty-bourgeois views are tenacious", but nobody seems to find this alarming any more; rather, it is simply understood that it takes time to make grand changes in what we in the West call the political culture.[23]

The Hungarian party's attitude toward religion reflects this tolerant approach. Seeing in the churches a continuing source of influence, the party has gone to considerable lengths to support "progressive" churchmen and to work out a fairly compatible church-state relationship. Party spokesmen still believe that Marxism-Leninism will one day triumph over religious creeds, but in the meantime the building of a developed socialist society entails cooperation between party members and churchgoers. Kádár's "pilgrimage" to Rome in 1977 should be seen as a symbolic reflection of a policy that not only the party, but at least some religious leaders as well, consider mutually advantageous.[24]

This live-and-let-live attitude contrasts with the continuing tension between church and state in Czechoslovakia. Despite the partial rapprochement in 1977 that facilitated the elevation of Prague's Bishop František Tomásek to Cardinal, anti-religion campaigns continue and churchgoers in some cases jeopardize their careers if they send their children to religious instruction. By 1981, a number of priests had become victims of a new wave of persecution, aimed at those who dared to protest the state's tough anti-religion policies.[25]

In their toleration of divergent ideological outlooks, Hungary's leaders sometimes appear to be making a virtue out of existing social contradictions that are beyond their control. In the words of György Aczél, an influential member of the Politburo, "Socialist construction is not free of contradictions, but far from undermining socialist society, their exposure and resolution strengthen and develop it."[26] Thus, dialectically, the party should not deny the existence of problems, nor should it dogmatically seek to suppress every citizen whose outlook is not in line with the communist vision. Rather, a patient attitude combined with effective methods of ideological persuasion will yield the proper results in the long run. In the meantime, there is much to be learned by confronting and resolving the contradictions.

Evaluating all these factors as indicators of progress is obviously full of ambiguities. If the Soviet Union is indeed a qualitatively more advanced socialist society than Czechoslovakia or Hungary, it is difficult to judge exactly what it is that makes it so. This leaves us wondering what, precisely, must transpire between now and the time when the two smaller countries will cross the threshold into the new stage themselves. In the meantime, the ambiguity of the defining characteristics leaves the door open for divergent policy lines on many important issues. Perhaps nowhere is this more evident than in the approaches taken by the HSWP and the CPC to the question of socialist democracy.

MANAGEMENT, ADMINISTRATION, AND SOCIALIST DEMOCRACY

Central to the institutional development foreseen in the new historical phase are the twin goals of improving management techniques and "perfecting" socialist democracy. More advanced forms of management and administration, as well as intensified citizen participation in political and administrative functions, dovetail in the Soviet view of developed socialism. In no sense does this imply a lessening of control or any "withering away" of the state; instead, it involves a strengthening of state institutions as well as measures consciously aimed at linking state and society ever more closely together.[27] Judging from the Soviet example, the process is to continue, perhaps indefinitely, as society moves toward communism.

Responding to the promise of the scientific-technological revolution, the Soviet theorists emphasize the need to control the productive environment, utilize the new methods and tools of modern technology to their fullest extent, and thereby harness the creative powers of human society to the optimal benefit of socialist development. The new era requires complex but efficient organizational structures, highly trained management specialists, and, to ensure the consistent coordination of economic and political aims, continued guidance by the party. These goals are often expounded together with the idea that more and more tasks are to devolve to lower administrative levels, increasing the role of workers in some decisions as well. To the extent that the Soviets are explicit about the further improvement of socialist democracy, it is stated in terms of these devolving responsibilities and decision-making areas.

There is an inherent tension between efficient management and control over the productive environment, on the one hand, and the furtherance of socialist democracy, on the other. The tension can be seen quite strikingly in the Czechoslovak and Hungarian approaches to this aspect of developed socialism. In principle, there is no disagreement on the need to "perfect" organs of administration, management, and citizen participation, but the two regimes differ substantially on the relative importance they attach to the participatory question as well as their approach to several aspects of the management-administration question.

Institutional Structure and Socialist Democracy

The regime in Prague has not deviated from the Soviet approach to economic organization, despite a flirtation with the decentralizing, partially market-oriented ideas of Ota Šik during the Novotný-Dubček years. In the seventies there has been no relaxation of central control over economic planning, and neither has there been any question about the primacy of political goals over economic. To this day, technological progress is seriously affected by the removal of many highly skilled persons from scientific and managerial positions in the years 1969-71 for political reasons. In Hungary, on the contrary, the New Economic Mechanism (NEM) adopted in 1968 has since been modified and compromised somewhat, but the system is nevertheless a relatively decentralized one run by a dispersed managerial elite that sometimes finds itself in conflict with the political elite. In Hungary, at least, managers and economists can openly complain when political considerations impinge upon economic rationality.[28]

The Hungarian NEM gave substance to a pragmatism on the part of the Kádár regime that has often reflected an unconcern with the rigors of ideology and a preference for that which works. Yet, the Hungarian approach to developed socialism has its own ideological rationale; ever since the adoption of the NEM, the Hungarians have sought to improve their institutional structures so as to further both economic efficiency and socialist democracy. In fact, the momentum of change in this direction preceded the emergence of the developed socialism theory and has, in a sense, absorbed the latter. Rather than being the practical application of Brezhnev's theory in a Hungarian setting, the reforms of the NEM period and beyond have co-opted the rationale of the new theoretical orthodoxy. The changes flowing out of the NEM, initially reflecting a rather radical departure from the "internationalist" (i.e., Soviet) economic model, now find a convenient justification in the new theory of developed socialism. Ironically, the Hungarians have thus found that the Soviets' new theoretical model could be applied quite nicely to the institutional forms already evolving in Hungary -- forms that were initially greeted with some reservations by the Soviets.

The decentralization of the economic management system has come to be explained as a logical step in bringing the locus of decision-making authority closer to the workers, thereby making it possible to work toward the next logical reform: bringing the workers themselves directly into the decision-making process.[29]

Likewise, a new emphasis has been placed on governmental decentralization, focusing primarily on the enhancement of local councils as the basis of wider political participation. The 1972 constitution granted local councils a wide range of new powers at the expense of higher governmental bodies. Like the economic reforms, these too have come to be described, ex post facto, as another example of Hungarian society's continued evolution toward developed socialism. Multiple-candidate elections in some parliamentary districts are cited as still another example.[30]

Czechoslovakia has resisted changes in any of these directions since the debacle of 1968-69, when one of the central reform issues revolved around questions of socialist democracy and citizens' participation. The party leaders have been very defensive about the institutional system as it is; President Husák has insisted that "Our state, an instrument of the working class and other working people, is genuinely democratic".[31] Lip service is repeatedly given to such vaguely worded goals as "perfecting what may be described as people's state self-administration", "educating and training the masses in the work of management", and so on, but there have been no major institutional reforms since 1969.[32] Rather, when referring to future efforts at increasing socialist democracy, existing structures are reemphasized -- the organs of the National Front (trade unions, youth league, and others), the national committees, and other conventional institutions -- and there are no implications that these organizations will change their style of activity.[33] With respect to democracy on the shop floor, the most important instruments are production conferences, meetings in the factories at which workers are informed about matters of plant policy and given a chance to make suggestions. Explicitly rejected is any return to actively oriented workers' councils on the Yugoslav model or on the model of the councils that sprang into being in Czechoslovakia in 1968.[34] Regarding the structure of economic planning, the Czechs and Slovaks have renounced the decentralizing ideas of Ota Šik and the other reformers of the 1960s and returned to a centrally planned model. Admitting that it will be difficult to "achieve an optimal blend of centralism and democracy," the leaders have nevertheless strongly reaffirmed a high degree of central control, and in language that might suggest an implicit criticism of Hungary's model.[35]

One further difference emerges in the two countries' policies on socialist democracy. This concerns the role of trade unions. There is no indication in any of the Czechoslovak discussions that the trade unions are to be made more representative of their constituencies' interests than they have been traditionally. From Hungarian sources, in contrast, one finds a lively debate about the trade unions and their possible future evolution. Sándor Gaspar, the General Secretary of the All-Hungary Council of Trade Unions, argued in 1978 that the trade unions have a dual role entailing obligations to the state, on the one hand, and to the workers, on the other. Implicit in the argument is the suggestion that the two interests may very well be in conflict at times. Elaborating on this implication, Gaspar argued that one function of the trade unions is "defending the interests of the working class and other categories of the working people" by striving for justice, opposing arbitrary actions, eliminating excessive red tape, and pushing for a more direct role in enterprise decisions concerning profit sharing, investments, and other matters.[36]

Already in the 1970s, Hungarian trade unions had begun to exercise this function cautiously but with some effect on policy, both at the plant level and in the national parliament.[37] It remains to be seen to what degree the unions will become truly democratic representatives of their large constituencies, but the subject continues to be discussed in the 1980s. In response to the formation of an independent labor union in Poland, Hungarian authorities began to consider ways of making their official unions more autonomous from other economic and political institutions.[38] Still more interestingly, the Hungarian trade unions sent an official letter to Solidarity, the Polish independent union, during the latter's congress in October 1981 responding to Solidarity's invitation (addressed to all the official trade unions of the Warsaw Pact countries) to dialogue. Gaspar himself declined to enter into open talks with Solidarity, noting official Hungarian misgivings about the increasing politicization of the Polish union, but appeared to leave the door open for further contacts.[39] It is perhaps too much to speculate that this indicates the Hungarians' eagerness to learn from Solidarity's example, but the cautious and measured Hungarian response to the situation in Poland certainly contrasts with that of the other bloc regimes (especially Prague, whose response has bordered on hysteria).

Democracy versus Control

Official Hungarian statements on the subject of socialist democracy have a ring of seriousness to them that may not be fully born out in practice but sound more persuasive than Czechoslovak statements. Since 1968, Czechoslovakia's rulers are aware that the question of democracy is terribly sensitive in their society, and the last time the question was raised in a substantial way, the results were not something today's leadership would care to repeat. Any real efforts to bring the workers into a meaningful decision-making role would expose the underlying political tensions in society and destabilize the party's rule. In Hungary, on the contrary, some officials -- those associated with the more "liberal" wing of the HSWP -- believe that there are no political tensions in their society severe enough to justify the indefinite postponement of democratizing measures.[40] The Hungarian leadership is rather divided on the issue, however; Kádár himself has taken a cautious approach to the broadening of political participation, setting the tone for a controlled transition to a more democratic system.

The different official attitudes highlight the continuing instability of the regime's authority in Czechoslovakia, as compared to the relative self-confidence of the Kádár regime, and draw our attention to a problem facing every communist government: how can the regime realize its oft-proclaimed objective of truly integrating the workers into the decision-making apparatus while at the same time ensuring that the correct decisions will be made? That is, how can the political system become truly democratic while still guaranteeing that the party will continue to guide, if not control, the governing of society?

IMPLICATIONS

In strictly theoretical terms, one finds no apparent disagreement in either Prague or Budapest with the Soviets' general conception of developed socialism. Both the Czechoslovak and the Hungarian leaderships have accepted Brezhnev's theoretical innovation and incorporated it into their party lines. Both regimes are eager to solidify their societies' socialist basis, develop their economies further and in a more well-rounded fashion, and strive for further progress toward the universal evolution of socialist man by continually improving the worker's material and spiritual environment.

Beyond this general consensus, there are some notable differences in the Czechoslovak and Hungarian interpretations of the specific policy implications. In embracing the idea of developed socialism, Czechoslovakia's leaders have fallen completely into line behind the Soviet leadership, associating the building of developed socialism with a centralized economic command structure and attempts to silence dissenters. The Hungarians, on the contrary, find in the theory of developed socialism a justification for just the opposite -- economic decentralization and a moderate tolerance of ideological deviation within certain boundaries. Both profess their intention to perfect or improve upon the institutions of socialist democracy, but only the Hungarians have made any moves toward meaningful changes in practice.

The Czechoslovak regime's position on socialist democracy happens to be thoroughly consistent with that of the CPSU, but it is in fact dictated every bit as much by the regime's weakness _vis à vis_ its subjects as by its sense of being in tune with the imperatives of the scientific-technological revolution. The Prague regime cannot afford to relax its grip for one minute lest it risk another 1968, and, therefore, "socialist democracy" must remain only an empty slogan. Hungary's rather more serious approach to socialist democracy, in contrast, derives from the Kádár regime's basic stability -- perhaps an "uneasy stability," in the words of George Schöpflin, but a palpable stability.[41] In contrast to the defensiveness evident in Prague, the view in Budapest is confident and forward-looking, tempered, of course, by the party's insistence on maintaining its unchallenged political leadership. One should not idealize the Hungarian regime's interpretation of socialist democracy, for it is a vision of a "democracy" qualified by firm party control; but neither should one overlook the subtle distinctions between the Kádár approach and the Brezhnev-Husák formula.[42]

Given the novel Hungarian blend of control and tolerance, economic planning and decentralized management, one might raise the question of a distinct Hungarian "model" of developed socialism. The Hungarians themselves would offer a curious answer: while denying that their policies constitute a specific model, they are quick to add that Hungary's particular national conditions call for policies that specifically speak to those conditions. In accordance with the standard Soviet-bloc doctrine, they reject "the theories of different 'models' of socialism, 'different' Marxisms, 'pluralist' Marxism, etc., at one time current in Hungary too."[43] In Kádár's carefully chosen words, the Hungarian party must "take account both of our specific national conditions and of the common international regularities of building socialism." Lest there be any doubt about what that means, he adds:

> Drawing on the experience of others is not the same as mechanical copying and does not impair a party's independence. For each party is responsible for what experience it draws on and how it uses it. Our own party makes it a point of applying the commonly valid doctrine of Marxism-Leninism with full account to Hungary's historical, political, economic, and other peculiarities...[44]

The cases of Czechoslovakia and Hungary suggest that the guiding ideology retains the relative malleability it has always had. Soviet theorists have argued that national peculiarities will fade away during the period of developed socialism,[45] but the contrasting policy approaches in Prague and Budapest -- not to mention Belgrade and Warsaw -- suggest that developed socialism might look and feel quite different from one country to another. In both the Hungarian and Czechoslovak cases, the theory has been interpreted to fit prevailing policies. In the one instance, those policies are nearly identical to the Soviets'; in the other, they are very different. One must wonder, therefore, exactly what Brezhnev's theoretical innovation really means for policy makers in Eastern Europe. One is tempted to conclude that it is little more than a rationalization of prevailing policies.

There is perhaps one further element in the question, and this brings us back to the point with which this chapter began. The concept of developed socialism has become firmly established in the ideological orthodoxy of the Soviet bloc. The legitimacy of the bloc regimes is in large part derived from their adherence to the norms of this ideological orthodoxy, and their adherence to the orthodoxy entails (in part) the use of an officially sanctioned vocabulary. By couching their current policy discussions in terms of striving to create developed socialism, the Czechoslovak and Hungarian regimes enhance their legitimacy in the eyes of Moscow -- an "external" legitimacy imposed by geopolitical reality. The Hungarians have found the concept sufficiently malleable to fit their particular brand of reformism despite the moderately divergent nuances of their policies. In turn, their reformist policies, carefully aimed at defusing any impulses within Hungarian society toward rebellion or serious opposition, help to establish the regime's legitimacy at home. The Hungarian regime thus rests on a reasonably well-balanced combination of external and internal legitimacy. One should not be tempted to predict the longevity of this balance in an era of volatile economic trends, nor should one forget that the prime architect of the current system, First Secretary Kádár, is an old man with no heir apparent. On the other hand, one should not underestimate the capacity of the system to perpetuate and renew itself, assuming that pragmatism continues to hold strong among the party elite.

As for Prague, the regime has ironically "liberated" itself from concern about its legitimacy in the eyes of Czechoslovak workers. The legitimacy of the current Czechoslovak regime is a matter only for the well-purged party elite and its friends in Moscow. To be sure, the regime wishes to minimize discontent among the workers through sound economic policies and material incentives, but minimizing discontent has in effect replaced the goal of positive legitimation for at least the time being. Meanwhile, the leadership can feel secure of its position, legitimized by Soviet power. It is likely that the current leaders themselves agree fully with the standard Soviet interpretation of developed socialism, but their position is naturally fortified by their reliance on Soviet force to keep them in power.

As a final point, it must be mentioned that harsh economic realities looming in the 1980s could have a devastating effect on both countries as they attempt to move toward developed socialism. By the end of the 1970s it had become apparent that the economic progress of the preceding decade was seriously threatened by the world energy crisis and by the prospect of dwindling raw materials in the Soviet bloc. Moving into the 1980s, Hungary and Czechoslovakia both faced serious inflationary pressures overall, spiraling increases in the cost of energy, and occasional shortages of fuel. Foreign trade deficits mounted in the late 1970s; Hungary seemed to have brought this problem under control by 1980, but Czechoslovakia continued to run deficits in its accounts. Both governments found it necessary to pass their economic problems on to consumers in the form of higher prices, thereby endangering the goal of an ever-improving standard of living.

This could have serious implications for the future. In Hungary, rising consumer expectations have contributed to the stability of the party's rule; if the economy fails to satisfy these expectations, it is possible that the party will lose public support and find it impracticable to achieve any meaningful democratization.[46] In autumn 1981, the regime began to plan new reforms in industrial management, showed an interest in joining the International Monetary Fund, and let it be known that it hoped to achieve full convertibility of the forint.[47] These were not radical steps, perhaps, but they underscored an official determination to stabilize an economic situation that was displaying some unmistakable signs of weakness.

In Czechoslovakia, where the leadership has preferred to define developed socialism in purely economic terms, the impact of a protracted economic crisis could be even more portentous, perhaps leading to strikes and other forms of confrontation between the workers and the regime.[48] With the Polish example just across the border, Czechoslovakia's leaders have had reason to be nervous as they have struggled to adjust the policies of the seventh five-year plan (1981-85) to counter the hard times ahead. However, they unveiled no new approaches at the Sixteenth Party Congress (April 6-10, 1981), preferring to stress continuity in their policies along with the virtue of hard work.[49]

In either case, the outlook in the early 1980s was hardly one of inevitable prosperity. As in other countries of Eastern Europe, the vision of a developed socialism characterized by an inherent stability threatened to become an illusion. If developed socialism is defined by the least common denominator among the numerous formulas extant, it refers to a highly advanced socialist society capable of managing its own evolution. Czechoslovakia and Hungary may be further away from the threshold than their leaders would like to admit, for they face an immediate future that is filled with uncertainties.

NOTES

1. I.V. Dudinskiĭ, "Kommunisticheskie i rabochie partii ob ekonomicheskikh problemach razvitovo sotsializma," Voprosy istorii, no. 10 (1971), pp. 3-22; Konstantin Katushev, "Tendency and Objective Necessity for Closer Unity of Socialist Countries," World Marxist Review 16, no. 8 (August 1973), pp. 3-14. (Hereafter, this journal will be referred to as WMR.)

2. Pyotr Demichev, "Developed Socialism - Stage on the Way to Communism," WMR 16, no. 1 (January 1973), p. 11. For a concise list of indices proposed for defining the nature of developed socialism, see the comments of the Polish theorist Stanisław Widerszpil in an international symposium on "Characteristics of Developed Socialism," WMR 18, no. 1 (January 1975), p. 86.

3. See, e.g., the comments of Květoslav Roubal and György Borsányi in "Economics and Politics under Developed Socialism: Theoretical Conference," WMR 20, no. 3 (March 1977), pp. 64, 66-67.

4. Widerszpil, ibid.

5. I have eschewed the term "developing" in preference for "maturing" in this context, because the word "developing" connotes an association with Third-World countries and, in the opinions of most Soviet-bloc theorists, is inappropriate when used with reference to Eastern Europe. Romanian theorists, it should be noted, disagree with this general proposition and do not hesitate to apply the term "developing" to their own society. (See, e.g., the discussion in WMR 18, no. 1 (January 1975), especially the exchange between the Romanian participant (B. Zaharescu) and his comrades from Bulgaria, Hungary, and the Soviet Union.)

6. Gertrude Schroeder, "Consumer Problems and Prospects," Problems of Communism 22, no. 2 (March-April 1973), p. 11.

7. Richard Kosolapov, "The Approach to the Study of Developed Socialism," WMR 17, no. 9 (September 1974), pp. 63-67.

8. Otto Ulč, Politics in Czechoslovakia (San Francisco: W.H. Freeman, 1974), p. 47; also "The Czechoslovak Economy: Achievements, Problems, Prospects (Roundtable Discussion)," WMR 16, no. 8 (August 1973), p. 66.

9. György Aczél, "On the Approaches to Developed Socialism," WMR 19, no. 3 (March 1976), p. 14.

10. Alfred B. Evans, Jr., "Developed Socialism in Soviet Ideology," Soviet Studies 29, no. 3 (July 1977), pp. 419-21.

11. T. Anthony Jones, "Modernization and Education in the U.S.S.R.," Social Forces 5, no. 2 (December 1978), pp. 522-46.

12. Ivan Volgyes, "Modernization, Stratification and Elite Development in Hungary," Social Forces 57, no. 2 (December 1978), pp. 500-21; cf. Mária Markus and András Hegedüs, "The Role of Values in the Long-Range Planning of Distribution and Consumption," in Hegedüs et al., The Humanisation of Socialism; Writings of the Budapest School (London: Allison and Busby, 1976), p. 147ff. For the characterization of Hungary as "socially heterogeneous," see the remarks of the Imre Pozgay in WMR 16, no. 6 (June, 1973), p. 27 and, especially, József Bálint, "Effectiveness, Planning, Growth," ibid., p. 21.

13. Otto Ulč, "Some Aspects of Czechoslovak Society since 1968," Social Forces 57, no. 2 (December 1978), p. 425, citing a 1975 study by František Charvat. Czechoslovak society was pictured as being even more complex by the most far-reaching sociological study of Czechoslovakia undertaken in the post-1945 era, that of Pavel Machonin et al., Československá spoločnosť (Bratislava: Epocha, 1969). The Machonin approach has been rejected by the post-1969 leadership as ideologically unacceptable. For analysis and commentary, see Ulč, Politics in Czechoslovakia, p. 53; David W. Paul, The Cultural Limits of Revolutionary Politics; Change and Continuity in Socialist Czechoslovakia (Boulder, Colo. and New York: East European Quarterly and Columbia University Press, 1979), pp. 159-71; and Ernest Gellner, "The Pluralist Anti-Levellers of Prague," Government and Opposition 7, no. 1 (Winter 1972), pp. 20-37.

14. Volgyes, op. cit., pp. 505-06ff.

15. From a speech of December 1972, cited by Evans, op. cit., p. 421.

16. For example, Ellen Jones and Fred W. Grupp have argued that non-Russians are being effectively assimilated into the economic and political life of the USSR, but they are not being assimilated socially and culturally. (Jones and Grupp, "Dimensions of Ethnic Assimilation in the Soviet Union," paper presented at the Eleventh National Convention of the American Association for the Advancement of Slavic Studies, New Haven, Connecticut: October 1979.) For a dissenting argument, see Teresa Rakowska-Harmstone, "Ethnicity and Change in the Soviet Union," in Rakowska-Harmstone, ed., Perspectives for Change in Communist Societies (Boulder, Colo: Westview Press, 1979), pp. 167-88.

17. Official statistics show a steady increase in Slovakia's contribution to Czechoslovakia's total national income, social product, and industrial production. For a summary, see "The Czechoslovak Economy: Achievements, Problems, Prospects (Roundtable Discussion)," WMR 16, no. 8 (August 1973), pp. 57-79; also Jozef Lenárt, "The Economy and Democracy," WMR 21, no. 7 (July 1978) p. 8ff.

18. See, e.g., Ľudovít Pezlár's comment in WMR 16, no. 8 August 1973), p. 68.

19. Even the officially-sponsored organization for the Hungarian minority, Csemadok, sought to go its own way in 1968 and demanded that the status of the Hungarians in Czechoslovakia be

seriously reexamined. See H. Gordon Skilling, *Czechoslovakia's Interrupted Revolution* (Princeton University Press, 1976), pp. 606-609.

20. Demichev, *op. cit.*, p. 20.

21. See H. Gordon Skilling, *Charter 77 and Human Rights* (London: Allen and Unwin, 1981).

22. See, e.g., the comment of Oldřich Švestka in the proceedings of an international theoretical conference on "The Present-Day Problems of Socialist Democracy and Its Perspective," *WMR* 18, no. 2 (February 1975), p. 78. During the weeks leading up to the tenth anniversary of the Soviet-led intervention, the regime went to great lengths to discredit the 1968 reformers, linking them to American subversive activities. The New York Times News Service surveyed the propaganda barrage in a dispatch by David Andelman (August 15, 1978). For a direct example, see "Reakční úloha revizionismu ve světle zkušeností KSČ," *Rudé Právo*, August 19, 1978.

23. Miklós Óvári, "New Stage in Building Developed Socialism," *WMR* 18, no. 8 (August 1975), p. 27.

24. János Kádár, "Some Lessons of Socialist Construction in Hungary," *WMR* 20, no. 1 (January 1977), p. 11. Kádár reiterated his party's satisfaction with church-state relations in his address to the Twelfth Party Congress in March 1980. For a statement by a Roman Catholic clergyman sympathetic to the regime, see Msgr. József Cserháti, "Open Gates," *The New Hungarian Quarterly* 18, no. 67 (Autumn 1977), pp. 48-62.

25. For discussions of the contrasting Czechoslovak and Hungarian policies toward religion, see Radio Free Europe Research, Situation Reports: Hungary/31 (September 1, 1976) and Czechoslovakia/41 (November 23, 1977). On the 1981 events, see *Czechoslovak Newsletter* 6, no. 9 (September 1981), published by the Council of Free Czechoslovakia, New York, pp. 5-6; also *The New York Times*, September 21, 1981, p. 5.

26. Aczél, *op. cit.*, p. 16.

27. Evans, *op. cit.*, pp. 421-23. The task of bringing citizens into a more participatory role corresponds to what Kenneth Jowitt has described as "inclusion." See Jowitt, "Inclusion and Mobilization in European Leninist Regimes," in Jan F. Triska and Paul Cocks, ed., *Political Development in Eastern Europe* (New York and London: Praeger, 1977), pp. 93-118.

28. The prominent economist György Varga, for example, has openly chided managers for pandering to state administrators rather than making decisions on the basis of economic considerations. (Reported in Radio Free Europe Research, Situation Report: Hungary/31 (December 13, 1978), p. 5.

29. Pozgay, *op. cit.*, p. 29; Béla Biszku, "Promoting Socialist Statehood and Democracy," *WMR* 16, no. 10 (October 1973), pp. 14-17.

30. Biszku, *ibid.*, p. 15; also Pál Romany, in "The Present-Day Problems of Socialist Democracy," pp. 80-81; and Dezső Nemes, "The Socialist Political System in Hungary," *WMR* 21, no. 11 (November 1978), pp. 22-23. Cf. Peter A. Toma and Ivan Volgyes, *Politics in Hungary* (San Francisco: W.H. Freeman, 1976), pp. 52, 70. It is interesting to note that the number of multiple-candidate

districts was reduced in the 1975 elections from that of 1970, the year they were first introduced.

31. Gustáv Husák, "Confidently and Creatively along the Leninist Road," WMR, 19, no. 6 (June 1976), p. 11. (Emphasis added.)

32. Lenárt, op. cit., p. 9, 12.

33. Ibid., pp. 9-10.

34. Lenárt, ibid., p. 13; K. Roubal, in "The Czechoslovak Economy; Achievements...," p. 79. Cf. Ulč, Politics in Czechoslovakia, pp. 81-84.

35. Lenárt, pp. 13-14. In 1975 a conservative reform of the economic system was put into effect, creating a middle tier of managers between the central planners at the top and the plant directors. The new structure is similar in concept to that first adopted in the German Democratic Republic, as the managers of the so-called production-economic units have wide-ranging responsibilities but are still subordinate to the central planners.

36. Sándor Gaspar, "Builders of Developed Socialism," WMR 21, no. 1 (January 1978), pp. 48-58, cited from p. 49.

37. Ibid., pp. 52-53; Toma and Volgyes, p. 68ff.

38. See the report by Dusko Doder in the Washington Post, September 19, 1980, pp. A1, A24.

39. The Christian Science Monitor, October 5, 1981, p. 2. A dispatch by United Press International, published by the Seattle Post-Intelligencer on October 4, 1981, reported the Hungarian message to have been openly more friendly.

40. See, e.g., Péter Varkonyi in Társadalmi Szemle (April 1977), summarized in Radio Free Europe Research, Situation Reports: Hungary/15 (April 26, 1977). Cf. V. Benke, in Népszabadság, November 28, 1978.

41. George Schöpflin, "Hungary: An Uneasy Stability," in Archie Brown and Jack Gray, eds., Political Culture and Political Change in Communist States (London: Macmillan and New York: Holmes and Meier, 1977), pp. 131-58. Recent reports of opposition within Hungary confirm that the regime's critics are not yet an organized political threat, but their activities have increased since the emergence of Solidarity in Poland. For one report, see The Wall Street Journal, December 16, 1980, pp. 1,20.

42. The Hungarian approach would seem to constitute a conservative argument for the more literal interpretation of socialist democracy, based on the premise that a stable government enjoying the placid acceptance of the masses can afford to open its decision-making processes to a broader public participation. The Polish reformers, discussed in Maurice Simon's chapter elsewhere in this book, would seem to be taking the opposite tack, arguing that the very instability of the Polish political system requires a broadening of the support base and a move toward the inclusion of more diverse social elements in the decision-making processes.

43. Aczél, op. cit., p. 16.

44. Kádár, op. cit., pp. 6-7.

45. See, e.g., Katushev, op. cit., pp. 7-8.

46. Kádár's carefully worded remarks at the Twelfth Party Congress were aimed at bracing the population for hard times ahead. Although he stressed the regime's intention to maintain the standard

of living, he warned that further price increases were likely and wages would be increasingly dependent on productivity levels (Népszabadság, March 25, 1980, pp. 5-7 and March 28, 1980, pp. 4-5). Just as some price increases were about to become effective, however, the Polish strikes occurred. The immediate response in Hungary was to rescind the price increases (The Wall Street Journal, December 16, 1980, pp. 1, 20).

47. A rather optimistic report on Hungary's exports appeared in Business Week, no. 2705 (September 14, 1981), p. 50.

48. Nor is this mere speculation. Strikes reportedly broke out among the miners of Ostrava in 1979 and were violently suppressed by the state militia. It was not surprising that the Czechoslovak leadership reacted to the events in Poland the following year by expressing their horrified condemnation, no doubt fearing that their own workers might also be tempted to test their power against that of the regime.

49. The Sixteenth Congress of the CPC was analyzed in detail in Radio Free Europe, Situation Reports: Czechoslovakia/7 (April 30, 1981).

4
Developing Socialism and Worker-Party Conflict

Daniel N. Nelson

THE CONFLICTUAL IMPLICATIONS OF DEVELOPMENT FOR COMMUNIST SYSTEMS

Ruling communist parties seek socioeconomic "development" through public policies, in part, because their Marxist roots require building and maintaining the "objective conditions of socialism". Development is also at the core of such regimes' policies because their Leninist origins require ever-greater systemic performance by which to legitimize their elitist and hierarchical rule. Political capital is thus heavily invested in the pursuit of development.

The legitimacy of communist party government, defined by both ideological and system-performance criteria, rests on the socioeconomic and political conditions implied by the term "development". Paradoxically, however, the policies by which communist regimes try to achieve or assure development endanger their political control.

Recognition of conflict between policy and polity in communist states is critical to an understanding of such systems' political futures. More precisely, the outcomes of developmental policies include consequences which undermine the Party's control.

The concept "developed socialism" incorporates the incompatability of policy and polity in communist systems. Offered first by the Soviet leadership to denote achievements of CPSU rule, developed socialism implies an advanced stage of socioeconomic and political evolution; it suggests that economic growth, distributive equality and participatory expansion have taken place, bringing the system to a quantitative and qualitative stage above socialism per se. Allegedly, the processes of change leading to developed socialism are orderly and nonconflictual, carefully defined by the Party.

But, as I have argued elsewhere,[1] policies designed to achieve developed socialism have brought conflict as they promoted growth and competition as they distributed resources. Such conflict and competition, furthermore, mean that changes implied by developed socialism are not likely to be held within the boundaries of the political control guarded by the Party.

Evidence of conflictual processes inherent to developed socialism is somewhat more difficult to identify than in relatively more "open" systems. But one arena in which dramatic events, and relatively good data have allowed us to observe conflictual processes within communist states is worker-Party relations. Within the stratum of industrial labor--i.e., the stratum integral to ideological and system-performance criteria for legitimacy--one can see clearly alienation from Party rule on material and political grounds. The profound irony of communist rule is, indeed, that workers have been the most consistent opponents of regimes which allegedly rule in their interest; the presumed beneficiaries of developed socialism have exhibited their disillusionment with policies meant to achieve such an end.

Policies which allocate a disproportionate share of a nation's resources to heavy industry, while both redistributing little wealth to an expanding industrial labor force and maintaining limitations on the channels for participation in workplace governance, have consequences that weaken the bases of Party control. Poland has been, during the past decades, the most clear example of confrontation between workers and Party arising from policies of the PUWP. By 1980-81, Polish workers would no longer accept the political status quo and were willing to engage in conflict to obtain structural change. But the conflictual processes can be documented elsewhere.

In Romania, industrial labor has begun to question Party hegemony, broadly expressing its dissatisfaction via opinions which diverge from accepted PCR (Partidul Comunist Roman) priorities. Some strike action has been undertaken in the Jiu Valley among miners in August 1977, a more limited work stoppage at the "23 August" enterprise in Bucharest during 1980, and October, 1981 violence again in the Jiu Valley. That Romanian industrial labor is at an earlier point in its awareness of self-interest, is less organized, and has fewer potential "allies" (no staunchly independent Church, for instance) cannot be doubted. Precisely because a large industrial labor stratum is new in Romania, and because it lacks skills, education, trade union history and material expectations that one finds in Polish labor, the Romanian case is an important arena in which to examine the genesis of worker-Party conflict. As the PCR persists in its policy goals of <u>dezvoltare multilateral</u> (multilateral development), will the growing stratum of industrial labor, required to be increasingly productive in an environment of residual socioeconomic inequalities and political constraints, be a source of political instability as in Poland? To what extent may we expect the PCR to come into conflict with its own policies via confrontations with workers?

A "DEVELOPING SOCIALIST STATE"--CONCEPT AND IMPLICATIONS

Romanian leaders and its economic planners argue that their nation is "developing" as opposed to "developed." They utilize these terms, furthermore, in a sense that duplicates their Western usage--i.e., to connote wide-spread systemic changes like industrialization, urbanization, growth in literacy, mechanization of agriculture, etc. One member of the Romanian Academy of Social and Political Science writes, for instance, that

> Romania still shows a great discrepancy when compared to the economically developed countries, as regards the level of the national income, the per capita output of some main products, her economic pattern, the level of labor productivity, of foreign trade, etc. When compared to other countries, the Romanian economy shows features typical of the developing countries. In 1970, the gross national product per head of population was within the limits registered in certain developing countries which are acknowledged to belong to this category, for it amounted to about 50 percent of the working population is employed in agriculture and the per capita yield...is approximately half the figure obtained in the developed countries.[2]

Party leader Ceausescu emphasizes the need for development and modernization at every opportunity as well. Achieving the social equality of a Marxist-Leninist state presupposes, Ceausescu has argued, the "impetuous development of the forces of production" and the Party's complete attention to industrialization and agriculture modernization to create a strong economic base.[3]

Covertly since the late 1950s when the first of several five-year plans was revealed that emphasized heavy industrialization, the Romanian regime has been engaged in an intensive effort to push, at breakneck speed, what was later denoted by Party General Secretary Nicolae Ceausescu as "multilateral development." April, 1964, marked the Romanian Communist Party's declaration of independence[4] (as it has subsequently been called) from CMEA and, thereby, Soviet plans for Romania's future, which had called for an agricultural and natural resource orientation for Romania's economy in a planned-for division of labor among socialist countries. Foreign policy deviation from Warsaw Pact norms during the 1960s and 1970s envinced the continued intention of Romania's leaders to pursue their autarkic economic goals coupled with a re-emergent nationalism.

Ceausescu's pronouncements on the subject of "development" now occupy volumes of published works under the general title of Romania on the Way of Building up the Multilaterally Developed Socialist Society.[5]

The concept of "multilateral development" was first employed in the late 1960s by Ceausescu, and was made an integral part of the Party's program at the Tenth Congress in August of 1969. Thereafter, the term was used with ever-increasing frequency. A decade later, "multilateral development" was intoned to subsume virtually all socioeconomic and political changes desired by the Party leadership, from specific tasks such as quality control of all products to the vague notion of "raising the general level of civilization..." By implication, Nicolae Ceausescu is credited with ideological originality for his use of the concept. The broad scope of "multilateral development," of course, provides a carte blanche for Party leadership; only a political organization as pervasive as the Party can implement a plan over decades designed to "ensure the assertion of...socialist principles in all compartments of economic and social life, the fullest assertion of human personality, and the harmonious blending of personal interests with the general aspiration of the entire society."[6] Furthermore, very few people are likely to oppose such universal goals connoted by "multilateral development."

So intense is Romanian devotion to an identity as a "developing state" that its relations with the so-called Third World have been cultivated with great care. Accepted as a member of the Group of 77, and with permanent observer status at meetings of the non-aligned movement since 1976, Romania is the only European state which proclaims its "developing" status to the point of seeking integration with the Third World. General Secretary Ceausescu, in efforts to solidify and expand such links, visited 37 African, Asian and Latin American states between 1970 and 1977.[7]

Many advantages accrue to Romania as a result of its self-classification as a developing state. International connotations of developing status are numerous and important. Since the concept of "developed socialism" emanated from the U.S.S.R. in the mid-1960s, the degree to which Romania demurs from being similarly categorized can be viewed as part of an overall effort to maintain independence from the Soviets. To be "developing" as opposed to "developed" helps to rationalize lower defense expenditures as when Ceausescu refused to raise military outlays at the November 1978 Warsaw Pact Political Consultative Committee Meeting in Moscow. Romania's different trade pattern, exhibiting proportionately greater exports to and imports from non-CMEA countries than any other East European state, is also defended in light of the developing status of Romania's economy.

Domestic purposes are served as well. Sacrifices and delayed material gratification can, one might suspect, be better tolerated when understood as part of a larger plan for socioeconomic development. While appeals for collective values and socialist consciousness in lieu of monetary reward may "get old," there is nevertheless greater rationale for sacrifice in a "developing" environment than in a presumably higher socioeconomic state.

But the status of a developing state may, concomitant with the advantages which accrue to a country thus classified, raise an acute dilemma for a socialist polity. If the pursuit of developed socialism risks "unleashing" forces with political implications, then where the structures and processes of government are not firmly rooted in tradition and popular legitimacy, the chance of systemic political change increases. Where such processes reveal illegitimacy of a ruling party or elite, the polity itself is incompatible with the consequences of its own policies.[8] The PCR has not, then, avoided the challenges to its political control by adopting the identity of a "developing" state.

SOCIOECONOMIC CHANGE AND POLITICAL ALIENATION OF INDUSTRIAL LABOR

Socioeconomic change in Romania was rapid and fundamental for most of the 1960s and 1970s. The transformation of an agricultural economy and largely peasant society into an industrial and urban system was a political decision by the Romanian Communist Party, as was the strenuous effort to become identified as a "developing" state. There is no need here to recite in detail from Romanian or international sources the impressive achievements of those two decades. A few examples, however, might best illustrate the degree of socioeconomic transformation.

Romania's annual rate of growth in GNP per capita (in constant prices) has been, through the 1960s and 1970s, among the highest in communist Europe as well as in the world. From 1970-75, the mean annual rate of growth in GNP was 8.7 percent (see Table 4.1), which exceeded by a comfortable margin the growth rates of other CMEA countries, and was twice that of Hungary and Czechoslovakia. Its industrial output grew faster than other CMEA members during 1971-75 as well. Meanwhile, longitudinal comparisons with Romania's recent socioeconomic past suggest dramatic movements of population to urban areas, lower infant mortality and longer life expectancies, and expanding enrollment in higher education (Table 4.2) while many economic indicators (Table 4.3) reveal equally great increases in industrial production.

TABLE 4.1
Romanian Socioeconomic Change in Comparative Perspective

	1970-75 Average Annual Rates of Growth of GNP per capita (constant prices)	1971-75 Growth of Industrial Output (constant prices)
Bulgaria	7.1	9.0
Czechoslovakia	4.4	6.7
East Germany	4.8	6.3
Hungary	4.1	6.3
Poland	6.8	10.5
Romania	8.7	13.0

SOURCES: Industrial output for 1971-75 from Kraje RWPG, 1960-1975 (Warsaw: Glowny Urzad Statystyczny, 1976), p. 48. U.S. Central Intelligency Agency, Research Aid: Handbook of Economic Statistics (Washington, D.C., 1976) and T.P. Alton, "Economic Growth and Resource Allocation in Eastern Europe", U.S. Congress, Joint Economic Committee, Reorientation and Commercial Relations of the Economies of Eastern Europe (Washington, GPO, 1974).

TABLE 4.2
Demographic/Social Indicators

	1950	1960	1970	1 July 1979 (est.)
I. Urban Population	25.4	32.1	40.8	48.7
II. Infant Mortality (Deaths under 1 year per 1,000 live births)	116.7	74.6	49.4	31.6
III. Life Expectancy at Birth (Male and Female Combined)	63.2	66.0	68.5	69.8
IV. Portion of Population Enrolled in Higher Education (%)	0.3	0.4	0.7 (1971-72)	.9
V. Hospital Beds per 1,000 Inhabitants	4.2	7.3	8.3	9.4

SOURCES: Anuarul Statistic al Republicii Socialiste Romania, 1972, 1979, 1980 (Bucuresti: Directia Centrala de Statistica, 1972, 1979); Demographic and Statistical Yearbooks of the UN (New York, United Nations 1950-1979).

TABLE 4.3
Economic Indicators

	1950	1960	1971	1979
I. Industrial Employment as % of All Employed	12.0	15.1	24.7	34.7
II. Agricultural Employment as % of Total	74.1	65.4	46.4	30.7
III. Share of Industry in National Income (%)	44.0	44.1	60.3 (1970)	58.5
IV. % of Roads Modernized (i.e., paved)	4.8 (1956)	6.7 (1959)	15.1 (1971)	19.6
V. Electrical Energy Produced (KW hrs/capita)	129.5	415.7	1,927.4	2,945.0
VI. Motor Vehicle Production (all kinds)	none	12,123	74,360	128,847
VII. Radio Production	none	167,000	484,000	757,000
VIII. Television Production	none	15,000	300,000	574,000
IX. Refrigerators	none	10,548	191,619	446,000

SOURCE: Anuarul Statistic al Republicii Romania, 1972, 1979, 1980 (Bucuresti: Directia Centrala de Statistica, 1972, 1979, 1980).

Notwithstanding mounting hard currency debt, trade imbalances, and labor-based difficulties that emerged in the late 1970s and early 1980s, the PCR has pledged to continue its drive towards the status of a developed socialist state by 1990.[9] The demands on worker productivity to fuel such continued industrial expansion are great, while the rate of investments is being maintained at very high levels.[10] The capital of such a still-poor country (by European standards), then, will continue to be channeled narrowly as workers and other citizens are called upon to sacrifice and defer consumption.

Nicolae Ceasuescu's regime invests not only financial resources but political capital as well in its reach for developed status by 1990. The fusion of socioeconomic and political changes connoted by the Party's use of "developing socialism" means that the PCR seeks and expects dynamic processes to be within the bounds of its political control. But the material promise of egalatarian socialism is not evident in Romania. Neither has the participatory promise of socialist democracy been implemented thus far. Because the Party's goals are thus out of step with the principal expectations of developed socialism, developmental policies become potentially destabilizing for communist party government.

Although Romania remains distant from such instability, the political antithesis of Party hegemony, namely pluralism, cannot be separated from the country's increasing complexity and capacity as reflected by demographic and economic indicators. As the parochialism of pre-1950 Romania (or even, perhaps, pre-1960) wanes under the impact of developmental policies, indicators of pluralism have become apparent. These "outcroppings" which challenge the Party's hegemony have been especially evidenced among workers, but are not confined to that stratum.

The diversification of opinions, viewpoints, values and interpretations in a system rapidly becoming more complex can best be seen, of course, with longitudinal data, ideally following the same individuals through time or by sampling techniques at several points in time. These techniques have not been available in Romania.[11] Nevertheless, a variety of more limited data enable us to assemble a view of nascent pluralization.

We know from Romanian data, for example, that usage of electronic media has spread, that people rely primarily on television for news,[12] and that news events are interpreted from different perspectives.[13] This is particularly true for younger, less educated, urban workers who, as a group, are "most likely to use electronic media" in all of Eastern Europe.[14] Whereas parochials make few judgments about the quality of their social, economic or political existence, we can presume that electronic media not only distribute information more rapidly but have the potential to do so more widely, paving the way for a broader range of interpretations. Some data from Romanian sources reveal such phenomena--citizens relying more on television as long ago as 1970 for knowledge about events of national importance[15] and, for the most part, decreasing their reading after television was introduced into the home.[16] Romanian citizens, meanwhile, do not adhere to patterns of interpretations exhibited by "elites"; samples among citizens typically are more interested in non-political events and a broad range of non-collectivist values.[17] The Party's control over media content does not appear to have assured a uniformity of interpretations in an environment of increasing socioeconomic diversity and complexity.

Other forms of data reveal not only typical societal "growing pains", but the lack of uniform, controlled change. The impact of higher expectations is suggested when only 8.6 percent of peasant children are interested in remaining in rural areas[18] while in urban areas, where most industrial labor resides, hooliganism (or "anti-social behavior") and interpersonal violence are rising,[19] as citizens disagree regarding how to react.[20] Such indices are not conclusive, but appear to suggest that the complexity of socioeconomic life is concomitant with people in all walks of life thinking less in a narrow spectrum, being less deferential to elites and to tradition or statutes. Politically-induced changes ostensibly toward developed socialism, then, provide a volatile and fertile milieu for conflictual processes.

There is ample evidence that Romania's path to developed socialism already incorporates sizeable elements of working class disenchantment with their material and political conditions. From a survey of over six thousand young workers (aged 14-30) in the early 1970s, one can obtain an in-depth portrait of the conflictual processes underway in a developing socialist polity. Half of those interviewed wanted to change jobs; almost a fourth had already shifted jobs at least once. Young workers argued that their productivity could be most increased by improving the "co-interest system", i.e., by making a stronger connection between pay and productivity.[21] A plurality of workers of all age groups in another survey, and 58 percent of the 40-49 year old category, were dissatisfied with pay.[22] Overall job dissatisfaction, focusing on the material aspects of employment, and the resulting low productivity and "fluxuation" of the work-force from job to job, are severe and persistent problems for the Romanian path to developed socialism. Workers are not reluctant to complain, and are doing so with greater frequency.

The reasons for material dissatisfaction among Romanian workers are not that they dispute the PCR's goal of "development" (how could one favor stagnation?). Instead, their complaints emphasize the distribution of resources within the country and their inability to find quality consumer products on which to spend Romanian currency as their wages rise. Few circumstances motivate discontent more than being called upon to defer material or other values without the sense that sacrifice is spread evenly in society. In democratic capitalist societies, where the ethos is one of equal opportunity not an equal distribution of wealth, disaffection from the political system because of inequalities will be present, of course, but a government's legitimacy is not premised on a commitment to serve the interests of working people by eliminating socioeconomic differences. A communist party government, on the other hand, has the added ideological burden of equalizing the distribution of wealth. It follows that deferred consumption, capital accumulation and investment in heavy industry--all part of the Romanian vision of development--should imply sacrifices distributed evenly within Romanian society. To be labeled a "developing state", in other words, might aid the Party in its relations with the citizenry insofar as sacrifices are more reasonable. But the same classification could harm a communist party's legitimacy (more than a non-socialist government) were socioeconomic change undertaken in an environment of inequality.

Perceptions of socioeconomic well-being among workers are most likely sensitive to inequalities between occupational categories and between neighborhoods. Put simply, the most salient inequalities are those evident where one works and where one lives. Not unlike his counterpart in other cultures, the Romanian worker has found material sacrifices he is called upon to make for the sake of development and modernization to be placed disproportionately on the shoulders of industrial labor. Moreover, neighborhoods where workers live have not measured up to the images of urban life held by millions of erstwhile peasants qua first-generation factory labor. "Developing socialism", then, has not seen the material concerns of industrial labor satisfied by a government which speaks the rhetoric of workers' interests.

There is no shortage of impressionistic evidence to support allegations of socioeconomic inequalities at the workplace and within urban areas. Unfortunately there are few published statistics to corroborate such impressions. A hierarchy of wages within factors creates a 3:1 ratio between the base pay of lower management personnel and line workers. A median wage for an unskilled manual factory worker hovers around 200 lei/ month (about $180), whereas the director of a factory's quality control would receive in the vicinity of 6000 lei. But salary is a poor indicator of socioeconomic differences. Privilege and access are key concepts for understanding social inequalities in communist systems.[23] Party membership in the factory unlocks some doors for workers, but the upper reaches of Party elites at local levels have privileged access to goods and services worth far more than salary increments. The best products, rapid service, higher quality housing with little or no delay, and assured action on needs and requests are earmarks of inequality much more than salary differences. People for whom special shops and clinics are available, where no lines exist, and for whom bureaucracy responds are those of status--status which usually, but not necessarily, coincides with higher income. Accounterments of status in communist societies, are nevertheless, quite material. Sections of county capital cities as well as Bucharest are recognized as elite enclaves, while chauffeur-driven limousines, often a Mercedez-Benz, denote such status on the road.

If there has been a re-distribution of wealth during the post-war socialism of Eastern Europe, workers understand that the commitment to equality has been less than total, that significant distinctions not only remain but are becoming more evident, and that sacrifices are still demanded of them. Perhaps these conditions would be more easily accpeted were a country such as Romania to have a large surplus of labor. But Romania's workforce is expanding very slowly, and there are signs of labor shortages in the 1980s and beyond given current demographic trends.[24] While over 11 million people were employed in Romania's workforce by the late 1970s, only East Germany exhibited a more negative labor outlook (having an almost static number of employed people). In a market economy, the increased demand for labor during rapid industrialization and general economic expansion coupled with a slowly growing workforce would suggest a substantial rise in living standards for factory labor. Instead, faced with a threatening neighbor, increasingly uncertain energy supplies, and many other international variables, Nicolae Ceausescu continues to demand that Romanian laborers defer their material concerns, and satisfy themselves with visions of future prosperity:

> Any reduction in accumulations, any slackening of the development rate in the conditions of the current technical-scientific revolution can only condemn our nation to long-term backwardness, and can only jeopardize the people's present as well as their future. Our people are fully conscious of the fact that their welfare and happiness exclusively depend on the work they perform, being the fruit of the efforts of their hands and minds. That is why they carry out with perfect conviction the Party's policy for developing the economy at a fast tempo for devoting a substantial percentage of the national revenue to accumulation, ...to increasing and

> modernizing the country's productive forces, being perfectly conscious it is only this that can ensure the welfare and happiness of our entire nation, an ever brighter future for all our people.[25]

Given the consumer societies of neighboring Yugoslavia and Hungary, however, such appeals make less sense as time goes on in the minds of Romanian labor.

Romanian industrial labor has political as well as material grievances. The differentiation of their priorities, opinions and interpretations in the political realm is not seen, of course, in forms familiar to Western experience (legislative lobbying by independent trade unions, support for competitive parties, etc.). At the enterprise level, however, workplace governance becomes an arena in which the political concerns of workers can be observed and, to some degree, measured. General Assemblies of Enterprises, and particularly their executive organs called Workers' Councils (Consiliilor Oamenilor Muncii or COM) were offered by a 1971 statute as the organizational basis for worker participation. These structures, however, merely perpetuated the domination of a "politically reliable, somewhat older, predominately non-worker cohors"--i.e., the "same cast of characters who head Party, State and mass organizations in the local area."[26]

As a result of the non-representative aura which surrounds COM, the councils and general assemblies receive minimal interest from production-line workers across ages, industries and other intervening variables. Party cadres control meetings, agendas,[27] workers' council elected members are not well known by employees,[28] and they are rarely consulted by workers to deal with a problem at the workplace.[29] In a previous study, such indicators led me to conclude that "workers do not identify with or rely upon these councils or the system of self-management to represent their interests."[30]

Because such official outlets for worker involvement have lacked credibility as participatory mechanisms,[31] and are thus viewed as Party efforts to mitigate the dynamics of political change, the gap between worker and Party grows. The mixture of coercive measures and minor structural and procedural modifications characteristics of PCR policy towards workers since the early 1970s remained clearly in place through the end of the decade; the Jiu Valley miners' uprising in August 1977, for example, was met with both the movement of troops into the region and a 1978 campaign for workers' self-management (autoconducerea) which ostensibly reinvigorated the COM mechanism. The 1979 effort to form a free trade union in

Romania, however, suggested both the persistence of disaffection from the Party and the continued negative reaction from the PCR to pluralistic voices. The Twelfth Party Congress in 1979 gave little to workers, delaying further the reduction of the work week and offering modest pay increases while demanding ever greater productivity.[32]

Coupled with techniques to reinforce vertical integration meant to dampen local interests,[33] coercion and procedural adjustments have slowed, not stopped, outcroppings of pluralism which challenge PCR hegemony. There are indications that, in the 1980s, Romanian leadership must turn to other policies if the PCR hopes to limit the demands of industrial labor on the Romanian political system into the 1990s. Tolerating or even accepting dynamic processes within the society it rules may be a tactic that would, for some time, give the PCR greater political control. Continued emphasis on workers' self-management, and the continuation and extension of multiple candidacies in elections for people's councils and the Grand National Assembly can be utilized as symbols of the Party's tolerance for pluralism. That such a pre-emptive strategy is contemplated by the Ceausescu regime may have been suggested by the General Secretary's June 24, 1981 speech to the Congress of Working People in which he proposed that Romania replace the concept of proletarian dictatorship with that of a "workers' democracy". This manipulation of theoretical concepts serves both an international aim (distinguishing Romania from Soviet orthodoxy) and the domestic need to retain the Party's political "balance" amid the dialectics of developing socialism. It appears that PCR leaders have recognized that the Party much soon "shift its weight", as it were, to confront other issues which are uncovered by developmental policies. We should not expect Romania, in the 1980s, to become pluralistic in the sense of Poland during the 1970s (with KOR, ROPiCO, a strongly politicized Church, etc., and numerous underground publications). Nevertheless, there appears enough circumstantial evidence to suggest that issues are being raised by industrial labor that are (or will) change Romanian political life, that the PCR is cognizant of such change, and that the mix of its reactions to political dynamics will also be in flux. Central to these processes, of course, is worker-Party conflict; most often, issues which arise from the pursuit of developed socialism will be evident at the workplace and environs.

CONCLUSION

Because data are fragmentary, the risks of drawing longitudinal conclusions about one case, much less at the comparative level, are considerable. Nevertheless, I think it is not unwarranted (given what evidence is available) to suggest that paths to developed socialism have not involved industrialization, urbanization or other signs of increased complexity and capacity while omitting the diversification of opinions, viewpoints, values and interpretations. And, contrary to the expectation that rule by a communist party would eliminate the economic bases for differing interests (by ending private ownership and eliminating residual inequalities), we do not see workers and societies writ large at peace with their own conditions. Instead, there is a willingness to air material grievances, and a rejection of sanctioned channels for involvement in workplace governance. Even in a system such as Romania, as yet not replicating the volatile conditions of Polish society, the signs of worker discontent and a restive society are to be seen in empirical research. That we can generalize little from the Romanian case is clear; neither it nor Poland are "typical" of communist systems. But in these dissimilar contexts, both communist governments have had to respond to similar conflictual undercurrents of change.

To be, or to become, a "developed socialist state", then, does not connote the slow-paced, limited emergence of new social and political forms which communist party leaders suggest. That scenerio, in which a change of productive relationships would be a correlate of continued Party hegemony, centralization and stability,[34] is contradicted by the experience of Poland and limited data from other European communist systems including Romania. The model of limited and careful modernization under Party suzerainty--in which the European communist leaders have invested their political capital--is not, however, benign. Inherent to developed socialism are the seeds of issues which countervail Party authority--the antitheses of its political control. If, as some analysts have suggested, "developed socialism" was offered by Brezhnev and others as an effort to "contain and manage certain kinds of conflict while...providing greater space for limited reform,"[35] then Party leaders wrongly believed that the mere conceptualization of conflictual processes could halt them. Instead, Party efforts to oppose or mitigate change via the use of a term such as developed socialism merely conceptualizes their core political dilemma. Had Leonid Brezhnev said nothing about razvityi sotsializm in 1967, or omitted its elaboration at the Twenty-Fourth Party Congress,[36] challenges to Party hegemony would have nevertheless arisen.

Worker-Party conflict thus occurs against the backdrop of much wider and ongoing processes of change. Neither Solidarity nor the nascent grievances of Romanian labor can be viewed in isolation from developed socialism. Communist policies meant to achieve greater complexity and capacity will be correlates of antitheses of Party control. The worker-Party conflict we have seen in Poland for over two decades will thus not "spread" in communist Europe, for similar processes are already underway.

NOTES

1. See my "Worker-Party Conflict and the Dialectics of Developed Socialism", presented at the American Political Science Association Annual Meeting, New York City, September 1981.

2. Vasile Rausser, "Romania's Economic Relations with the Developing Countries", in Revue Roumaine des Sciences Sociales: Serie de Sciences Economiques Tome 16, no. 2, 1972, p. 195.

3. Nicolae Ceausescu, Raport la Conferinta Nationala a Partidului Comunist Roman, Iuliu 1972 (Bucuresti: Editura Politica, 1972), p. 98.

4. "Declaratie cu privire la pozitia Partidului Muncitoresc Roman in Problemele miscarii Comuniste si Muncitoresti internationale, adoptala de Plenara largita a C.C. al P.M.R. din Aprilie, 1964" (Bucuresti: Editura Politica, 1964).

5. Nicolae Ceausescu, Romania pe drumul construirii societatii socialiste multilateral dezvoltate, vols. I-XVI (Bucuresti: Editura Politica, 1968-78).

6. Program of the Romanian Communist Party (Bucharest: Agerpres, 1975), p. 74.

7. Leonte Tismaneau and Rolica Zaharia, Present and Prospect in Romania's Social and Economic Development (Bucharest: Meridiane, 1977), p. 71.

8. This point is discussed further by Zvi Gitelman "Development, Institutionalization and Elite-Mass Relations in Poland" in Jan F. Triska and Paul M. Cocks, eds., Political Development in Eastern Europe (New York: Praeger, 1977).

9. A thorough description of the Romanian plans for development through the 1980s can be found in Marvin R. Jackson, "Perspectives on Romania's Economic Development in the 1980s", in Daniel N. Nelson, ed., Romania in the 1980s (Boulder: Westview Press, 1981), pp. 254-305.

10. Romania has been, during the 1970s and into the 1980s, investing most of its growth in national income--a rate which has risen to an astonishing 35-40 percent. See Jackson, p. 275.

11. Reasons for this lack of empirical research are discussed in Daniel N. Nelson, "Romania", in William A. Welsh, ed., Survey Research and Public Attitudes in Eastern Europe and the Soviet Union (New York: Pergamon, 1981), especially pp. 436-443.

12. Argentina Firuta, "Schimbari in Modul de Viata al Clasei Muncitoare", Viitorul Social 7, no. 1 (1978), pp. 75-81.

13. See Pavel Campeanu, "Evaluarea Informatiei de Actualitate", Viitorul Social 7, no. 1 (1978), pp. 97-99.

14. William Welsh, "Summary and Conclusion" in William Welsh, ed., Survey Research and Public Attitudes in Eastern Europe and the Soviet Union (New York: Pergamon, 1981), p. 483.

15. See Table 8.1 in Nelson, "Romania", p. 444.

16. See Table 8.2 in Ibid.

17. The original research for such findings was conducted by Pavel Campeanu, op.cit., especially pp. 97-99.

18. Achim Mihu and Voicu Lascus, "Pentru Care Profesiuni Opteaza Tineretul Scolar?", Era Socialista no. 7 (1973), p. 38.

19. Liviu Damian and E. Dobrescu, "Noile Ansambluri de Locuinte Ameliorarea Relatiilor Umane", Viitorul Social 3, no. 2 (1974), p. 399.

20. Mircea Preda and Ioan Vida, "Interferente ale Eticului, Politicului si Juridicului la Nivelul Constiintei Individuale", Viitorul Social IV. no. 2 (1975), pp. 322-330.

21. Ovidiu Badina and Catalin Mamali, "Indicatori Tehnici si Umani ai Integrarii Tinerilor in Munca", in Badina and Mamali, eds., Tineret Industrial (Bucuresti: Editura Academiei, 1973), p. 66.

22. Mariana Sirbu, "Integrarea in Munca si Participarea Politica in Procesul Dezvoltarii Constiintei Socialiste", in Constantin Potinga and Vasile Popescu, eds., Constiinta Socialista si Participare Sociala (Bucuresti: Editura Academiei, 1977), p. 37.

23. Perhaps the best effort to treat such concepts from an empirical perspective is Mervyn Matthews, Privilege in the Soviet Union (London: Allen and Unwin, 1978). The Polish case was thoroughly examined in a volume edited by Kazimierz Slomczynski and Tadeusz Krauze, Class Structure and Social Mobility in Poland (White Plains, NY: M.E. Sharpe, 1978).

24. See projections in Era Socialista (5 June 1979).

25. Nicolae Ceausescu as quoted in Leonte Tismeau and Rolica Zaharia, p. 90.

26. Daniel N. Nelson, "The Worker and Political Alienation in Communist Europe", paper presented at the Midwestern Political Science Association meeting, Cincinnati, Ohio (April 1981), p. 15.

27. Mariana Sirbu, op.cit., p. 43.

28. Ion Petrescu, Psihosociologia Conducerii Colectiva a Intreprinderii Industriale (Craiova: Scrisul Romanesc, 1977), p. 56.

29. Petrescu, p. 79.

30. Nelson, "The Worker and Political Alienation...", p. 18.

31. Aspaturian discusses the non-participatory involvement characteristic of European communist systems in "Political Participation in Eastern Europe...", passim.

32. See Jackson in Nelson, p. 285 regarding the work week and pp. 289-295 concerning economic incentives for productivity.

33. Nelson, "Vertical Integration...", discusses the reassertion of central authority vs. local interests.

34. Donald R. Kelley explains this scenerio in "The Soviet Image of the Future", in Robert Wesson, ed., The Soviet Union: Problems and Prospects (Stanford: Hoover Institution Press, 1979).

35. Donald Kelley as quoted by Valerie Bunce and John Echols, "Soviet Politics in the Brezhnev Era: 'Pluralism' or 'Corporatism'" in Donald Kelley, ed., Soviet Politics in the Brezhnev Era (New York: Praeger, 1980), p. 10.

36. Leonid Brezhnev, Speech to the Twenty-Fourth Party Congress, Pravda, March 31, 1971.

5
Developed Socialism in Yugoslavia: Socialist Self-Managed Pluralist Democracy

Jim Seroka

INTRODUCTION

"Developed Socialism" in Yugoslavia provides a construct through which piecemeal, moderate reform can be discussed and debated by political participants. Yugoslav developed socialism, however, has different socio-cultural roots and a different socio-history than the other states of Eastern Europe and the Soviet Union. Therefore, its agenda is radically different, and it is likely that Yugoslav developed socialism may enjoy a fate different from that of its neighbors. This chapter deals with the unique background of Yugoslavia's developed socialism and its distinctive programmatic components. In addition, this chapter will include an analysis of the advantages and disadvantages of the program to determine whether the Yugoslav system is capable of handling the stresses and strains of its society in transition.

Nearly every society creates its own political lexicon to accommodate changes, to institutionalize the process of reform, and to legitimize political conflict. As seen earlier, the rhetoric of "developed socialism" is part of that political lexicon for many of the states of Eastern Europe and for the Soviet Union. In Yugoslavia, the analagous role is played by the concept of "Socialist Self-managed Pluralist Democracy." This concept furnishes the core framework for legitimizing reform in the Yugoslav state, and I will briefly analyze the history and role of this concept.

Yugoslavia's social and political system can be considered an anomaly in the contemporary world. The conjunction of nonalignment with a ruling communist party, a planned economy and economic self-management, and a decentralized political system combined with a latent inter-nationality conflict conspire to place Yugoslavia in a most perilous and delicate international and domestic situation.

To avoid the chaos from unmanaged conflict, Yugoslavia's political leaders must be able to adapt and to adopt their policies quickly and responsibly to changing circumstances. The Yugoslavs, more than any other East European state, must develop and institutionalize a system for expediting reform and legitimizing and limiting political conflict.

The management of incremental political change in Yugoslavia is channeled through the social institutions which have evolved from Yugoslavia's "Socialist Self-managed Pluralist Democracy." Proposals for change within Yugoslavia are characterized by such language, and successful proposals are cloaked in the rhetoric of this form of developed socialism. Conversely, a proposal which fails to be interpreted in the prevailing political lexicon will not be adopted. Thus, a rigorous analysis of the vocabulary of political debates in Yugoslavia and a careful attention to the nuances of "Socialist Self-managed Pluralist Democracy" are essential tools to an understanding of the Yugoslav political environment.

A DISTINCTIVE MODEL

Yugoslavia's developed socialism is distinctive in background and usage from the other socialist states discussed in this book. It has not been externally imposed, and it encourages a much wider range of activities. In addition, socialist self-managed pluralist democracy needs to operate in an atmosphere of great social risk and with an agenda radically different from that of its neighboring states.

Unlike the other states of Eastern Europe, Yugoslavia's commitment to developed socialism grew independently of events in the Soviet Union; nevertheless, there are striking parallels to the development of a similar doctrine in the Soviet Union. In the first place, in Yugoslavia, "Socialist Self-managed Pluralist Democracy" was formulated largely as an attempt to confirm President Tito's lasting contribution to socialist thought. In the Soviet Union one detects an analogous motivation underlying Chairman Brezhnev's involvement with "Developed Socialism." A second common parallel is that both doctrines were enunciated to respond, in part, to a series of economic difficulties and a growth rate that was slower than anticipated. A third common linkage was the concern to revitalize the interest of the domestic sectors of both societies in socialist reform, and to introduce an environment conducive to the promotion of qualitative change without concomitant social conflict.

In spite of these three common characteristics, Yugoslavia's vision of developed socialism is not completely analagous to the experience of Eastern Europe. First, Yugoslav "Socialist Self-managed Pluralist Democracy" was an indigenous development and was not imposed upon Yugoslavia. The Hungarian, Czech, Polish, and Romanian versions of "developed socialism" trace their roots to Brezhnev's speech at the 24th Party Congress of the C.P.S.U. Such a difference, therefore, can lead to radically different policy outcomes and political processes in Yugoslavia as opposed to the other states of Eastern Europe.

Yugoslavia's developed socialism also differs fundamentally from the Soviet version because the objective needs and circumstances of Yugoslavia are radically different from those of her socialist neighbors. If nothing else, Yugoslavs enjoy a much more open society and are exposed to an immeasurably greater number of outside pressures. In a sense, Yugoslavia experiences a much more realistic world environment and is under great compulsion to develop a revised political ideology that meets its complex set of objective needs and circumstances.

The most visible point of departure between Yugoslavia and her neighbors is the content of Yugoslavia's developed socialism. The intellectual heritage of socialist self-managed democratic pluralism is different from the Soviet and satellite versions. Its agenda is different, and its procedures for institutionalizing the status quo are quite unique. In addition, the processes for party revitalization, the avoidance of social fragmentation and the muzzling of opposition all tend to indicate that Yugoslavia's self-managed pluralist democracy framework is not a pale imitation of the Soviet example.

The purpose of this chapter is to illustrate the unique characteristics of the Yugoslav model. In particular, I will present its history and its conceptual framework. This will be followed by an assessment of the probable direction of change and chances for eventual success.

BACKGROUND TO YUGOSLAV DEVELOPED SOCIALISM

Yugoslavia's concept of socialist self-managed pluralist democracy rests upon a different historical tradition and a much longer social history than does the movement towards developed socialism in the Soviet Union and Eastern Europe. The tradition of Yugoslav developed socialism is an amalgamation of various historical trends including the experience of a guerilla war for liberation, the emotional and political isolation following the break with Stalin, the constant adjustments in policy in search of a political equilibrium, the recent need to reestablish discipline, and finally, the movement to institutionalize Titoism for a post-Tito society.

The experience of the Communist Party of Yugoslavia during World War II has had a fundamental imprint on Yugoslavia's approach to socialism. During World War II it was necessary to decentralize the Party, to encourage local initiatives, and to promote national consciousness to prosecute successfully a war of liberation. To a great extent, the standard operating procedures of the Party established through the war, facilitated the development of a Party independent of outside pressures and reliant on its own members.

The postwar development of the myth of the wartime role of the Party was perhaps more important in shaping the approach to developed socialism than the actual events of the war. The official postwar mythology of the wartime period stressed decentralism, democracy, pluralism of interests, united front movements, nationalism and trust in the people. The accepted mythology of the past did much to set into concrete the ideal norm for the Yugoslav Party and society in the future.

The maverick tendencies of the wartime years and mythology were intensified during the 1948 break with Stalin. The isolation of the Yugoslavs from the socialist camp during this period resocialized the Party and populace within a framework of self-reliance. It also forced the party to develop a model antithetical to Stalinist totalitarianism, and a model that extolled the values which subsequently became associated with developed socialism. Most importantly, it forced committed communists to reevaluate their past behavior and to begin to formulate a paradigm for a new society.[1]

The third factor influencing the evolution of Yugoslav developed socialism was the experience of the 1953-1968 period during which self-management was adopted, government was decentralized, and the foreign policy of nonalignment was implemented. Of greater importance, however, was the success of the Party (renamed to the League of Communists) in establishing limits to social changes; first by the elimination of Djilas and other liberal elements from positions of power; and later by the purge of Rankovic and his conservative faction. The major impact of both movements should not be evaluated by their immediate impact upon policy, but rather by the qualitative new role which they gave to the League of Communists, namely, a duty to maintain the social equilibrium. The Party's new function was to guard against the threat from the liberals and conservatives and to readjust policies periodically with that objective in mind. During this period most of the theoretical underpinnings for Yugoslav developed socialism were formulated.

The nationality disturbances of the early 1970's and the impending need to institutionalize the Yugoslav system before Tito's death are the last of the remaining historical trends affecting the development of Yugoslavia's Socialist Self-managed Pluralist Democracy. The former stressed the need to reestablish discipline and the hegemony of the party to preserve the legacy of President Tito and much of the postwar experience. The events of the early 1970's underlined the importance in developing a Titoist ideology after Tito. Yugoslav "Socialist Self-managed Pluralist Democracy" became that ideological formulation.

THE YUGOSLAV REFORMIST AGENDA

Throughout the post-war period, the League of Communists tended to be obsessed with the need to institutionalize the process of reform and to establish every imaginable safeguard to limit the range and extent of potential reforms. The underlying concern has been to perfect an institutional system which can accommodate social change and protect Tito's legacy.

Yugoslav political theorists and decision-makers are well aware of the potential risks involved in neglecting the conflict between economic development and socio-political change as well as their dynamics of change. Jovan Dordevic, a noted Yugoslav constitutional lawyer, presents this point quite clearly:

> Every political system is simultaneously harmonious and fractious, rational and irrational, full of possibilities and surprises. The logic of the system is in these antagonisms and possible conflicts. They simultaneously define and limit the political system. There is not a scientific system of politics if it does not recognize and analyze these opposing structures. . . . Every political system in socialism is in the process of change, in harmony with the constant thesis to overcome the old forms of underdevelopment and domination and to

> uncover new paths. Its structure is not only incomplete, but it is also never closed.[2]

In this view, the basic challenge for developed socialism is to devise political structures that can promote and facilitate stable resolution of the conflict, yet flexible enough to meet new and unforeseen needs. According to Najdan Pašić, former Dean of the College of Political Science in Belgrade,

> It is desirable, in fact essential, that these factors, and especially the holder of governmental authority, have an active role in channeling the direction of society, which means that they should be involved in the sense of encouraging and supporting some tendencies and interests and discouraging others.[3]

Probably the most obvious manifestation of the intensity with which political structural solutions have been applied to the basic disharmony between economic development and social change is that there have been four constitutions in postwar Yugoslavia, the most recent enacted in 1974. All these constitutional changes were made to help make the Yugoslav political system congruent with economic and social realities.[4]

Throughout the postwar period, two guiding principles have been steadfastly held. One was the need to alter policy to meet the changing social circumstances and economic conflict, and the second was to permit sufficient flexibility to accommodate the variability of circumstances in the country. The notion of a guided, but open society is conscientiously supported, even though these objectives may be, at times, contradictory.

The direction for change is invariably provided by the Leagus of Communists, while much of the ideological substance of these changes is based on the theory of self-management. Self-management has gradually expanded from the relatively limited confines of industrial management to include nearly every aspect of social, economic, and political life in Yugoslavia today.[5]

Although other socialist systems claim direction of society, flexibility, and a strong ideological party, Yugoslavia may now be unique in the sense that much of its behavior can be classified as preventive rather than as reactive. The League of Communists appears to be actively engaged in short, medium, and long-range planning for social problems, all under the rubric of "self-management democracy." Thus, plans are made and implemented often before the social problem manifests itself or grows into crisis proportions.

A recent example of this preventive activity is the monograph "About the Further Development of Our Political System and the Tasks of the League of Communists," written by Edvard Kardelj and adopted as the basis of discussion for the 11th Party congress held in 1978.[6] The monograph is a detailed theoretical conceptualization of the meaning of developed socialism in Yugoslavia for the next several years.[7] The Kardelj presentation is significant because it set the stage for considerable debate over the political, economic, and social priorities of Socialist development in Yugoslavia in 1977-78.

As a result, an analysis of this period of debate will indicate not only the meaning of Yugoslav developed socialism, but also the interaction of various groups in society with it, as well as its prospects and significance for the future.

DEVELOPED SOCIALISM IN YUGOSLAVIA: SELF-MANAGEMENT SOCIALIST DEMOCRACY

To understand the debate over developed socialism in Yugoslavia one must first define social self-management and explain its role in Yugoslav society. The reason is obvious in the Yugoslav context: Yugoslav self-management is defined as a system that promotes simultaneously two objectives: "Elements that secure an optimal degree of democracy in daily life and measures which secure the optimal development of productive forces."[8]

As is evident, "Self-management" is a relative term, the operational meaning of which changes according to circumstances. What the Yugoslavs mean by the concept in political terminology is the development of a rational and effective system of mass participation in decision-making. It is neither party politics in the western model,[9] nor a state bureaucracy in the Soviet model,[10] nor an anarchistic or mass society.[11] Moreover, Yugoslav political decision-makers are quite conscious of what self-management is not supposed to become, and they actively try to prevent the transformation of Yugoslav society into any of the above antithetical forms.

Four characteristics seem to provide the commonality of time and circumstances for Yugoslav self-management. They will now be enumerated and explained.

Recognition of Diversity of Interests. Unlike other Marxist-Leninist societies in Yugoslavia, conflicts of interests are accepted as natural political events.[12] No pretense is made that a developing society can exist without conflict or stress. In fact, the appearance of conflict is perceived to be a healthy sign for the society.[13]

This diversity, although recognized and legitimized, is institutionalized differently than in Western societies. In Yugoslavia, division in society is dealt with at the lowest possible political unit, such as the factory branch or neighborhood. The divisions are handled without the benefit of other political parties or legitimized quasi-political interest groups.

Active Participation of the affected citizenry in the decision-making process is the second constant principle of Yugoslav self-management. The encouragement of and dependence upon participation has been extended gradually from socio-political organizations as well as worker councils and to neighborhood assemblies, and, most recently, to legislative bodies at all governmental levels. Participation is considered the most vital factor in the measurement of success of the Yugoslav political system.[14]

Decentralism is the third essential factor. In both the economic and political arenas decisions are being made in, and autonomy has been granted to, smaller and smaller organizational units. In the political sphere the commune seems to be growing in importance at the expense of the republic and federation.[15] In economic life, the basic factory division (OOUR) has replaced the enterprise (OUR), which previously supplanted the industry as the most significant decision-making unit. This change in emphasis, although slow, is now nearly complete.[16]

The Directive Role of the League of Communists is the fourth element. The League of Communists (SKJ) has primary responsibility for directing the entire process and for making adjustments, as well as for setting the specific policy issue agenda. Although its techniques for accomplishing these goals may have changed over time, the primary objectives have not been altered.[17]

Thus, from an ideological perspective, Yugoslav self-management is an attempt to combine in one set of institutions and procedures two primary Marxist-Leninist principles; the dictatorship of the proletariat, and the withering away of the state.

Yugoslav self-management is also important from a political perspective. The intent of the system appears to be to fractionalize conflict to the lowest possible decision-making level. It also seems to promote cross-cutting cleavages along occupational, educational, generational, and even class lines in order to contain the more destructive nationality cleavages. Finally, it seeks to provide regional and individual economic equality without concomitantly endangering basic freedoms.

The Yugoslav system of self-management is difficult to administer. It calls upon the decision-maker to exercise self-restraint constantly,[18] it must be modified frequently, and it depends upon individual support. In such a system the outcome must always be pareto-optimal.[19] If it is not, it is quite possible that the nationality-cultural cleavages of Yugoslavia could again threaten the basic social fabric.

The position of self-management in relationship to the basic conflicts noted above can be represented schematically. Figure 1 illustrates the role of self-management in relation to the conflict between economic and social development. Figure 2 provides a basic outline of the equality-freedom conflict.

Figure 5.1
Typology of Modern Social Systems According to Conflict Between Economic Growth and Political Participation

		Economic Growth	
		YES	NO
Political Participation	YES	Self-management	anarcho-liberalism
	NO	bureaucratic-technocratism	system breakdown

Figure 5.2
Typology of Modern Social Systems According to Conflict Between Equality and Freedom

		Equality: YES	Equality: NO
Freedom	YES	Self-management	anarcho-liberalism
	NO	bureaucratic-technocratism	system breakdown

The terms "anarcho-liberalism" and "bureaucratic-technocratism" in both figures are the theoretical and political opposites of self-management. "Anarcho-liberalism" is a system that resembles the undirected competitive party system in western societies.[20] "Bureaucratic-technocratism" is identified with the overly directed state managed society of the Soviet bloc.[21] The fourth cell, "system breakdown," indicates a situation in which the political system collapses from failure to provide any social value.

Figures 5.1 and 5.2 emphasize the fact that much of the language of the postwar political debates in Yugoslavia is understandable from this perspective. The terms allow one to make projections about future policy and political decisions. For example, the early 1960 campaign against bureaucratic-technocratism signalled an opening up of the political system that was conducive to participation and freedom, although with the risk of slower growth and greater inequalities. The campaign against anarcho-liberalism later in the decade correspondingly signalled the adoption of policy measures promoting economic growth and equality, but with the risk of less widespread participation and less freedom.

THE KARDELJ INITIATIVE AND ITS ACCOMPANYING DEBATE

The movement to develop an instutionalized procedure for social change led directly to Edvard Kardelj's sweeping vision of socialist humanism. The debate which his plan created can be divided into three stages. Stage 1 is the introduction and initial acceptance of the Kardelj plan; Stage 2 describes the escalation of resistance; and Stage 3 outlines the format of the final compromise.

Prelude: Kardelj's Vision of Socialist Humanism

On June 13, 1977 the presidency of the Central Committee of the League of Communists of Yugoslavia heard and approved the contents of a speech delivered by Edvard Kardelj, a member of that body and one of the most influential individuals in Yugoslavia. That speech, entitled, "The new areas for human freedom and democracy," was adopted by the Presidency of the Party at the 30th session as the working document and guidelines for debate for the then forthcoming 11th Congress of the League of Communists.[22] The speech was later expanded into book length form for the more intense and detailed discussion which the role of being the guidelines for party debate thrust upon it.[23]

The debate which the Kardelj speech and writings initiated set the tone of public discussion on a relatively high level. The two basic questions were: what should be the primary vlaues for the political system, and how should the political system resolve the conflict. Hence, the speech signalled the renegotiation of the future policy tradeoffs between economic development and social development, and the formation of the precise nature of developed socialism in Yugoslavia's future.

The Kardelj address rested upon three premises: first stability is essential, second intra-societal variation must be tolerated; and third, society can and should be directed. The premise that stability is essential is a restatement of the basic conflict between economic and socio-political development that was noted earlier. According to Kardelj,

> The social-economic content and stability of productive relations of every society has the determining role in the character and formation of its political system and in its social and political stability.[24]

The second premise became very important in the later development of the debate because it posed many practical questions. Fully stated, Kardelj's assumption is that political and ideological systems must be very flexible in order to accommodate variation in society[25] and that this social variation requires both a political and an economic solution.[26]

The third premise that society should be directed, is much less controversial and is generally accepted.[27]

Kardelj employed these three principles to develop a framework for socialist development. The framework became the center of extended debate, which can be summarized in five basic points.

1. First Kardelj accepts the principle of "democratic self-management pluralism." He realizes that interests in a developing society diverge and they become difficult to resolve.

Inevitably they lead to conflict which must be resolved by self-management decision-making processes rather than by multi-party politics. In Kardelj's phrasing:

> In our society there exists, in addition to the previously mentioned class conflict, other ideological and political differences and conflicts, but these are conflicts based upon socialist social relationships. These differences and conflicts affect ques-

> tions such as the further development of socialist society, resolution of actual economic, social, culturel, and other problems, the direction and tempo of the further development of socioeconomic, political and other relationships, and ideological and political differences which appear in connection with such problems, etc. However, such conflicts and differences are not resolved in a political struggle for power, but in a system of self-managed democracy.[28]

Obviously, such a principle could be interpreted as emphasizing the dimension of participation at the expense of growth, and freedom at the expense of equality, and both positions are reminiscent of unacceptable anarcho-liberalism.

2. Second, conflicts resulting from pluarlism must be resolved at the lowest possible decision making level. As Kardelj put it:

> Therefore, our system of self-management democracy, and especially our delegate system, is entirely able not only to express the plurality of self-management interests, but to resolve them by democratic means . . . but contemporary conditions of our self-managed society the resolution of these conflicts is not possible except on very narrow areas.[29]

This principle became the subject of considerable controversy, not so much for its ideological meaning, but for the attendant difficulties in its implementation.

3. The third principle calls for a more intensive adoption democratic procedures. Edvard Kardelj asserted that:

> Socialist self-management cannot continue to function if it does not develop further as a democratic system. Its general political result can be nothing other than the constant expansion of the freedom of man.[30]

Certainly, the objections that applied to the first principle can apply to this one as well.

4. The League of Communists and other socio-political organizations should influence self-management socialist development, but they should not assume full control of the process nor impede democratic procedures. This is the fourth principle. Kardelj expressed it in this manner:

> Our concept of the leadership role of the League of Communists in our social life was never identical to the concept of a political monopoly on state power or with the concept of a one-party system. The League of Communists as an ideological and political vanguard of the working class is an expression of the specific complex of ideological and political interests

> of this class and of all working people, and according to this is a constituent part of the democratic pluralism of self-managed interests, and not some political force above or outside those interests.[31]

This principle definitely expresses a desire to move away from the bureaucratic-technical cell in Figures 5.1 and 5.2. It weakens considerably the traditional Marxist-Leninist role of the Party in society and directly affects the power of much of the political leadership.

5. The fifth principle is a recognition of the delicate nature of the self-managed democratic system. Kardelj called for the adoption of policies that could promote stability and depoliticize issues. He pleaded for political and social tolerance, as suggested in this part of his speech:

> Therefore, in a system of self-managed democratic pluralism the majority of problems can be resolved by self-managed agreements and only a small fraction by political decision making or by the arbitration of governmental organs. In fact, self-management means democratic decision making about social functions in which every conflict of interest is transformed into a struggle for political power.[32]

Again, as is true for most of the other principles, the fifth principle can be perceived as an attempt to exchange more participation for economic and social efficiency and more freedom at the possible expense of equality.

Thus, one can see that the Kardelj initiative, if implemented, would imply a drastic change in socio-political relations, a deterioration in the power of the Party and government, major decentralization, a marked increase in liberalism, and tolerance of competing interests. The essence of Kardelj's position could be summarized as "socialist humanism."[33]

Stage 1: Initial Acceptance (June-September, 1977)

The 30th session of the Presidency of the Party on June 13, 1977 was well publicized and the Kardelj speech was published in full in Kommunist, the Party weekly. It was also given extensive coverage in the daily newspapers.[34] The pressure for acceptance was strong. One notable example of this was the June 27th issue of Kommunist which reported the attack by non-Yugoslav Communist parties charging that the Kardelj document had strong bourgeois tendencies.[35] The intent was to indicate that if other non-self-managed Parties were attacking the document, then common patriotism, if nothing else, demanded support and encouragement.

A second example of the strength of the initial pressure for acceptance was the reports of pledges by important non-political individuals from the scientific and cultural communities.[36] The intent behind this was to demonstrate widely based, informed support for the program.

By late August, testimonials of support from Party dignitaries began to appear,[37] and a campaign was initiated for mass involvement in the debate and discussion.[38] The campaign included the heavy endorsement and publication of the Kardelj book which was based upon the June 13th document.[39] This campaign also included an informational aspect in which important points of the Kardelj initiative were explained,[40] sometimes by Kardelj himself.[41] Appeals were made for support from other socio-political organizations, most notably the Socialist Alliance and Syndicate of trade unions.[42]

This initial period, nevertheless, involved several anomalies that were quite indicative of future developments. For example, Tito maintained silence. None of the six Republic Central Committees gave the speech unconditional endorsement. Many of the local Party organizations treated the Kardelj initiative in a very circumscribed manner, regarding it as a way of reforming the delegate system and not a societal transformation. Finally, and most importantly, the pluralistic dimension was dropped almost completely from public discussion, and public explanations began to take a defensive tone. Quite certainly, large and important social groups within Yugoslavia either had strong reservations or were actually opposed to various aspects of the Kardelj's document.

Stage 2: Development of Resistance (October, 1977-February, 1978)

Beginning in October, 1977 the public debate began to take a more strident and much more critical approach. On October 3, 1977 Kardelj's interview with the Washington Post was widely reprinted in which Kardelj was asked the following question:

> In your newest book about "The Direction and Development of the Political System of Socialist Self-management," you speak about self-managed pluralism. There are those who wish to interpret this as a return to the '60's, that is, on the road which leads to liberalism.[43]

In effect, Kardelj was being asked to defend his program from the charge of anarcho-liberalism. This was a clear sign that the battle had been joined, and it indicated the grounds on which it would be fought. In brief, those favoring the Kardelj program faced the label of "anarcho-liberalism," while those opposed faced the charge of "bureaucratic-technocratism."

Throughout October, 1977, the Kardelj program was attacked on a wide number of fronts from within the country. The Socialist Alliance of Bosnia-Hercegovina expressed concern about the problem of implementation and the avoidance of a return to anarcho-liberalism.[44] The Serbian League of Communists deferred commitment until further study.[45] The printed media tended to ignore the collective nature of the decision of the Presidency of the Party and referred to the self-management democracy as Kardelj's plan rather than the Party's plan. There appeared to be widespread concern in the Party about democratic centralism. This term became the password for the opposition and summarized their fears of a return to anarcho-liberalism.

A strong attack on the Kardelj plan came on October 21, 1977 from a group of Croatian party theoreticians. This attack was reprinted in Naše Teme, an influential Croatian monthly.[46] The article appeared to be the result of an attempt to redefine the debate and to take the initiative away from Kardelj and his supporters. The charges were quite extensive, and the most serious are listed below.

1. There is insufficient conceptual and practical delineation of self-managed pluralism from anarcho-liberal pluralism.[47]
2. The potential for unrestrained conflict is too high.[48]
3. The Kardelj plan ignores the power of bureaucratic-technocratic forces in society.[49]
4. The plan is too idealistic and could inadvertantly lead to corruption by anarcho-liberal or bureaucratic-technocratic forces.[50]
5. The plan does not give sufficient authority to the Party to direct society.[51]

These charges were representative of the particular points of resistance to the Kardelj program. If allowed to stand unchallenged, the charges would have gutted the Kardelj plan or exposed it to transformation by anarcho-liberal or bureaucratic-technocratic forces.

Beginning in late October, Kardelj and others began to defend themselves from many of these charges. The delegate system, a source of strength for the opposition, was severely criticized[52] and it was intimated that the present system was too strongly under the thumb of technocratic forces,[53] especially on the local and regional levels.[54] In November, Kardelj, speaking before the Socialist Alliance of Croatia, warned of the danger from technocratism[55] and charged that the delegate system was the brake upon the entire plan of self-management democracy.[56] He further advised that the League of Communists, Socialist Alliance, and trade union movement must become more democratic and work more within the system and not upon it.[57]

In effect, by November, the Kardelj forces were actively recruiting support from the other non-Party socio-political organizations. Support from the trade union movement came in January,[58] from influential academics in December,[59] and from the Congress of Self-Management[60] and Socialist Alliance in February.[61]

Of more concern, however, was the behavior of the Party leadership. In January, Stane Dolanc proposed a compromise that, in effect, limited the Kardelj initiative to the delegate system.[62] At the 34th session of the Party Presidency, the first following the Kardelj initiative, the entire problem, was sidestepped,[63] at least publicly, and in early February Jure Bilić, Secretary of the Executive Committee of the Party, obliquely criticized the Kardelj initiative by stressing that the Party must not become "solely an internal revolutionary force for social transformation."[64] What he meant was that the League must not permit society to degenerate into anarcho-liberalism.

Stage 3: Compromise (February-June, 1978)

The events of the earlier period indicated that neither side could claim complete victory, without the direct intervention of President Tito.[65] The eventual result was a compromise that was approved, but not fashioned, by President Tito before the opening of the fifth session of the Central Committee in February.[66] Elements of both socialist humanism and democratic centralism were merged together at the fifth session of the Central Committee.[67] The agreement was solidified at the 36th session of the Presidency of the Party later that month[68] and ratified in the Party statutes in March.[69] Finally, it was legitimized by Tito at the 11th Party Congress in June.[70]

The Compromise gave solace to both sides in the dispute. The major advantages for each side are as follows:[71]

Socialist Humanists

1. Agreement to reform the delegate system and political process through more democratization.[72]
2. A stronger focus on Party democracy, especially at the cell level.
3. Continuation of efforts against "bureaucratic-technocratism."
4. Agreement that the Party works primarily within the system and not upon it.
5. The Socialist Alliance and trade unions will assume a larger share of responsibility in policy-making.
6. Continued decentralization of conflict.

Democratic Centralists

1. Strong emphasis on discipline within the Party.
2. Major emphasis on economic growth.
3. Deemphasis of the pluralism thesis as the goal and cornerstone of political life.[73]
4. Stress on the needs to balance ideals with practical realities.

Neither camp could claim complete victory from the result, but both could live with it. More importantly, however, the compromise fashioned here may have set several precedents for the future, but it could well suffer from several sources of instability and points of conflict. All parties at least agreed that, even though a perfect stage of self-management had not been reached, the twin evils of bureaucratic-technocratism and anarcho-liberalism had been avoided.

Since the events of 1977 and 1978, both the major actors, namely Tito and Kardelj, have died, yet the process continues and promises to become the keystone of the forthcoming 12th Party congress in 1982. One section of the process in particular entitled the "Tito Initiative" continues to be very controversial and may become the rallying point for a second social debate on this issue. The Tito initiative is a plan to rotate all political and government officials every year. The intent is to reduce the threat of techno-bureaucratism and to increase participation in government.

One can conclude that, although Tito has died, Titoism lives. His legacy is entitled Socialist Self-managed Pluralist Democracy. It has now become the institutional framework for change and reform in the Yugoslav state.

ASSESSMENT

A most vexing question facing "socialist self-managed pluralist democracy" concerns its ability to handle the stresses and strains of a society satisfactorily without the leadership of President Tito and without the guidance of Eduard Kardelj. It is evident that the system of developed socialism in Yugoslavia is complex. Furthermore, it is not rooted in a firm set of practical policy programs. Both characteristics make it very difficult to guide programs, to assess direction, and to evaluate progress. Nevertheless, it is possible to draw some tentative conclusions about the general behavior of the program and to compare the advantages and disadvantages of Yugoslav developed socialism in the context of the 1980's.

The system of socialist self-managed pluralist democracy provides two major advantages for the Yugoslavia of the 1980's. First, conflict is introduced and managed at very low institutional levels. Second, this system depersonalizes responsibility, thereby raising the threshold for risk. Taken together, both of these advantages tend to reduce the overall intensity of conflict and to create an atmosphere for institutional, incremental reform.

The process of decentralization and the encouragement of participation within the Kardeljian framework are well designed to legitimize and routinize conflict into narrow and circumscribed areas. The system, therefore, creates a framework for discussion, change, and reform. The change is necessarily incremental, and, over time, a greater number of individuals become coopted by or committed to the system. Thus, the encouragement of decentralization and participation within a reform structure as envisioned by Kardelj tends to provide stability in an otherwise unstable system, and the recent rapid multiplication of self-management organs is probably the best single indicator of the success of the program.

In practice Yugoslav developed socialism tends to spread out responsibility for programs among all members of the self-managed system, because each member participates in the decision-making process. This devolution of responsibility, although possessing negative features, tends to support the development of incremental reform and the system takes on the appearance of being responsive and equitable. A major advantage of the collective responsibility is that innovative approaches and procedures posing an element of risk can be adopted because responsibility is shared collectively, and because no one person will be blamed if there is failure. In Yugoslavia's present social situation, the advantages which this system provides to overall systemic stability are self evident.

The contemporary environment and the Kardeljian vision of developed socialism confront each other along a number of fronts, thereby introducing three disadvantages to the system. There are the problems of a slower growth rate in the economy and the serious demographic imbalances throughout the society. Additionally, since Tito's illness and death, Yugoslavia suffers from a lack of direction and diffusion of authority. Third, compounding all the above problems, is the persistence and seeming tolerance of social and economic inequalities.

A no-growth economy exacerbates the internal contradictions within a self-managed pluralist democracy. Conflict is increased and the growing demands of individuals upon society can only be met at the expense of other individuals and groups. The competition for economic resources encouraged by the pluralistic tendencies of developed socialism potentially can degenerate into conflict and into demands that higher level authorities adjudicate more disputes. The potential for conflict has been realized in contemporary post-Tito Yugoslavia. Demands upon the economic and social system for redistribution of capital and investment capacity have become intensive and threaten to paralyze the national level legislative process process.[74]

The demographic problem further compounds this situation and exacerbates even further the potential for intra-societal conflict. While the rate of economic growth has slackened, the number of new and, in many cases more educated, entrants into the labor market creates considerable new stress. Responsible job positions for the new entrants are becoming increasingly rare and the prospects for promotion are becoming even more dismal. Thus, while the system of socialist self-managed pluralist democracy encourages group participation in basic decision-making, it may lead to frustration and hostility under the present economic and demographic circumstances. Events in the Kosovo province in the Spring of 1981 clearly demonstrate the seriousness of the situation and the latent threat which exists against the Kardeljian vision of society.

Since Tito's illness and death, a new challenge to the Yugoslav developed socialism system has emerged, namely a breakdown in authoritative decision-making. Presently, no individual or programmatically cohesive group exists which is in the position to make binding decisions. Tito's place in the decision-making process has not been filled. Consequently, conflict once initiated may never be terminated. So far, the negative features of this threat have not been realized because there appears to be a widespread reluctance on the part of most decision-makers to initiate conflict that has the potential to be self-consuming. Yet, the reluctance to introduce conflictual issues will gradually undermine the flexibility of the system and potentially make socialist self-managed pluralist democracy irrelevant to the future concerns and needs of Yugoslav society.

A final disturbing feature of Yugoslav life endangering the system of developed socialism has been the persistence of social and economic inequalities. These inequalities (i.e. national, income, education, etc.) create a climate that constantly inflates the size of the policy agenda with which developed socialism must deal. The system promises relief from considerable inequalities; yet there is a gap, possibly growing, between expectations and performance. The end result is the persistence of a growing list of potentially explosive social problems, thereby possibly overburdening the system at a time when it is least capable of providing solutions.

With respect to an overall assessment of the prospects for continued success of the system of socialist self-managed pluralist democracy, one can be mildly optimistic. First, despite the Kardeljian claim, the system can be characterized as one which is "muddling through." As such, it is very adaptive to change and very flexible when under pressure. Second, the system is also conservative in outlook and results, even though it is very liberal in terms of appearance and values. Thus, within the same structural format, all the major value positions can be represented. Third, the system is now legitimized; no individual may be committed to each and every aspect of the program, but nearly every citizen is committed to some part of the system. Thus, one may conclude confidently that Titoism can survive Tito and that developed socialism can become an institutionalized system of limited reform and change.

NOTES

1. See Eduard Kardelj, Sećanje: Borba za Priznanje: Nezavisnost Nove Jugoslavije 1944-1957 (Radnička Štampa, Beograd, 1980).

2. Jovan Dordević, Politički Sistem: Prilog Nauci o Čoveku i Samoupravlanju. Privredni Pregled, Belgrade, 1973, p. 320.

3. Najdan Pašić, Političko Organizovanje Samoupravnog Društva, Belgrade: Komunist, 1974.

4. For a theoretical treatment of this thesis see Jakov Blažević, Aktualnosti Revolucije: O Novom Ustavu Socijalističke Samoupravne Demokracije (Čakovec: Zrinski, 1973).

5. Andelko Veljić, Društveno Samoupravljanje u Jugoslaviji, (Sarajevo: Veselin Masleša, 1973).

6. Edvard Kardelj, "Sloboda i Demokratija Samoupravnog Socijalizma," Politika (June 14, 1977).

7. The selection of issues is taken from Ivan Perić, "Diskusija o Studiji Eduarda Kardelja: Pravci Razvoja Političkog Sistema Socijalističkog Samoupravljanja," Naše Teme, Vol. 21, No. 12, 1977, p. 2606.

8. Milan Ramljak, "Razvoj Socijalističkih Samoupravnih Društveni venih Odnosa u Jugoslaviji" in Željko Pavić (et al.) Samoupravljanje, (Zagreb: Školska Knjiga, 1974), p. 50.

9. For an apt description see E.E. Schattsneider, Party Government (New York: Holt, Rinehart and Winston, 1942).

10. A good description can be found in David Lane, Politics and Society in the USSR (New York: Random House, 1970).

11. See William Kornhauser, The Politics of Mass Society (New York: Free Press, 1959), and Radovan Pavičević, Država Kao Konfederacija Komuna: Kritika Prudonovih Shvatanja (Beograd: Institute za Medunarodni Radnički Pokret, 1969).

12. See Jovan Mirić, Interesne Grupe i Politicka Moć (Čakovec: Zrinski, 1973).

13. The six volume study coordinated by Stojan Tomić,

Komunalni Konflikti, Institut za Društvena Istraživanja (Sarajevo, 1973), provides ample documentation of this point.

14. See Stojan Tomić, "Institucionalni Sistemi Participacija i Samoupravljanje," Socijalizam, Vol. 18, No. 4, 1975, pp. 452-467.

15. For an elaboration of this point see James Seroka, "Local Socio-political Organizations and Public Policy Decision-Making in Yugoslavia," in Kenneth Naylor (ed.), Balkanistica II (Cambridge, Mass.: Slavica Publishers, 1975).

16. See Jovan Marjanović, Delegatski Sistem i Politička Reprezentacija (Belgrade: Institut za Političke Studije, 1974).

17. See Rade Aleksic (et al.), SKJ i Socijalistička Revolucija Jugoslavije (Zagreb: Centar za Aktualni Politicki Studiji, 1973).

18. One arena in which this self-restraint is most obvious is the legislature. For an incisive analysis of this point see Lenard Cohen, Revolutionary Socialism: The Political Institutionalization of the Yugoslav Assembly System, 1963-1973 (Unpublished doctoral dissertation, Columbia University, 1978).

19. Pareto-optimality is the best possible solution that does not hurt anyone.

20. See Radoslav Ratković, "Liberalizam i Partija" in Šta je Liberalizam? (Beograd: Institut za Političke Studije, 1973).

21. The connection of these terms with nonalignment should be stressed. Foreign policy and domestic politics have many such links.

22. For the entire text see Politika (June 14, 1977) on Komunist (June 20, 1977).

23. The book is Edvard Kardelj, Pravci Razvoja Političkog Sistema Socijalističkog Samoupravljanja (Belgrade: Komunist, 1977).

24. Ibid., p. 15.

25. Ibid., p. 22.

26. Ibid., p. 24.

27. Ibid., pp. 22-23.

28. Ibid., p. 86.

29. Ibid., p. 98.

30. Ibid. p. 135.

31. Ibid., p. 177.

32. Ibid., p. 96.

33. The term is not my own. See Komunist (August 29, 1977), p. 6.

34. Komunist (June 20, 1977) and Politika (June 14, 1977).

35. Komunist (June 27, 1977), p. 6.

36. Komunist (July 18, 1977), p. 1.

37. Komunist (August 29, 1977).

38. Politika (August 18, 1977), p. 6.

39. Politika (September 22, 1977), p. 6.

40. Komunist (September 19, 1977), p. 1.

41. Komunist (September 19, 1977), pp. 4-6.

42. Komunist (September 26, 1977), p. 3 and Politika (Sep (September 5, 1977), p. 8.

43. Komunist (October 3, 1977), p. 6.

44. Komunist (October 17, 1977), p. 2.

45. Politika (October 11, 1977), p. 6.

46. Ivan Peric (et al.), 1977, op. cit. pp. 2603-2654.

47. Ibid., pp. 2611-2613.

48. Ibid., p. 2618.
49. Ibid., p. 2621.
50. Ibid., p. 2622.
51. Ibid., p. 2631.
52. Politika (October 12, 1977), p. 9. For an explanation of the delegate system in Yugoslavia see James Seroka, "Legislative Recruitment and Political Change in Yugoslavia," Legislative Studies Quarterly, Vol. 4, No. 1 (February, 1979).
53. Politika (October 24, 1977), p. 5.
54. Politika (November 7, 1977), p. 9.
55. Politika (November 11, 1977), p. 7.
56. Politika (November 12, 1977), p. 5.
57. Komunist (November 21, 1977), p. 6.
58. Komunist (January 2, 1978), p. 3.
59. Politika (December 16, 1977), p. 6.
60. Politika (February 16, 1978), p. 6.
61. Politika (February 26, 1978), p. 6.
62. Komunist (January 16, 1978), p. 3.
63. Komunist (January 30, 1978), p. 3.
64. Komunist (February 6, 1978), p. 5.
65. A precedent for this did exist in Tito's famous Letter in 1971.
66. Komunist (February 13, 1978), p. 3.
67. Komunist (February 13, 1978).
68. Politika (February 28, 1977).
69. Komunist (March 27, 1978), pp. 5-7.
70. Komunist (June 21, 1978), p. 3.
71. See Tito's speech to the 11th Party Congress reprinted in Yugoslav Survey, Vol. 19, No. 3 (August, 1978), pp. 5-58.
72. In practice this meant that participation by citizens, socialist alliance members, and trade union members would be encouraged more, and that the League would refrain from dominating the selection process and the behavior of the delegates.
73. Some mention is made in part two of the Resolution of the 11th Congress of the League of Communists, "Uloga i Zadaci Saveza Komunista Jugoslavije u Borbi za Razvoj Socijalističkog Samoupravljanja i za Materijalni i Društveni Napredak Zemlje," Jugoslovenski Pregled, Vol. 22, No. 6, 1978, p. 242.
74. See my paper to the British Political Studies Association annual meeting in Hull, England (March, 1981) entitled "Yugoslav Budgetary Processes and Implications for Succession, Federalism, and the Distribution of Political Power."

6
Developed Socialism and the Polish Crisis*

Maurice D. Simon

THE POLITICAL CONTEXT

The vocabulary and imagery of Polish politics since 1970 reflected the hopes and fears generated by rapid and intense socio-economic and political change. The December 1970 workers' disorders which toppled Wladyslaw Gomulka from power brought forth bright slogans and promises of "a new political style."[1] First Secretary Edward Gierek and his associates proclaimed "We are building a second Poland" and hailed the transition to "mature" or "developed socialism." By the mid-1970s, however, such optimism appeared unwarranted and seemed designed instead "to reassure both the elites and the masses about the maintenance and survival of a system faced with the unforeseen and unpredictable consequences of reaching the postindustrial stage."[2] The confrontations and convulsions of 1980-1981 again raised possibilities for reform and "renewal," but these objectives were subverted by the imposition of martial law recently announced by General Wojciech Jaruzelski on December 13, 1981. Jaruzelski's claim that Poland had moved to "the edge of the abyss" provided a stark contrast to the connotations of the developed socialism doctrine that dominated political discourse during the 1970s.[3]

In light of this kaleidoscopic swirl of events, it is useful to examine the role of the developed socialism doctrine in the political development of Poland during the past decade. It is clear that by 1973 developed socialism had been ideologically sanctioned as the doctrinal expression of Gierek's program of reconciliation between the communist party and the public. Developed socialism emphasized that more advanced socio-economic conditions in the country necessitated alterations in the political institutions. Throughout Gierek's tenure as First Secretary, the Polish United Workers' Party (PUWP) contended that the emergence of new forces in society--primarily the scientific-technological revolution, the crystallization of new economic and social interests, the intensification of group claims for new reforms of political participation, and public pressures for more flexible and innovative political institutions--would be taken into account in the formulation and implementation of public policies. In theory, at least, developed socialism

*See explanatory note p. 114.

denoted accommodation to social pluralism through consultation and cooperation.

In retrospect, the discussions of the doctrine by high-ranking party officials ring hollow. The symbolic and propaganda uses of the doctrine were manipulated by the party authorities to good advantage.[4] Indeed, the standard Polish considerations of developed socialism hardly deviated from Soviet interpretations.[5] In a typical exercise, two PUWP spokesman mimicked the Soviet line by arguing that the transition to developed socialism requires: 1) the complete diffusion of socialist relations in all areas of social and economic life; 2) a high level of development of material forces, application of the attainments of the scientific-technological revolution, rational and complete harnessing of the creative potential of the people and the natural wealth of the country; 3) strengthening the unity of the people around the working class and its party and establishing socialist ideology in the social consciousness; 4) achieving realization of the socialist bases of social justice and intensifying the process of equalizing conditions of life, reducing relative differences between urban and rural areas and between manual and non-manual labor; and 5) developing socialist democracy by constantly improving the activities of the state, its institutions and organs in order to better serve the socialist development of the country and to assure the needs of its citizens.[6] While such goals undoubtedly had considerable mass appeal, these conventional treatments of the doctrine typically failed to explore what policies would fulfill these objectives. The practical issues and implications of the developed socialism doctrine were virtually ignored. Consideration of how existing public policies incorporated the aims of developed socialism was minimal, which meant that indirect or direct criticism of current practices was absent. In short, the PUWP leadership attempted to utilize the doctrine to defend and justify the status quo.

If the discussion of developed socialism had been restricted to these conventional presentations, there would be little utility in examining the Polish version of the doctrine. But this is not the case. Once the high-level discussions of developed socialism were sanctioned and entered the public domain, other reform-minded analysts proceeded to offer more innovative and daring interpretations. In the more tolerant and relaxed political atmosphere of the 1970s, these analysts perceived that the ambiguous doctrine of developed socialism would permit a fuller and more critical assessment of developmental trends and the nature of the political order. The most sophisticated and challenging explorations of the doctrine were conducted by leading sociologists who had been concerned with constructing theories of socialist development. The participation of acknowledged sociological figures such as Wlodzimierz Wesolowski, Jan Szczepanski, Jerzy Wiatr, Stanislaw Widerszpil, and Sylwester Zawadzki lent depth and credibility to the analysis of the doctrine. In both scholarly and politically-oriented journals (among the latter were Polityka and Nowe Drogi), their observations and diagnoses offered the necessary substance and controversy for a serious consideration of the doctrine. In contrast to the propagandistic treatments by orthodox party spokesmen, these analyses provided ideological justification for actual policy reforms. Through these efforts, serious policy and ideological issues were placed more prominently in the public domain.

In the following sections, I will seek to identify and explore some of the main dimensions of these sociologists' discussions of developed socialism. In doing so, I will examine: 1) economic and technological factors; 2) social structural factors; 3) political factors, especially those related to citizen participation; and 4) the call for a macro-societal approach to social analysis and collective decision-making. In the final section, I will evaluate how these interpretations of the doctrine are related to the Polish crisis of 1980-1981.

ECONOMIC AND TECHNOLOGICAL FACTORS

Virtually all of the orthodox discussions of the "transition to developed socialism" placed heavy emphasis on strengthening the economic base and the material forces of production in Poland. The list of economic and technological imperatives for development usually included the harnessing of scientific and technological innovations in the production process, the adoption of more effective organizational and managerial techniques, the improvement of centralized planning through more careful allocation of resources and close supervision of production activities, and increasing the productivity of employees by utilizing them more effectively. In essence, this list affirmed the traditional central command perspective with the qualification that there was a greater emphasis on rational administration and increased concern with the application of advanced technology.[7]

The main implication of such central command approaches is that "technical economic considerations" should be given first priority in order to boost the material forces of production. The strategy of "intensive economic development" followed by Poland during the 1970s placed a premium on productivity and efficiency directed by scientific management.[8] The problem with such views is that they tend to underemphasize non-economic, subjective factors that have a crucial role in the developmental process.

A prime example of the political consequences of overemphasizing technical economic considerations and mistakenly playing down non-economic, subjective factors was the decision to reform the industrial wage system which contributed to the outbreak of the workers' protests of December 1970. As de Weydenthal points out, the decision made sense in efficiency and productivity terms. However, failure to explain the policy to workers and to involve workers' organizations in the policy formulation process had disastrous results: "...the growing isolation of the party top leadership from the workers whose anxieties at the prospects of unemployment and economic scarcity would gradually crystallize around specific events, finding in them a convenient rallying point."[9] In both 1976 and 1980, the economic measures adopted by the authorities (including centralized control of the wage fund and price manipulation) made some sense in economic terms, but were insufficiently understood and agreed upon by the industrial working class.[10] Workers' protests and strikes underscored the fact that purely technical approaches to the problems of the Polish economy could create social disorder on a massive scale.

In contrast to the orthodox spokesmen of developed socialism, the reform-oriented analysts sought to avert such mistakes. They attempted to do so by taking greater account of the unplanned, less controllable factors of social life which were perceived as adversely affecting economic performance. For example, the influential political sociologist Jerzy Wiatr argued that political factors should be weighed carefully in formulating economic policy. Wiatr held that in making economic decisions, differentiated interests should be recognized and it must be asked how such interests "modify behavior." For Wiatr, the essential non-economic, non-technical questions concern: "In what way do economic interests become political interests in socialism (that is in conditions of far-reaching concurrence of politics and economics)?" Wiatr emphasized that failure to recognize differing economic claims may be "a projection, undoubtedly unconscious, of the interests of those social groups which, wielding sufficient power, need no particular protection to look after their interests satisfactorily."[11]

The implications of this approach to developed socialism are clear. Economic decisions cannot be made strictly in administrative, resource allocation, and developmental terms. Societal interests and public opinion must be measured and evaluated, with citizens being given some systematic and meaningful input into the policy formulation process. As Poland makes the transition to developed socialism, decision-making must more systematically incorporate a consideration of how political and social factors affect performance. As sociologist Andrzej Kaminski observed, economic planning and implementation must tackle the "problematics of societal organization, the structure of power connected with it, and the structure of social interests."[12]

The critics of the traditional central command approach toward socialist economic development often termed these highly rational, economic efficiency oriented approaches as being "technocratic-elitist" in nature. Adopting this position, Sylwester Zawadzki (a noted expert on state and law) argued that proponents of the centralized model erred by promoting a one-sided interpretation of the social consequences of technological progress which mechanistically extended the developmental tendencies of capitalist states to the socialist system.[13] Zawadzki suggested that advanced technology and administrative techniques utilized in the West would be ineffective in Poland unless social and motivational factors were taken into account by decision-makers. The representation of citizen interests (he did not specify such organs as trade unions) was cited as a method for combating the "bureaucratism" which can emerge when "technocratic-elitist" policies are followed.

Wlodzimierz Wesolowski (a renowned authority on class and stratification in socialist societies) argued that economic development under socialism "politicized" citizens and that the improvement of the system of economic administration would fundamentally depend upon directly involving citizens in the functioning of economic institutions and in setting economic policy. While Wesolowski did not specifically mention the workers' protests of 1970 and 1976, these obviously played a role in his call for the development of work-place democracy as an element of developed socialism. Workers' councils, youth organizations, and party units in factories, he pointed out, could be agencies for economic and political education, as well as permitting workers to express their concrete aspirations. Workplace self-government, he contended, could prevent tendencies toward "demoralization" if workers were given a real forum for discussion and to make proposals. Thus, Wesolowski noted a need for better economic and political communication between workers and decision-makers.[14] A quote from sociologist Stanislaw Widerszpil is in the same vein:

> In the conditions of constructing an advanced socialist society, there appears the problem of the socio-economic effectiveness of production and the rationality of operation. This is a concept fundamentally different from economic efficiency understood technocratically. It is self-evident that the economy is not simply just one branch of social life, but forms the base of society. But to an increasing extent results depend on how all the other spheres of a uniform social system are developing.[15]

In other words, drawing on the negative experiences of 1970 and 1976, these analysts stressed that economic decision-makers should avoid the isolation from social and political realities that comes through overemphasis of central control and technological solutions to complex problems.

This contrasting emphasis between those who advocated essentially administrative-technocratic approaches to socialist economic development and those who called for greater consideration of socio-political and subjective factors also found expression in a debate over decentralization of the Polish economy.[16] Witold Ratynski, a social scientist with hard-line party connections, accused Mieczyslaw Rakowski, the reform oriented editor-in-chief of Polityka, of heading in the direction of "revisionism" by advocating decentralization of the economy. Rakowski, who enjoyed support from managers and engineers who desired more far-reaching economic reforms and a greater devolution of decision-making authority in the economic realm, denied that decentralization is inconsistent with mature socialism.

SOCIAL STRUCTURAL FACTORS

During the 1970s there was an outburst of sociological studies dealing with the changing nature of the political social structure. These extensive and sophisticated analyses of the evolution of social class and strata, patterns of stratification, and authority relationships were undertaken mainly by the Social Structure Section of the Institute of Philosophy and Sociology of the Polish Academy of Sciences.[17] The main objective was to determine whether, in the long run, the increasingly complex division of labor produced by socialist industrialization integrally affected the distribution of such attributes of social position as professional qualifications, education, income, authority, and prestige. These studies also sought to delineate to what degree the traditional class-type groupings (the working class, the peasantry, and white-collar workers) retained traits developed under capitalism and to what degree they took on new characteristics under socialism.[18] The degree of integration of these class groupings into socialist society was also a topic of particular interest. Finally, these studies focused on social differentiation in terms of socio-occupational status and its influence upon social development. Understandably, many of these analyses figured in the discussions of the developed socialism doctrine.[19]

A most interesting aspect of these analyses was the description and analysis of "structural collisions of interests" capable of leading to "articulated conflicts." According to sociologists Kazimierz Slomczynski and Wlodzimierz Wesolowski, the scarcity of many consumer goods and the operation of the system of distribution under contemporary socialism is "bound to produce conflict of interests between various socio-occupational groups to which goods are unevenly distributed."[20] Contradictions or conflicts of interests could be generated by the uneven distribution of key consumer goods (primarily housing and foods), income differences associated with differentiated educational attainments (raising the meritocracy versus egalitarianism dilemma), unequal provision of social services (health care, education, transportation, access to cultural facilities), and differences in positions in the authority structure affecting citizens' abilities to influence policy decisions (party versus non-party members). With such factors in mind, the sociologist Andrzej Tyszka argued for "following and defining the types of conflicts and questioned economic and social interests; bringing to light the causes of these conflicts; (and) analyzing methods and outcomes of arbitration of conflicts and tensions."[21] Thus, understanding the dynamics of the transition to developed socialism would require the acknowledgement of competitive interests as an element of socialist societies and necessitate serious discussion of the role of politics in conflict resolution.

Significantly, the reform oriented analysts emphasized that the transition to developed socialism would not permit the easy resolution of these contradictions. Wesolowski warned against any "technological determinism" that predicts the domination of society by experts, but also stressed that the future social structure of socialist society could have many possible variations and that there would be policy conflicts over which variations should prevail.[22] He also argued that a socially just structure could only emerge through the promotion of policies that would bring a more equal set of objective living conditions, increased citizen participation, and the formation of a "socialist ethos" supportive of a socialist value system. From this perspective, the social structure of developed socialism must evolve through planning which demonstrates a deep sensitivity to the needs and perceptions of citizens. Such planning would be flexible, allowing for a variety of means and a variety of end results.

The recognition of conflicts of interests generated by an increasingly complex socialist society also produced calls for the regulation of such conflicts. In a characteristic set of statements, Tyszka pointed out:

> These conflicts are not always clearly visible. They are, however, potentially present in the form of contradicting or unreconciliable interests.
>
> Socialist society has at its disposal instruments for regulating conflicts and contradictions. . . There are mechanisms for reconciling divergent interests as well as personal and group interests with macrosocial ones.
>
> The presence of a conflict substratum and of a range of regulating means together make for the process of new social structure development.[23]

These statements indicated that developed socialism would require intervention by the political system to resolve conflicts of interest that threaten social harmony. Put somewhat differently, the doctrine of developed socialism must view divergent interests as a normal feature of society. Under developed socialism, effective compromises between conflicting groups would have to be worked out through political mechanisms. By extension, this would mean giving various organizations which had served as transmission belts of communist party policy in the past (e.g., the trade unions, the minor political parties, the national legislature or Sejm, etc.) some real influence in the formulation and implementation of policy.

Although in the standard Soviet and Polish party versions of developed socialism there were some indications of a greater sensitivity to this growing social complexity and its political implications, the reform-oriented Polish analysts went much further in seeking to define its dimensions and to sanction its political expression. They argued that developed socialism requires formal recognition of the diversity and complexity of the Polish social structure through the establishment of institutional mechanisms for conflict resolution.

POLITICAL FACTORS

Those who emphasized the role of socio-economic development in generating a more structurally complex society offered strong arguments in favor of defining plural interests as natural and legitimate socio-political forces.[24] Sociologist Jerzy Wiatr wrote extensively on this subject and his position was frequently expressed by reformers:

> It is essential that the socialist political system acts as an efficient medium for the representation and articulation of the interests of various groups

> and sections of the working masses, one in which disparate though basically non-antagonistic interests are politically adjusted... The system's effectiveness is to a large extent dependent on the degree to which it is capable of releasing the energy of the masses, and this in turn requires proper stimulation of the process of articulating interests, representing aspirations, and mobilizing the enterprise of all classes, strata, and socio-occupational categories of the world of labor.[25]

The significance of these remarks was the claim that developed socialism requires the forging of compromises between various social groupings, compromises that would convince them that their needs would be properly heard, heeded, and transformed into policies. Wiatr's remarks clearly implied that the integrative "hegemonic" communist party had been deficient in these areas and that other institutions would have to function more effectively to improve political communication and decision-making.

In the liberal weekly Polityka, Wiatr elaborated further, discussing the attributes of political wisdom.[26] He emphasized that the "crux of the matter lies not so much in wisdom of the authorities wielding power, but rather in the establishment of a mechanism of rule of a type capable of providing for flow of information on the factual state of affairs that would reach the leaders freely, without unnecessary changes and without 'improvements.'" He stressed the importance of receiving divergent viewpoints, permitting the expression of alternative policy formulations, and maintaining political flexibility:

> One can govern wisely only when one consults different, alternative viewpoints on each prospective solution, before making a final decision, and only when one allows the supporters of different options to present their opinions ... In part, this depends on the psychological characteristics of the man who makes the decision--his ability really to listen to others, his readiness to compare his own views with those of others. But it is also a problem of creating mechanisms of such types that they would make these comparisons easier and surer.[27]

Wiatr's position clearly advocated the recognition of plural interests and opinions and the development of institutional means for expressing and reconciling them in policy formation and implementation.

Along similar lines, Sylwester Zawadzki (a respected analyst of state and law) identified four criteria for the development of "socialist democracy" during the transition to developed socialism:

1. Citizen influence over state decisions through the provision of direct and indirect representation.
2. Realization of civil rights and freedoms for citizens as guaranteed in the socialist constitution.

3. Realization of equal legal treatment and equality for citizens in political, economic, and social life.
4. Observance of due process for citizens in social life.[28]

Zawadzki contended that these criteria are inextricably interrelated and that undermining any single criterion would detract from the development of socialist democracy as a whole.

Both Zawadzki and Wiatr, prominent party sociologists who published regularly in mass circulation journals, consistently argued that the development of political institutions guaranteeing the direct and indirect representation of citizen's interests would enhance the goal of social integration and contribute to the overall effectiveness of the political system. A weakly developed set of political structures would not be able to accommodate the growing diversity of interests occurring during the transition to developed socialism and would ultimately contribute to spontaneous disruptive outbursts.

The future of socialist democracy, Zawadzki argued, requires the following institutional developments:

1. The ruling Marxist-Leninist party must continue to exercise its leadership role in society, but at the same time it must strengthen its own internal democratic processes. In dealing with other non-communist parties in the Polish system, it must observe correct inter-party relationships.
2. The position of representative organs in socialist society must be strengthened through improving the electoral process, providing constituents with better capacities to influence their representatives, and increasing the influence of these organs over the administrative agencies of the state.
3. Social organizations, such as the trade unions, must be made more effective by increasing internal organizational democracy and making them more responsive to their members' interests.
4. The role of self-governing organizations (workers' self-management councils, peasant cooperatives, residential self-government units, and professional associations) must be increased.
5. Direct forms of democracy, such as national and local referenda, consultations by leaders with special citizens' groups, and the creation of select problem-oriented commissions that have citizen representation should be developed.[29]

One concrete example of this support for strengthening socialist democracy was demonstrated by the growing interest in the functions and activities of the national parliament, the Sejm.[30] Analyses of the activities of the Polish Sejm during the 1970s indicated that while it had yet to gain the capacity to either formulate or initiate broad policy discussions, it did play a more extensive role in the policy process. Working within the policy established by other political agencies (primarily the PUWP and the Council of Ministers), its primary concerns were the quality and effectiveness of legislation formulated elsewhere. Thus, it acted to detect flaws in proposed policies, to make amendments, to clarify goals and means of implementation, to anticipate citizens' reactions to policy, and to facilitate the expression of various interests. Even before the 1980 crisis, the strengthening of the internal composition and organization of the Sejm gave it the structural capacity and potential to fulfill representative, interest articulation, interest aggregation, and political communication functions--as had been advocated by Zawadzki and other reformists analysts of socialist development. Similarly, local people's councils[31] and the system of workers self-management,[32] received considerable attention from the reformist analysts.

In keeping with the position that developed socialism would require greater possibilities for the expression of divergent views, some analysts openly called for greater toleration of dissent. Stanislaw Widerszpil, a sociologist prominent for his studies of social change, presented a characteristic position on this matter:

> It is wrong to treat all contradictions between different social groups and the institutions of government as conflicts between socialist and anti-socialist forces... Many contradictions arise within the socialist ranks and are of a non-antagonistic nature. They should be aired in time to be resolved by removing their causes and by means of discussion and persuasion.[33]

In this view, social tensions should be channeled through institutions where bargaining and compromise would produce social harmony. Thus, Mieczyslaw Rakowski, the editor of Polityka, voiced his disagreement with the program of the Polish dissidents, but contended that they could not be viewed as a "disaster or a plague." He argued that "in their publications they make use of what is published in the official press" and that they "challenge certain phenomena which I criticize too." In sum, he admitted that Poland's social and economic situation had produced politically "polemical and heated discussions" which should be viewed as "an entirely normal phenomenon."[34] The views of Rakowski and other reformist analysts were certainly more tolerant of dissent than those of party spokesmen (e.g., Rybicki and Werblan),[35] and seemingly had some impact on party policies. During the 1970s, the party leadership acted with relative moderation in its dealings with the dissident movement.[36]

THE MACRO-SOCIETAL PERSPECTIVE

One of the crucial elements in the discussion of developed socialism was the call for the adoption of macro-societal perspectives in both social science analysis and in collective decision-making. In essence, this reflected the position that the three main elements discussed above (harnessing the forces of economic, scientific, and technological progress; recognizing the growing complexity of the social structure; accepting plural interests and fostering socialist democracy) are interdependent.

In this vein, Jan Szczepanski, the highly-respected sociologist who has played an active role as a policy advisor, urged in his writings that a synthetic (or comprehensive) picture of the development of Polish society until the year 2000 be worked out.[37] His arguments, in essence, called for recognition of, and sensitivity to, the highly organic and integrated nature of advanced industrial societies. His main concern was to show that economic and political decisionmakers have concentrated their attentions on the material and human resources available for industrial development without sufficiently investigating the societal factors which determine their effective usage. The guidance of an advanced industrial society toward collective goals would require fuller recognition of the complex interaction of the various components of society which he outlined as:[38]

1. The basic systems, defined as society's natural resources, its demographic profile, and the international context (political, economic, and military) within which it must operate.
2. The social structure of society, defined as the existing social classes and strata and their interrelationships, including such factors as educational training, professional aspirations, the status system, and social consciousness.
3. The system of central control, meaning the ruling party, governmental, and economic institutions of the society and the physical and organizational capacities they possess.
4. Directly and centrally controlled systems, primarily the main sectors of the socialist economy, the mass communications network, transportation system, administration of justice, and the national security establishment.
5. Indirectly controlled systems, such as the non-nationalized sector of agriculture, the private services sector, the mass culture, the scientific establishment, and the mass voluntary organizations.
6. Relatively independent systems, such as the Catholic Church, which exert some influence on social life.
7. Spontaneously developing systems, meaning public attitudes and opinions, which constitute micro-societal responses to the activities and decisions of public authorities.[39]

This outline of the interacting elements of socialist society provided only a sketch of factors which might be taken into account in social and policy analysis. Other comprehensive or global approaches to Polish society shared this same defect.[40] Yet, the main objective was politically significant: to redirect policymakers away from the over-optimistic, simplified social engineering of the past. Szczepanski criticized decisions made on the basis of single-factor explanations or single-method solutions:

> Numerous examples demonstrate how these methods and theories concentrating exclusively on the factors under their investigation, caused negative results, since it led to neglect of other factors actively contributing to the problems which were to be solved. To 'absolutize' one method necessarily leads to onesided actions, which aggravates the situation by leaving elements of reality without control of correction.[41]

A developed socialist society, Szczepanski suggested, must recognize that its highly complex nature will produce tensions and irregularities. Solutions to problems must be comprehensive rather than partial, with policymakers avoiding the mistaken impression that "if social mechanisms are misaligned...it is sufficient to align or treat the mechanism...for it to go on effectively and function well."[42]

He cautioned social scientists and policymakers alike to be aware of the fact that social problems that are in the process of being resolved can, in fact, generate new problems:

> ...social problems may, very well, emerge from the very process of development and...their appearance is neither a pathology in need of cure nor alignment, but rather a state of tension has been reached between elements within the social system...The second point is equally important; the solution of social problems always creates new situations; it is not a return to a previous norm. Thus, the solution of one problem arising in one state of society always leads to the creation of a new state, in which new problems are, of necessity, unavoidable.[43]

Szczepanski thus placed heavy emphasis on the system of social control--the party and governmental institutions--in stimulating progress toward developed socialism. What is significant was his implied call for greater sophistication on the part of the party and governmental institutions in tackling existing problems. Given the complexity and interdependent nature of society, he argued that the central control institutions would have to be more responsive to various subsystems, "finding ways of liberating social energy, methods of setting in motion the motor factors of development, and at the same time of eliminating efficiently the factors of stagnation, passivity, and routine which creep easily into formalized organisms, if the latter do not include mechanisms for automatic improvement."[44]

Thus, Szczepanski called upon the central party and governmental institutions to respond to the complexity of exercising power in an advanced socialist industrial society. This call for the adoption of a macro-societal perspective in social science analysis and collective decision making was, in essence, a call for the party and government to be more flexible in their institutional arrangements and practices. It was also a warning against excessive optimism in social engineering, recognizing that this is a highly complex and tension producing task in societies moving toward developed socialism. Szczepanski, who served as chairman of an expert commission that proposed comprehensive reforms of the Polish educational system, did not mention that experience, but apparently he drew on that set of events when he observed that the transition to developed socialism requires both increased competence from those who attempt to guide the processes of change, and patient understanding when unexpected disorders occur. The essence of the adoption of a macro-societal perspective might therefore be summarized as: expect the unexpected and do not grasp for easy solutions. Implicitly, this conveyed criticism of the technocratically optimistic tone expressed in conventional party treatments of developed socialism.

PERSPECTIVES ON THE CRISIS OF 1980-1981

The public discussion of developed socialism during the 1970s was restricted to party ideologists who represented the orthodox line and prominent intellectuals who functioned as establishment critics. Given restrictions on public debate, their analyses and implied policy directions did not fully reflect the issues and controversies which spawned the crisis of 1980-1981. The intellectual opposition which emerged in the 1970s went further by offering much more severe criticism of the system in their "underground" publications, striking an increasingly responsive chord among the population as conditions deteriorated.[45] With the outbreak of the waves of strikes in July and August of 1980, workers offered the most devastating condemnations of Polish socialism and its arrested development during the Gierek era.[46] In this situation, it became unnecessary to discuss developed socialism; the problem became how to resuscitate and revitalize the system in light of its failures.

For the orthodox proponents of the developed socialism doctrine, the events since July 1980 were a devastating blow to their claims of progress and stability. No success propaganda could contradict the facts: Poland was in a state of advanced economic, social, and political decay and disintegration. Party and governmental authorities were forced to be on the defensive in the face of overwhelming societal protest and alienation. In the words of one anonymous observer, "How can we discuss developed socialism anymore? What we have in our present system is neither developed, nor is it socialism."[47] The mounting discontent and organized confrontations swept Gierek from his political posts and required his successor, Stanislaw Kania, to reveal the errors of the system and to offer a process of "renewal" and social "partnership."[48]

In contrast, the reform-oriented analysts could find confirmation of their diagnoses of Polish development. As "establishment intellectuals" they were probably dismayed by the depth and intensity of citizens' grievances toward the system, but they certainly were not unaware of the need for profound changes in its institutions and policies.[49] In their writings, measured and calculated as they were, they had indicated that developed socialism requires economic decentralization and greater employer-employee cooperation or co-responsibility. They also called for fuller recognition of the complex social pluralism of a mature industrial state, more effective citizen participation in an array of social and political institutions, and adoption of more systematic and comprehensive frameworks for evaluating the functioning of a modern society. Their analyses of developed socialism displayed a sensitivity to the previous turmoil of 1956, 1968, 1970, and 1976 and contained implicit warnings that policy immobility and resistance to change threatened to provoke similar disorders.

Moreover, many of these establishment intellectuals were more critical and demanding behind closed doors. In private group discussions and publications, they had broached subjects and advocated positions that were rarely voiced in the public domain of the 1970s. The most widely known example of these critical activities is provided by the "Experience and the Future" Discussion Group whose reports of May 1979 and May 1980, gave evidence of the considerable ferment among the intelligentsia over the Gierek regime's misguided course. In these two documents, experts and professionals from a variety of fields detailed the dangerous situation of Polish society and offered general suggestions for producing social compromises.[50] Although it is beyond the scope of this discussion to delineate in detail the interconnections between the reformist developed socialism arguments and the "Experience and the Future" propositions, it is clear that they reflected substantially similar interpretations of social realities and that they offered compatible policy directions. Interestingly enough, in the "Experience and the Future" reports the formal doctrine of developed socialism was virtually ignored. This suggests that for these intellectuals the doctrine has been tainted by its propaganda uses by party ideologists and that it proved more fruitful to employ alternative formulations and analytical constructs. It appears that the doctrine provided a useful cover for public exploration of selected controversial issues during the 1970s, but its advantages were more limited when unrestricted candor was possible.

From August 1980 until the imposition of martial law, the developed socialism doctrine was superceded by the politics of "renewal" and "partnership." Following the Gdansk Agreements there was room for debate by workers, peasants, youth, and a host of other groups besides party ideologists and establishment intellectuals. Although there was profuse controversy over the nature of socialism and its evolutionary capacities, the crucial issues revolved around the implementation of the Gdansk accords. The most pressing items became the establishment of independent and self-governing trade unions possessing the right to strike, the creation of a national food program which would assure sufficient market supplies, the easing of censorship restrictions as well as provision of wider citizen access to the mass media, and the advancement of a dialogue between the Catholic Church and the state. A variety of other social, economic, and political issues were raised, making it clear that the system was in the throes of a momentous transformation. Under these circumstances, the doctrine of developed socialism seemed less useful as a political formulation, but it was clear that some other framework would have to take its place.

The post-Gdansk period witnessed the proliferation of political doctrines and discussions. Along with "partnership" and "renewal" came calls for "self-management" which would establish the basis for a "new social contract" and the "reconstitution of civil society."[51] These formulations were put forth by Solidarity activists and theorists as well as by establishment intellectuals, many of whom were party members. The proposals had much in common with the political thrust of the reform versions of developed socialism, for they emphasized that Polish society had become an entity which could no longer be centrally guided in an effective manner. Yet they were more radical in tone and more detailed in advocating policies. The developed socialism discussion was a sanctioned establishment debate. The consideration of civil society and self-management was an outgrowth of the confrontation between workers and the authorities. Now a sophisticated and aroused population sought co-participation in setting national policies and in making and implementing decisions in their places of employment. While the political formula for achieving these ends remained ambiguous and would have to be worked out through hard bargaining and compromises, many felt that accommodations could be reached. "Solidarity" as an organization and as an idea was seen as an instrument for guaranteeing that society would be able to self-manage and defend itself if the PUWP violated the social contrast.[52] In 1981, Abram Brumberg observed, "'Genuine pluralism' is no longer a slogan, a dream, or (to those who dread it) a nightmare, but part of evolving reality...and it is slowly becoming part of the country's collective consciousness."[53]

The declaration of martial law by the "Military Council for National Salvation" is the antithesis of what was envisioned by both the reformist analysts of developed socialism and those who advocated the civil society concept. It represents the imposition of an alien authority which distrusts popular participation. While Jarulzelski has promised that the renewal process will continue, his actions threaten to pit the military, the security forces, and the party-state apparatus against the Solidarity movement and the diverse social groups which have been struggling to reform and democratize the system. Martial law may result in the crushing of those who reacted against the political decay of the 1970s and who pressed for new conceptualizations of the policy, but it will not resolve Poland's economic problems and its spiritual malaise. In time, the authorities will have to reach some accommodation with a stubborn and resistant society in order to gain a modicum of support. Otherwise, Poland will not experience socialist development, but instead will undergo socialist atrophy.

NOTES

*This chapter was completed in December 1981, shortly after the declaration of martial law in Poland. An earlier version of the chapter entitled "Developed Socialism, Reformist Politics, and Participation in Poland" appears in Peter J. Potichnyj and Jane Shapiro Zacek, eds., Politics and Participation under Communist Rule (Elmsford, N.Y.: 1982). The author wishes to express his appreciation to the Research Council of the University of North Carolina at Greensboro for its support of his research and the preparation of this volume.

1. See Adam Bromke, "Poland under Gierek: A New Political Style," Problems of Communism, Vol. 21, No. 5 (September-October, 1972), pp. 1-19.

2. Andrzej Korbonski, "The 'Change to Change' in Eastern Europe," in Jan F. Triska and Paul M. Cocks, eds., Political Development in Eastern Europe (New York: Praeger Publishers, 1977), p. 23.

3. For Jaruzelski's remarks, see The New York Times, December 14, 1981. p. 8.

4. The term "success propaganda" became quite familiar during the 1970s in Poland. For many, "developed socialism" was part of the authorities' propaganda campaign. An excellent illustration of how the concept of "socialist democracy" and the doctrine of "developed socialism" were utilized by the regime during the 1970s can be seen in Sarah Meiklejohn Terry, "The Sejm as Symbol: Recent Polish Attitudes Toward Political Participation," in Maurice D. Simon and Roger E. Kanet, eds., Background to Crisis: Policy and Politics in Gierek's Poland (Boulder, Colorado: Westview Press, 1981), pp. 27-64.

5. The Soviet interpretation is analyzed in an article by Alfred B. Evans, Jr., "Developed Socialism in Soviet Ideology," Soviet Studies, Vol. 29, No. 3 (July, 1977), pp. 409-428. Also, see Adam Kosecki, Rozwiniete Spoleczenstwo Socjalistyczne (Warsaw: Wydawnictwo Ministerstwa Obrony Narodowej, 1977) for an official Polish party account of the background and content of "developed socialism" which differs little from the Soviet version.

6. Adolf Dobieszewski and Aleksander Owieczko, "Rola PZPR w kierowaniu procesami budowy rozwinietego spoleczenstwa socjalistyzcnego," in Materialy na Kurso-Konferencje Podstaw Nauk Politycznych (Warsaw: Centralny Osrodek Metodyczny Studiow Nauk Politycznych, 1976), p. 1.

7. Winicjusz Narojek, "The Planning Society," The Polish Sociological Bulletin, 30, No. 2 (1974), p. 40. For a fuller discussion of these points, see Narojek, Spoleczenstwo Planujace (Warsaw: Panstwowe Wydawnictwo Naukowe, 1973).

8. Kazimierz Secomski, "Sily wytwocze rozwinietego spoleczenstwo socjalistycznego," Kultura i Spoleczenstwo, No. 2 (1976), pp. 9-28.

9. Jan B. de Weydenthal, "The Workers' Dilemma of Polish Politics: A Case Study," East European Quarterly, Vol. 13, No. 1 (1979), p. 103

10. See Ian Shapiro, "Fiscal Crisis of the Polish State," Theory and Society, Vol. 10, No. 4 (July, 1981), pp. 485-491.

11. Jerzy Wiatr, Past and Present in Polish Sociology (Warsaw: Ossolineum, 1974), p. 47.

12. Antoni Kaminski, "Discussion of The Planning Society," The Polish Sociological Bulletin, No. 2 (1974), p. 56.

13. Sylwester Zawadzki, "Postep techniczny a rozwoj demokracji socjalistycznej," in J. Kowalski and L. Kisiakiewicz, eds., Panstwo, narod, demokracja socjalistyczna w PRL (Warsaw: Ksiazka i Wiedza, 1970), pp. 246-249. Zawadzki further develops these themes in "Demokracja a forma panstwa," in A. Lopatka and Z. Rykowski, eds., Formy panstwa socjalistycznego (Warsaw: Ossolineum, 1977), pp. 175-190 and in his own work, Z teorii i praktyki demokracji socjalistycznej (Warsaw: Ksiazka i Wiedza, 1980).

14. Wlodzimierz Wesolowski, "Rozwoj demokracji socjalistycznej a doskonalenie systemu zarzadzania," Gospodarka Planowa, No. 7-8 (1978), pp. 354-356.

15. Stanislaw Widerszpil, "The Advanced Socialist Society: An Analysis," Polish Perspectives, Vol. 21, No. 2 (February, 1978), p. 21. Widerszpil develops these points in his study, Refleksje nad rozwojem wspolczesnego spoleczenstwa polskiego (Warsaw: Instytut Wydawniczy CRZZ, 1979).

16. See Adam Bromke, "Poland at the Crossroads," The World Today, Vol. 34, No. 4 (April, 1978), pp. 153-154.

17. See the sources cited in Wlodzimierz Wesolowski and K.M. Slomczynski, Investigations on Class Structure and Social Stratification in Poland 1945-1975 (Warsaw: The Polish Academy of Sciences, 1977) and the Polish Sociological Association, Polish Sociology: Social Structure (Warsaw: Ossolineum, 1977).

18. Kazimierz Slomczynski and Tadeusz Krauze, Class Structure and Social Mobility in Poland (White Plains, N.Y.: M.E. Sharpe, Inc., 1978), p. 5.

19. See, for example, Wlodzimierz Wesolowski and Jerzy Wiatr, "Ewolucja struktury spolecznej jako przeslanka rozwoju socjalistycznego systemu politycznego," in A. Lopatka and J. Wawrzyniak, eds., Demokratyzm Socjalistycznego Systemu Politycznego PRL (Warsaw: Ksiazka i Wiedza, 1978), pp. 61-88.

20. See Polish Sociology: Social Structure, op. cit., p. 30.

21. Ibid., p. 48.

22. Wlodzimierz Wesolowski, "The Planning and Forecasting of Class Structure Transformation in Socialist Society," in Polska 2000, (Warsaw: Ossolineum, Special Edition, 1974), p. 58.

23. Andrzej Tyszka, "Diagnosis and Vision of the Structure of Socialist Society," in Polish Sociology: Social Structure, op. cit., pp. 50-51.

24. For a discussion of such arguments, see Sarah Meiklejohn Terry, "The Case for a 'Group' Approach to Polish Politics," Studies in Comparative Communist, Vol, XII, No. 1 (1979), pp. 28-34.

25. Jerzy J. Wiatr, "Lessons for the System," Polish Perspectives, Vol. 14, No. 11 (November, 1971), pp. 10-11.

26. See Jan B. de Weydenthal, "Poland's Politics: The Question of Power," RAD Background Report 22 (January 26, 1979), Radio Free Europe Research, pp. 6-7.

27. Ibid. Wiatr's most recent work, Przyczynek do zagadnienia rozwoju spolecznego w formacji socjalistycznej (Warsaw: Ksiazka i Wiedza, 1979), strongly favors creating political mechanisms to accommodate Poland's growing social pluralism.

28. Sylwester Zawadzki in Lopatka and Rykowski, op. cit., p. 183.

29. Ibid., pp. 187-189.

30. For further discussion, see Maurice D. Simon and David M. Olson, "Evolution of a Minimal Parliament: Membership and Committee Change in the Polish Sejm," Legislative Studies Quarterly, Vol. V, No. 2 (May, 1980), pp. 211-232.

31. For a discussion of people's councils, see Daniel N. Nelson, "Subnational Policy in Poland: The Dilemma of Vertical versus Horizontal Integration," in Simon and Kanet, op. cit., pp. 65-94.

32. For a discussion of the limited realization of workers' self-management, see Zvi Gitelman, "Development, Institutionalization, and Elite-Mass Relations in Poland," in Triska and Cocks, op. cit., pp. 119-146.

33. Widerszpil, "The Advanced Socialist Society," op. cit., p. 23.

34. "Polityka Editor See Contacts with Oppositionists as 'Normal'," Foreign Broadcast Information Services Reports (March 9, 1979), pp. 2-3.

35. Zygmunt Rybicki and Andrzej Werblan, "Historyczne Miejsce Demokracji Socjalistycznej," in Lopatka and Wawrzyniak, op. cit.

36. See the factors that account for this toleration in Adam Bromke. "The Opposition in Poland," Problems of Communism, Vol. 27, No. 5 (September-October, 1978), pp. 37-51.

37. Jan Szczepanski, "On Elaborating the Outline of a Synthetic Picture of the Development of the Polish Society until the Year 2000," in Polska 2000, op. cit., pp. 7-21.

38. Ibid., pp. 9-18.

39. In discussing the series of confrontations between the regime and society that has marked Polish post-war history, Szczepanski states, "I believe the key problem was the education of the young generation and the linking of this generation with the system. This process failed. The successive generations departed with disappointment from the system in its existing form, this being symbolized by the fact that the leaders of the policial emigration and of the opposition at home are mostly people who, as students, were 'the hope of the party' and the leaders of the party youth." He concludes, "The number of people is declining, who in the postwar period accepted the system and attempted to work in such a manner as to ensure, within the framework of this system, the development of the nation." See, Jan Szczepanski, "In Search for a Reasonable Way Out," Dialectics and Humanism, Vol. VII, No. 4 (Autumn, 1980), pp. 38-39.

40. See, for example, Adam Podgorecki, "The Global Analysis of Polish Society," The Polish Sociological Bulletin, No. 4 (1976), pp. 17-30.

41. Szczepanski, "The Social Sciences and Solutions to Practical Problems," in the Polish Sociological Association, Studies

in Methodology (Warsaw: Ossolineum, 1977), p. 20.

42. Ibid.

43. Ibid.

44. Szczepanski, "On Elaborating the Outline...," op. cit., p. 15.

45. For a discussion of the opposition in Poland, see: Adam Bromke, "The Opposition in Poland," Problems of Communism, Vol. 27, No. 5 (September-October, 1978); Walter D. Connor, "Dissent in Eastern Europe: A New Coalition," Problems of Communism, Vol. 29, No. 1 (January-February, 1980); Jacques Rupnik, "Dissent in Poland: 1968-1978: The End of Revisionism and the Rebirth of the Civil Society," in Rudolf L. Tokes, ed., Opposition in Eastern Europe (Baltimore: The Johns Hopkins Press, 1979).

46. See, for example, the selection of analyses and documents in William F. Robinson, ed., August 1980: The Strikes in Poland (Munich: Radio Free Europe Research, 1980). See, also, Jan B. de Weydenthal, "Workers and Party in Poland," Problems of Communism, Vol. 29, No. 6 (November-December, 1980); Jadwiga Staniszkis, "The Evolution of Forms of Working-Class Protest in Poland: Sociological Reflections on the Gdansk-Szczecin Case, August 1980," Soviet Studies, Vol. 33, No. 2 (April, 1981) and Abraham Brumberg, "The Revolt of the Workers," Dissent (Winter, 1981).

47. In private interviews, Polish social scientists sympathetic toward reform often indicated to me that the developed socialism doctrine was not very useful as a theoretical framework for explaining change, but that it did serve useful practical purposes by legitimizing discussion of alternative policies.

48. Useful recent discussions include: Abraham Brumberg, "Poland's Communists Reborn," The New Republic (June 6, 1981); F. Stephen Larrabee, "Poland, The Permanent Crisis," Orbis, Vol. 25, No. 2 (Spring, 1981); Adam Bromke, "Poland's Upheaval--An Interim Report," The World Today, Vol. 37, No. 6 (June, 1981); Pawel Spiewak, "Polish Reformer: A Long Way to Go," Vol. 25, No. 3 (Fall, 1981); George Kolankiewicz, "Renewal, Reform or Retreat: The Polish Communist Party after the Extraordinary Ninth Congress," The World Today, Vol. 37, No. 10 (October, 1981).

49. The term "establishment critics" is taken from an excellent unpublished manuscript by Jane Leftwich Curry and Joanna Preibisz, "The Polish Intelligentsia, 1980: The Missing Leaders," (1981). Curry and Preibisz provide valuable insights into how the reform-oriented intellectuals operated.

50. See Jack Bielasiak, ed., Poland Today: The State of the Republic (Armonk, N.Y.: M.E. Sharpe, Inc.).

51. See, for example, the selection of articles in the special section of Telos, No. 47 (Spring, 1981) entitled "Poland and the Future of Socialism."

52. For further discussion, see David W. Paul and Maurice D. Simon, "Poland Today and Czechoslovakia 1968," Problems of Communism, Vol. XXX, No. 5 (September-October, 1981); Abraham Brumberg, "Solidarity Forever," The New Republic, (March 21, 1981); Tadeusz Szafar, "Brinksmanship in Poland," Problems of Communism, Vol. XXIX, No. 3 (May-June, 1981).

53. Brumberg, "The Revolt of the Workers," op. cit., p. 27.

Part 2

Cross-National Perspectives

7
Party Leadership and Mass Participation in Developed Socialism

Jack Bielasiak

Two conflicting images have been dominant over the past decade in the Western perception of the Soviet Union and its allies in the socialist camp. The prevailing views have coalesced, on the one hand, around the belief that the centralized political structures of the socialist states are responsible for the socioeconomic problems everpresent in the European communist systems, and may even result in their decay. On the other hand, some scholars have looked upon varying forms of pluralism as descriptive of the present political reality in the socialist states. Both these perspectives stem from the belief that the diffusion and complexity characteristic of modern industrial societies cannot be governed effectively by a monolithic political organization, and that reforms in the system must prevail.

Neither decay nor pluralist explanations, quite naturally, have been accepted by the leaders of the socialist world. Nonetheless, communist politicians have had to respond to the socioeconomic problems apparent in their societies during the transition to industrialization. It is in this context that the theory of "developed socialism," a new stage on the road to the final communist society, was first announced by CPSU First Secretary Brezhnev in 1967. The theory created an all-encompassing analysis of the changes evident in the communist societies during their progression from extensive to intensive economies, and of the impact of these changes on the social and political conditions in the USSR and East Europe.[1]

Economic factors have helped to form the conceptualization of developed socialism. References to the shift from extensive to intensive development stress the necessity for greater economic efficiency. The scientific and technical revolution (STR) in production and management is to result in technological advances, increasingly rational management and gradual improvement in living standards. The consequent resolution of economic ills and the management of complex production forces will theoretically enable the maintenance of the essential structures of socialism and the directing role of the existing party institutions.

Soviet and East European ideologists claim that social transformation in the period of developed socialism is a dialectical process involving a gradual elimination of class distinctions and a drawing together of all the people. Concurrently, the growing diversification of economic life has an impact on the social structure of these societies which are characterized by the increasing differentiation of interests based primarily on occupational, residential, and cultural criteria.[2] The containment of the differences among the social strata, and the prevention of their emergence as major conflicts within society, are necessary tasks in the period of developed socialism. The goal is to be attained by the integration of diverse social interests on the basis of common beliefs and values. The function of political institutions and their cadres is to create cohesiveness among the different strata and to build social unity. Just as the growing complexity of the economy requires increasing coordination, so too social differentiation necessitates further efforts at controlled integration. For this reason, the role of political organizations and political elites must be intensified.

Changes in the political superstructure of mature socialist states are described primarily in terms of procedural improvements in policy-making. The maintenance of existing communist structures is assured by stressing the need for continued party guidance of socioeconomic development. At the same time, the sophistication of the modern industrial society requires the introduction of new methods in the decision making process. Soviet and East European theorists emphasize two ways of controlling societal forces: more advanced forms of administration and the creation of new channels for citizen participation. The first feature focuses on the application of rational administrative procedures in the wake of the scientific and technical revolution. The result is a scientification of decision making which streamlines the economic and social planning process, and enhances the dominance of central political organizations and personnel.[3] In practice this assures "the leading role of the party."

The second aspect is the intensification of socialist democracy, aimed at the expansion of popular participation. The focus here is on the local level, with increasing involvement of citizens in mass organizations, local Soviets and people's councils, and of workers in factories. The masses are expected to take a more active, albeit contained, role in the governing of society. The extension of participation remains in the lower organs, and is circumscribed by democratic centralism.

The theory of developed socialism postulates the capacity of political institutions to manage the economic and social changes evident in the Soviet and East European states. As such, the concept is an implicit rejection of Western claims that growing complexity necessitates the introduction of pluralistic modes of decision making in the polity.[4] The theorists of developed socialism do not envisage the breakdown and political decay of communist states predicted in the analysis of other Western observers.[5] On the contrary, the new stage in the evolution of socialist societies is described as part of the continuing progress of the USSR and the East European states along the road to communism. The advent of advanced industrialization in that part of the world is not the presage of continuing severe problems and crises, nor does it signal the transformation of communist countries into Western-style pluralist societies. Rather, further socioeconomic development signifies to the theorists the need to intensify the leading role of party institutions and citizens' participation.

Nonetheless, the political changes described in the literature on developed socialism are problematic. The emphasis on the leadership functions performed by the party institutions and political cadres does not fit easily with the laudatory descriptions of the intensification of socialist democracy. A tension is bound to exist between principles demanding an expansion in the functions of party organizations and the opening up of the political process to the masses of the working people. The question is how can socialist democracy based on the political participation of the people coexist with the dominance of the party as the controlling institution in all spheres of social activity? Furthermore, how is it possible for both mass participation and the leading role of the party to grow simultaneously in the period of mature socialism? Certainly the contradiction between the two prescripts is difficult to resolve, for how can the participation of the masses be strengthened when decisions are to be made by the party according to increasingly scientific criteria? Without doubt, it will be more and more difficult for citizens to surmount the claim that the party knows best.

This chapter examines the dilemma posed by the concurrent advocacy of socialist democracy and the leading role of the party in the political system of developed socialism. First, the focus is on the theoretical arguments presented by Soviet and East European specialists in regard to the two principal features of mature socialist states. Secondly, the tension between the extension of mass participation and the strengthening of party functions in political organizations and processes is explored. The final section deals with workers' participation and the party role in economic management.

THE THEORY OF SOCIALIST DEMOCRACY

The central feature in the discussions on the political system of developed socialism is the intensification of socialist democracy, which is described as the principal trend in the contemporary development of communist states.[6] In fact, the extension of democratic procedures is depicted as a condition of modernization. "Socialist democracy is the product of the socialist systems, but is also objectively necessary for its development. Socialist society cannot develop without the growth of democracy."[7] The introduction of more advanced forms of democratic participation is therefore a prerequisite to the continued growth of mature socialist societies, and as a consequence "is now a priority requirement."

Mass participation is supposedly manifested in the expansion of citizen involvement in already established "outputs" in policy implementation and supervision. Increases in popular participation in administrative public service are beneficial to the regimes not only because the process provides "voluntary" manpower, but also because it creates a closer identification between the people and the state. It is not surprising, therefore, that the communist leaders favor the extension of mass involvement in such activities. Increasingly, however, socialist democracy has become associated with the expansion of participant roles on the "input" side.

> The most important characteristic of socialist democracy and the main criterion of its development is the active participation of all employees, particularly manual workers, in the governing of the country and in the management of the national economy.[8]

Accordingly, the masses are to become more involved in policy deliberations and take a more active part in shaping the content of decisions.

The theoretical discussion of socialist democracy centers around three ways democratic procedures are invigorated.[9] The first concerns the improvement of already existing patterns of representative democracy. Here the emphasis is on the functioning of the state's legislative institutions, including activities of parliaments and local people's councils. This involves assurances to the people of responsibility and accountability by elected representatives, and the opening up of the selection of delegates. At the same time, socio-political organizations are to act more as representatives of the people's interests in the formulation of policy. A second method of democratization is said to be the expansion of direct participation through increasing involvement of citizens in public and state organizations, the institutionalization of direct consultations between leaders and the people, and the assumption of "control" functions by the masses over various state institutions. The third aspect is the development of workers' participation in the workplace through the promotion of various self-management mechanisms.

Problems of economic growth, social integration and political legitimacy in the communist states have led to the search for solutions, with the commitment to socialist democracy emerging as part of the response to these issues. The intent of the Soviet and East European governments is to resolve the current difficulties, at least in part, by involving to a greater extent their citizens in the affairs of state and thereby strengthening the understanding by the people of societal needs.

To a large degree, these needs are tied to economic performance. In the 1970s, the pressures resulting from the evolution of extensive into intensive economies, increasing demands in the consumer sector, and worsening international terms of trade contributed to a decline in the economic growth of communist societies.[10] The severity of the problems necessitated new steps to maintain economic progress and consumer satisfaction, without tampering with the basic centralized planning system. The attempted solution is to raise economic performance by improving industrial efficiency and productivity. To accomplish this goal, blue-collar workers must be motivated to improve their work efforts. The hope is that the involvement of workers in management issues will increase their understanding of the production process and therefore lead to greater worker responsibility, as well as enhance their satisfaction due to new opportunities for influence over working conditions and rewards. For that reason, "priority is being given to allowing the working people's councils more say in drawing up their own plans and budgets and extending their rights to make decisions or questions of socio-economic development of the enterprises."[11]

The extension of participatory roles to workers in the factory and citizens in the neighborhood is also aimed at creating greater social harmony. Efforts toward the latter are necessary due to the growing complexity of society, with the resulting increase in social and economic differentiation. The task is to reconcile the diverse social views through the recognition of each group's interests by providing them with the opportunity to participate in policy-making and implementation.[12] Social harmony is accomplished not only because various groups are presented with new means of expression, but also because the process of participation serves as a socializing device facilitating the mobilization of citizens in support of socialist values. Participation in the community and the workplace develops the "proper" social consciousness by exposing all citizens to a spirit of collectivism and cooperation.

The attainment of better social relations strengthens the political legitimacy of the communist regimes. This was especially important in the mid-1970s as a consequence of increasing manifestations of workers' discontent. The riots in Poland, strikes in Romania, and vocal demands in East Germany showed that the workers of East Europe had attained greater political awareness and solidarity. The leaderships of the communist states had to respond to this situation within the context of the Marxist definition of political rule. Political legitimacy of the communist parties is based on the claim that a congruence of interests exists between the masses and its vanguard, an argument difficult to uphold in the face of open workers' defiance. The communist regimes were forced to reestablish the identification of the party with the workers, promising to make workers' demands a greater part of decision making.[13] By upholding the primacy of the communist party, the new theoretical articulation also suggests that the aim of communist leaders is the development of symbolic rather than genuine participation.

THE LEADING ROLE OF THE PARTY

The leadership of society during developed socialism remains firmly vested in the communist party and its personnel. The party is the primary agent for the adaptation of socialism to the new scientific and technological era of human development, justifying not only the continued primacy of that institution but also the actual expansion of its functions throughout the periods leading to the establishment of communism. Theoretical arguments present three explanations for the intensification of the leading role of the party at this stage of development. First, as we have seen, the need for political guidance expands as economic and social processes become more complex. Second, the absorption of the scientific and technological revolution into the administrative practices of the party establishes political rule on a new rational footing. Third, the proliferation of non-antagonistic interests during developed socialism necessitates their integration into a common program. The party is perceived as the best possible agent for carrying out this task.

At this stage, the need is not for a mobilization of resources for the construction of socialism in an antagonistic environment. Rather, the party's function is to manage the economic and social transformations created by the scientific and technological revolution. The Romanian leader Radulescu, for example, states that:

> The vast scope of economic, political and social transformations in our country at the present historical stage of building a comprehensively developed socialist society . . . calls for more stress on the political factor in organizing and directing social activity and on the scientific principles of our leadership of society. More than ever before it is necessary to limit the sphere of action of spontaneous forces and create a socio-political climate and institutional framework for the successful use of the creativity of the masses.[14]

For that reason, the role of the communist party is "immensely greater than that of all the other elements of the political system."[15] The primacy of the party's leadership extends well into the future, for the impact of the STR on socialist societies creates increasingly more intricate social and economic conditions. In addition the leading role of the party is assured by the rapid pace of changes, over which constant political vigilance is required to assure the right course of socialist development.

The party's ability to set the correct path is enhanced by improvements in the policy-making and administrative processes of the political system. Changes in the party's own style of leadership are therefore a second major justification for the growth of its functions. The party's responsibility is not only to guide the evolution of the scientific and technological revolution in society, but also to absorb the laws of the STR in its own internal operations.[16] The introduction of new techniques in administrative and policy structures improves empirical information and processing, allows the identification of proper goals and necessary actions, and makes decision making a rational process. On this basis, the "essential conditions for scientific guidance of society and state" are created, reinforcing the claim that the party decides and acts in a scientific manner.[17] Thus the swiftest possible incorporation of rational methods into the party's policy setting and administrative functions is the current goal, for such action provides the best guarantee of the proper guidance of societies.

The stress on scientific decision making does not signify a reduction of policy formulation and implementation to a mechanistic application of rationality to the exclusion of political concerns. On the contrary, the primary responsibility of the party is "to reassert the primacy of politics over administrative efficiency, to assure that broader policy considerations and priorities are brought to the fore in decision making and implementation."[18] The optimization of effectiveness in policy during developed socialism is not to occur at the cost of political norms and party guidance. A leading Polish scholar, for instance, characterizes the political implications of the STR as follows:

> The technological revolution enhances rather than reduces the party's leading role. That is so because the social and political implications of every economic decision must be carefully weighed and measured against the value-criteria of the socialist system and the interests of the working people.[19]

Precisely because the means to set and implement decisions become more and more scientific, the party must ascertain the political reliability of these policies.

The party's political functions form the third justification for the leadership of the party under developed socialism. In this context, the task of the communist organization is to synthesize the diverse societal demands into a cohesive policy serving the needs of the entire population. Even though a community of interests exists in socialist states, diverse occupational, residential and cultural groups maintain their own special requirements. Moreover, the impact of the STR on the social and economic environment leads to the further proliferation of different strata in the mature socialist society. The party's policy aims at the political integration of the various interests advocated by these groups.

> Correct and timely assessment of their many different requirements, the order of their priority, harmonizing them with the overall interests of their society is a very important task, and a very complex one. . . . It can be accomplished only by the Communist Party, which represents the forward-looking elements of all classes and groups of Soviet society.[20]

In the conditions of developed socialism, then, the Party's political roles expand well beyond the mobilization functions it performed during the period of socialist construction. The communist party now acts as a political broker which takes into account and harmonizes differing interests into a unified, directed program determined by the superior political consciousness of the vanguard.

In summary, the ideological view of mature socialism stresses, first of all, the leading role of the communist party as a universal law in the construction of communist societies. Not only is the Party's primacy essential for the establishment and building of socialism, but its leading function is also a prerequisite for the successful passage of socialist states into the more advanced stages of developed socialism. The leadership of the communist party is said to grow logically due to the growing complexity of socialist development, the demands of the scientific and technological revolution, the acceleration of social and economic changes, and the resultant profusion of social relations. The response to these transformations is the expansion of the party's political management functions, so as to control and direct the process of societal change.

THE COMMUNIST PARTY: STATUS AND MEMBERSHIP

The ideology of mature socialism clearly recognizes the role of the communist party as far more significant than that of any other institution in the political system. Since the party's organizational capacity is required to integrate and lead society along the path of socialist development, the theorists of developed socialism are quite adamant about the increasing political status of the party in the new phase of socialism.

The enhanced status of the communist parties has been overtly recognized in the socialist countries through revisions of the state constitutions in the 1970s. The result is a codification of the leading role of the party for the entire society, and a new legal emphasis on the expansion of the party's tasks into all spheres of life. The 1977 Soviet constitution recognizes the major significance of the Communist Party in society--a role passed over in virtual silence in the 1936 constitution. In the new document, article 6 proclaims that "The Communist Party of the Soviet Union is the leading and directing force of Soviet society. It is the core of the political system and of all government and public organizations."[21] Similar language is found in the amendments to the East European constitutions, introduced as a result of the requirements arising from the entrance of the East European states into the period of building developed socialist societies. The formalization of the party's leadership function is put at the forefront of the constitutional principles. For example, a description of Bulgaria's political system states that:

> Article 1 of the Constitution proclaims the Communist Party as the guiding force in the state and society. The Constitution also points out that it is the Bulgarian Communist Party which directs the construction of a developed socialist society in the country. The leadership of the Communist Party is effected in both state and public life.[22]

The author goes on to stress that the Party's "role in this sphere takes a variety of forms but it is invariably a political leadership."

Clearly, then, the constitutional reforms introduced throughout the communist camp to mark the beginning of the new phase in socialist development emphasize the party's continuing dominance over society. The proclamation of this fact in the socialist constitutions, as well as unprecedented accentuation in the same documents of the leading role of the party institutions in all sectors of society, testify to the importance attached by the communist regimes to the highest possible official recognition of the party's growing activity. While it may be tempting to dismiss these constitutional steps as formal and meaningless, the fact remains that the incorporations of the "leading role of the Party" clause in the constitutions does sanction the commanding role of the party and places the rest of society in a position of legal subjugation to the party's directives. Perhaps the best recognition of the significance of this amendment came in the events surrounding the constitutional reforms in Poland during 1975-1976. There the specific mention of the leading role of the Polish United Workers' Party in the new document generated an outcry among the public, especially among the intellectual elite and the Church establishment.[23] Resistance to the clause produced many letters of denunciation and gave rise to an active political opposition in the country. Faced with this major discontent, the regime had to alter the amendment, making the party the "leading force in the construction of socialism" and not in the "state." Despite this reformulation, the dominant position of the communist party was nonetheless recognized in the supreme judicial document.

The constitutional changes of the 1970s in the Soviet and East European states make clear that despite the proliferation of socioeconomic groups, the intensification of socialist democracy, and the expansion of functions by state and public organizations, the communist parties retain their predominant role in the new era of socialist construction. However, a still unresolved issue concerns the nature of the party during the new period. The question is who will be given the opportunity to take part in party affairs, and thereby emerge as the leading elements in the mature socialist states? It is possible that the democratization of the political system described in the literature of developed socialism will extend to the ranks of the party, so that the resulting openness of the party will facilitate the involvement of the masses in the polity. In this sense, socialist democracy may emerge as an important feature in contemporary communist societies.

The nature and extent of political participation in communist systems has been a matter of considerable debate, for it is difficult to assess the full meaning of mass participation in the USSR and East Europe.[24] The basic problem concerns the evaluation of the quality of popular participation in the face of insufficient information about the actual involvement of citizens in political organizations, and their influence in public policy discussions. Some scholars have argued that mass participation in communist states fulfills important systemic functions, and therefore that participation roles are quite high. This claim is subject to considerable controversy for the exact meaning of such participation cannot be determined due to the lack of specific measures concerning citizens' involvement. However, we can rely on the extent and distribution of membership in political organizations as indicators of which groups in society have the opportunity to undertake participant roles in the polity. This does not mean that all such members are active participants with considerable impact on policy. Rather trends in the size and group representation of political organizations can provide some evidence of mass involvement and regimes' priorities concerning citizens' participation in politics.

A critical choice of the communist regimes during the transition to developed socialism has concerned the size of the ruling parties. The parties continued to expand steadily in the post-Stalin period, so that in the 1970s the Soviet and East European leaders faced "the dilemma of party growth."[25] The issue was whether to reduce recuritment and maintain a limit on party membership relative to the population, or whether to allow new entrants into the party to the point of enlarging significantly its ranks. The problem was intensified by competing images of the party in the new period. On the one hand, the traditional view of the party as the vanguard of the people was reinforced by new justifications for the intensification of the leading role of the party. To carry out these leadership functions, the communist organizations had to attract the most qualified candidates as well as to maintain their distinction as the best and the most advanced strata of society. On the other hand, the ruling parties were depicted as organizations increasingly representing all interests in society. In this vein, political statements foresaw the transformation of the parties into mass based institutions defined as "the party of all people."[26] The conflict between the "elite" and "mass" concepts of the party was a reflection of the divergent currents in the theory of developed socialism. It emphasized simultaneously the party's continuing dominance of society through its leadership role, and the democratization of society by the extension of mass participation.

The resolution of the dilemma appears to have been a middle course in most of the communist states. Table 1 reveals that the size of the parties has continued to increase in the 1970s both in absolute numbers and as a proportion of the national populations.

TABLE 7.1. Communist Party Memberships: Total (in thousands) and as % of Population

	1962	1966	1971	1976	1978
Bulgaria	528 6.6%	611 7.4%	699 8.1%	789 9.0%	812 9.2%
Czechoslovakia	1,680 12.1%	1,698 11.9%	1,173[c] 8.2%	1,382 9.3%	1,473 9.7%
GDR	1,610 9.4%	1,750[b] 10.3%	1,909 11.2%	2,043 12.0%	2,077 12.4%
Hungary	498 5.0%	584 5.7%	662[c] 6.4%	754[d] 7.2%	770 7.2%
Poland	1,270[a] 4.2%	1,848 5.8%	2,270 6.9%	2,500 7.3%	2,758 7.9%
Romania	900 4.8%	1,518[b] 7.8%	1,999[c] 9.9%	2,655 12.5%	2,747 12.6%
USSR	9,981 4.6%	12,357 5.3%	14,455 5.9%	15,694 6.2%	16,300 6.2%

a: 1961 b: 1965 c: 1970 d: 1975

Source: Official figures as reported by the East European and Soviet press.

In the second half of the decade, however, a stabilization of the membership is evident. It seems that while party ranks are to remain open to additional recruitment, there is also an attempt to maintain a more consistent level of party membership as measured by its population share. This is evident throughout the region, despite considerable variations in the proportional size of the ruling parties. The range is from 6.2% for the CPSU to over 12% for the Romanian (RCP) and East German (SDEP) parties. The latter two leaderships have adopted a recruitment policy which is aimed at demonstrating the mass character of their parties. Due primarily to the nationalistic content of the Romanian and German policies, this reflects the autonomy of Bucharest in foreign affairs and the SDEP's need to establish a separate identity from West Germany. In both cases, a broadly based party is taken as a symbol of significant popular support for the policies of the regimes.

The attempt to demonstrate increasing popular support for the leadership by involving a greater number of the people in the party is also evident from the rates of membership growth (Table 7.2). The data show that the average annual rates declined in all cases in the 1970s except for Czechoslovakia throughout the decade and Poland in the post-1976 period. The Czechoslovak party had been shattered and purged in the aftermath of the Prague Spring, and it was necessary to rebuild a party whose membership would be more supportive of the new regime. In Poland, the workers' demonstrations also required a response which would diffuse the discontent of the population. The opening up of the party ranks created at least a symbolic opportunity for the masses to take a more active political

TABLE 7.2. Communist Party Memberships: Average Annual Rates of Growth (%)

	1962-1966	1966-1971	1971-1976	1976-1978
Bulgaria	3.9	2.9	2.6	1.4
Czechoslovakia	0.1	-6.1[c]	3.0[e]	3.2
GDR	-2.9[a]	1.5[d]	1.4	0.8
Hungary	4.3	3.3	2.8[f]	0.7
Poland	9.1[b]	4.6	2.0	5.0
Romania	17.2	6.3[c]	5.5[e]	1.7
USSR	5.0	3.4	1.7	1.9

a: 1962-1965
b: 1961-1966
c: 1965-1970
d: 1965-1971
e: 1970-1976
f: 1970-1975

role within officially sanctioned channels. The faster expansion of popular participation in the party after 1976 was therefore part of the attempt to increase support for the Gierek regime.

In general, there is a decline in the party memberships' growth between the 1960s and the 1970s. Annual expansion rates, that had ranged around 4-5% and higher, have decreased to about 2%. The significant exception to that trend, the Czechoslovak party, suffered a major loss in membership in the post-1968 period and has as yet not regained its prior membership strength. Despite the growth of the other ruling parties, there is a clear trend towards limiting the rates of expansion. The former rapid inclusion of new members into party ranks has been slowed down in an effort to prevent the transformation of the party from a leading vanguard to an open, mass institution. The overriding concern in the period of developed socialism is still with the maintenance of the special status of the party and the recognition of its leadership role in society. To a large extent, this depends on safeguarding the party's image as an organization composed of "the best and brightest." In fear that the special authority of the ruling parties would be eroded as membership in them became commonplace, a curb in further <u>rapid</u> growth of the organizations has been implemented.[27] In practice, as in theory, the leading role of the party is dependent on a policy guarding the distinctiveness of its status as the vanguard of society.

The curbs on recruitment instituted in the 1970s have presented the communist leaders with another dilemma, this one concerning the social composition of party memberships. The problem in this regard centers around the tension posed by the need to recruit an elite of the best and the brightest, while conforming to the legitimation of party rule as the representative of the proletariat. In the first instance, in order to manage society, the communist party must admit into its ranks people with sufficient education and professional knowledge to cope with the requirements of a modern industrial state. As Hough has shown, the party membership saturation levels among the educated and white-collar strata are substantially higher than among the rest of the population.[28] In effect, the party rules through the administrative and technical elites and in order to lead effectively and maintain stability it must assimilate a large percentage of the best qualified elements of society. To accomplish this at a time when the scientific and technical revolution is giving rise to an increasing white-collar population, similar absorption rates require either an expansion in membership or a shift in the composition of the party to the detriment of blue-collar workers.

The first possibility, as was noted above, appears unacceptable to the communist leaders for it endangers the special vanguard status of the ruling parties. The second option, increased recruitment from white-collar strata, is bound to be at the cost of the masses of the working people, creating an erosion in the proletarian character of the parties. Such a development threatens the ideological legitimation of the party as the vanguard of the working class. For that reason, a decline in the proportion of workers within the party ranks is also an unacceptable solution. It has become especially so as a consequence of workers' disturbances in Poland and

Romania, and fear of the discontent of the laboring masses in the other countries of the socialist bloc. More than before the need is to demonstrate the close ties between the party and the working class, and to depict the party as the representative of industrial labor.

Commitments to a party of the proletariat were made by the Soviet and East European leaders despite the theoretical view that the communist party became the representative of all the groups in society during developed socialism. Policy statements stressed the working class character of the party and the need to attract more workers into its organization. The de-emphasis of the ideological concept of the "party of the whole people," and the strengthening of its class content, in fact extended the scope of mass participation, since the need to recruit blue-collar workers presented new opportunities for citizens' involvement in the polity. Political leaders made the theme of a workers' party and workers' control a keynote of their speeches in the latter half of the 1970s. For example, at the 25th CPSU Congress, Brezhnev affirmed that:

> Under the conditions of developed socialism, when the Communist Party has become the party of the whole people, it by no means loses its class character. In its nature the CPSU was and remains a party of the working class.[29]

The strengthening of the party's roots among the labor class and the extension of people's participation through socialist democracy was echoed by the East European communist leaders.[30] From the regimes' viewpoint, such a policy had the advantage of increasing the identification of the party with the interests of the proletariat at a time of increasing turbulence among the workers. At the same time, it facilitated the delineation of the party as a vanguard and helped to emphasize its status as the leader of the working class. The usefulness of the policy, however, depended on the implementation of measures reflecting the priority assigned to workers' participation.

Foremost among these steps was a drive to recruit a larger proportion of workers into the party. The result was a rapid increase in the percentage of workers admitted as members.[31] In the late 1960s, industrial laborers accounted for 48 to 52% of new recruits in the Soviet and East European communist organizations. A decade later, their number increased to about 60% or over among all party admissions. The fastest expansion occurred in Romania, where workers made up 72% of new members in 1977 and 84% in 1978. This deliberate attempt to alter the make-up of the party through shifts in recruitment has had an obvious effect on the social composition of the membership. Table 7.3 reveals that the share of workers has increased in all the communist organizations during the past decade. The changes have been of various degrees, with Romania, Poland, East Germany and Hungary exhibiting the greatest shift in favor of the working class. It is significant that the first three countries were subject to some form of vocal workers' discontent, and therefore adopted a strong policy favoring the inclusion of industrial labor in the political system. Hungary, although not subject to

TABLE 7.3. Social Composition of the Communist Parties (%)

	Bul.	Czech.	GDR	Hung.	Pol.	Rom.	USSR
	1962		1962		1964	1960	1961
Workers	37.2		33.8		40.2	51.0	34.5
Farmers	32.1		6.2		11.4	22.0	17.5
White-Collar	30.7		41.3		43.0	11.0	48.0
Others	--		18.7		5.4	16.0	--
	1966	1966		1966	1968	1965	1966
Workers	38.4	30.2		42.5	40.2	40.0	37.8
Farmers	29.2	8.1		6.0	11.4	32.0	16.2
White-Collar	32.4	30.5		51.5	43.0	22.0	46.0
Others	--	31.2		--	5.4	6.0	--
	1971	1973	1970	1970	1971	1971	1971
Workers	40.1	44.1	47.1	42.7	39.7	43.4	40.1
Farmers	26.1	4.7	5.8	--	10.6	26.6	15.1
White Collar	33.8	31.6	28.1	38.1	43.6	24.0	44.8
Others	--	19.6	19.0	19.2	6.1	6.0	--
	1976		1976	1975	1975	1976	1976
Workers	41.4		56.1	45.5	40.9	50.0	41.6
Farmers	23.0		5.2		9.5	20.0	13.9
White-Collar	35.6		31.5	46.1	43.2	22.0	44.5
Others	--		7.2	8.4	6.4	8.0	--
	1978	1977	1979	1979	1979	1978	1979
Workers	41.8	42.0	56.1	62.4	46.2	51.0	41.6
Farmers	22.4	5.3	5.2	10.8	9.4	19.0	13.9
White-Collar	30.2	35.2	31.5	25.3	33.0	22.0	ca.44
Others	--	17.5	7.2	1.5	11.4	8.0	--

Source: Official figures as reported by the East European and Soviet Press.

overt workers' discontent has favored a policy providing for workers' involvement in economic and political affairs as a means of attaining social cohesion and raising economic productivity. In all these cases, there was a practical need to bring the working people closer to the political authorities, resulting in a significant rise in the opportunity of workers to become part of the ruling parties. The extent of such opportunities was evidently less in the Soviet Union and Bulgaria, where the increase in the proportion of workers within the parties was less than 1% between 1971 and 1978. The latter occurred despite a substantial increase during the same time span of recruits with worker origins. The phenomenon of attrition between recruitment and actual party composition is also evident in the other East European states, but to a lesser extent.

The more stable patterns in the composition of the party vis-a-vis rapid changes in recruitment are likely due to two distinct processes. The first is that workers who enter the communist organizations have a higher attrition rate than their white-collar equivalents.[32] The demands of activism, study and responsibility are more difficult to keep up with for the industrial laborer than for the administrative or professional employee. The consequence is that many more workers are purged from party rolls than from the other social groups. This practice, however, does not seem to account for all the discrepancy between party recruitment and composition. Another trend is evident here: upward mobility of worker recruits into white-collar occupations. A large proportion of the working class being admitted into the political vanguard in the past few years has secondary education and makes use of further schooling opportunities offered through party membership.[33] In this way, workers are able to acquire new skills and upgrade their occupational status. For at least a section of the working class, then, the regimes' recent stress on party recruitment of the working masses has resulted in social mobility.

This policy is beneficial to the communist governments since it not only maintains recruitment from the working class, but it also provides the party with a better educated membership. This is confirmed by the fact that educational levels among members of the communist parties have improved steadily over the past decade, both among the working class recruits and among the more highly trained professional and technical elites.[34] The leadership has at its disposal a growing pool of well qualified personnel, who can guide society during the complex, strenuous conditions of developed socialism. The leading role of the party is thus maintained and facilitated, even while admission into the party favors the ideologically preferred working class. In effect, present recruitment policies have dual functions: by admitting a larger number of blue-collar employees, the political authorities can purge from the party ranks members who fail to meet the necessary criteria and retain those with the best potential for exercising political leadership. In this way, both concepts of the vanguard are served: the party appears as an organization of workers and an elite of the educated and best qualified to lead society.

The communist parties have been successful, over the last few years, in arresting the expansion of their membership vis-a-vis population growth. The party has retained its special status as a vanguard, where membership remains a privilege for selected individuals. Equally important, the downturn in the rates of growth has not had a negative impact on the social composition by eroding the proletarian character of the parties. This is largely due to the conscious policy of attracting workers into the organization at a level sufficient to offset the outward and upward mobility of manual labor.[35] Despite this mobility, the commitments of the communist regimes to a party of the proletariat have been translated into the actual inclusion of a greater number of workers into the party ranks. This is especially evident in the recruitment patterns in the late 1970s, as well as in the changes in the social composition of the ruling institutions (Table 7.3). At least as measured by party membership, then, popular participation in the political systems of the Soviet and East European states has increased in the past decade. The question that remains is how significant is such membership in terms of the actual participation of the masses in political activities.

PARTICIPATION IN POLITICS

Popular involvement in governance is described by political authorities as an important condition for effective leadership during the maturation of socialism. Rule through the dictates of the party as the representative of the people's interests is perceived as insufficient for the guidance of the scientific and technological society of developed socialism. Support for citizens' activism in politics has therefore emerged as an important ideological theme, reinforced by the social changes occurring during the transition to higher stages of socialist development.[36] In particular, the higher educational and professional qualifications of the people are taken as evidence that the masses can exercise more leadership functions. Indications are that steps to implement or extend socialist democracy, especially at the local level, have been taken over the past decade throughout the communist bloc. Better opportunities for popular inputs through citizens' access to local policy councils, the expansion of the functions of neighborhood government and public agencies, and increased direct contacts between the people and officials are features that provide the citizenry with the potential to step up their influence in policy deliberation and implementation.

Evidence of greater popular involvement in political action exists primarily in the activities of local state agencies. While the initial discussion on the transition to communism stressed the decline of state institutions in favor of public organizations and public self-administration, this has been reversed in subsequent descriptions of developed socialism.[37] Currently, local representative bodies are the embodiment of the popular will. The result has been the upgrading of the representational features of soviets and people's councils, both by offering the citizens some choice in the selection of their deputies and by allowing a greater number of councilors to come from the ranks of the working class. Poland, Hungary, and Romania have introduced the principle of multiple candidacies, where voters can exercise a limited amount of electoral preference from an approved list.[38] In the 1978 Polish local elections, there were thus some 160,000 candidates for approximately 100,000 seats on people's councils. Just as important was the activization of working people to leadership positions within the local organizations. The occupational status of deputies to local soviets in the USSR and people's councils in Poland, Bulgaria and Romania has shifted steadily in favor of the workers and, in general, to the detriment of white-collar representatives.[39] This has been paralleled by efforts to bring non-party people into political activities, and to provide them with responsible positions.

It is difficult to assess the meaning of these changes for the exercise of popular inputs into policy since we do not know how active the new deputies are in representing and advocating the interests of their fellow workers and non-party citizens. Presumably, however, information concerning the needs and demands of the masses will have a better chance of reaching local policy making institutions through the intervention of worker deputies. With this type of knowledge at the local administrative level, the interests of the masses may be increasingly reflected in decisions. This is especially so since people's councils and public organizations have, in recent years, expanded those activities touching most directly on the citizens' life and work.

The Soviets have been more active in assessing community needs and offering solutions to local problems, and have extended their control over budgetary matters and communal services.[40] The accretion of more responsibility to the neighborhood elective bodies has also occurred in the East European states, where citizens' opportunities for taking part in discussions of local councils have also increased.[41] In Romania, permanent national forums have been established (the Congress of People's Councils and the National Council of Working People) to further institutionalize mass participation in state institutions. In conjunction with the decentralization of the Hungarian economic system, greater autonomy was granted to people's councils to enable them to deal more effectively with local issues. The provision of wider powers to the local representative institutions and their presumed ability to affect more directly the living conditions of the people should encourage the greater activity of the masses in local politics.

Local public organizations also have been encouraged to meet their responsibilities as the representatives of the people and to fulfill citizens' demands. Trade-unions, young groups, and social organizations are viewed as organs of government which not only serve as links between the people and the authorities, but increasingly act as articulators of mass interests. In this manner, Hungarian trade-unions have been provided with a specific obligation to defend the rights of the workers to the extent of using a veto power to block measures detrimental to their constituencies. Other channels for the intensification of socialist democracy have centered around self-government in residential communities.[43] Bulgaria has thus instituted agro-industrial complexes and "systems of inhabited places" providing for greater organizational autonomy of the territorial regions, and administration through collective management, general assemblies, and specialized councils.

The provision of new participatory opportunities by means of organizational changes in the local community has been supplemented by the intensification of contacts in consultative forums between the political leadership and the masses.[44] This type of direct dialogue between the working class and party and state officials has progressed furthest in Poland and Romania in the wake of the labor strikes and riots in 1970, 1976, and 1977. Regular visits by the top leaders to factories and towns have become an important aspect of the political systems. The consultative exchanges have been further institutionalized through more direct contacts between the people and political and managerial staffs at their places of work and residence. The aim is to offer the citizens opportunities to express opinions to superiors, as well as to the highest officials of the country. In this way the needs and hopes of the masses are to become known to the leadership, who can take them into account in formulating national programs and thus avoid additional disturbances by the working class. For that reason, certainly, consultation has emerged as a major element in the activities of communist political institutions and has become a featured description of the merits of socialist democracy.[45] Direct consultations between leaders and various constituencies have provided at least a symbolic visibility to the people's increased involvement in the formulation of policies.

The procedural improvements in participatory mechanisms and the extension in the scope of state and public organizations' activities at the local level certainly provide greater stimulation for mass involvement in politics. The steps taken over the past decade to facilitate citizens' participation conform to the theme of intensifying democracy in the developed socialist society. We should recognize, however, that the new opportunities for participation provided throughout the communist camp are limited, both by structural arrangements and by the continuing assertions of the leading role of the party.[46] The participatory reforms concern primarily local representative councils and public organizations which continue to act in a centralized system subject to vertical integration, thereby limiting the competence of the local bodies. Many spheres of activity are beyond the jurisdiction of these institutions and are instead the prerogatives of local administrative organs responsible to central ministerial or party authorities. In addition, local councils and public institutions continue to be subject to executive committees and party organizations which intervene in the work of the participatory bodies. Citizens' activism, then, continues to be closely watched and supervised. Even in those instances where specific new functions are given to the public or people's organizations, old habits are difficult to break. The Soviets do not take the initiative in carrying out the additional tasks, which remain outside the influence of the masses and are instead dominated by the executive committees.[47] Hungarian trade-unions rarely make use of their new veto powers, and other rights, and then only after consultation with the enterprise party organization.[48] In Poland, the direct communication between the people and the leaders in consultative forums was often reduced to discussions between officials and the political aktifs. The result has been that information obtained in this manner is not reflective of popular feelings, with disastrous results for the country, as in June 1976 and July-August 1980.[49]

Limitations on the participatory opportunities emerging during developed socialism are reinforced by attempts to strengthen the leading role of the party. Even while promoting participation, the Soviet and East European regimes uphold the basic principle of the communist party's dominance and pursue policies to assure the leadership of party organs. There is no doubt that institutional and procedural rearrangements expanding the visibility of socialist democracy are subject to the traditional imposition of the communist party's guidance. To ascertain that reforms favoring popular participation do not overstep, and thus erode, the superior status of party organizations, campaigns affirming the directing role of party organs are evident. These directives provide party organizations with extended powers vis-a-vis their state and public counterparts, emphasize the activist role of party members in all sectors of society, and assure the proper training of party officials to fulfill these leadership roles.

Preeminence is assured by widening the powers of party institutions in the areas of decision making and supervision over policy implementation and performance.[50] Party influence in policy deliberations emanates from close control over agenda setting and information, arbitration in cases of conflict, and coordination of programs. Overall control in policy is guaranteed by the intervention of party departments in the work of other societal organizations. These powers have been extended in the 1970s by allowing primary party organizations to supervise state administrators and public employees even within the latter's areas of jurisdiction. In this way, the apparatus of the party has attained greater involvement in ministerial decision making, as well as in representative and administrative institutions throughout the hierarchy of the political system. Emphasis on the principle of democratic centralism provides further means for inclusive direction by the communist party over the policy tasks of state organs, people's councils, and public associations.

The fact that party members are leading activists in all state and public organizations represents an additional method of guaranteeing that the party sets the political line and supervises its implementation.[51] Membership in the communist organization carries the obligation of activism, and the "party group" in all institutions is required to provide political leadership. These functions are strengthened by the emphasis on commitment to the party line (partiinost) as the first principle in the work of officials, as well as by deliberate steps to expand the obligations of party activists in the contemporary period. In Romania and Poland, for instance, new positions of party organizer were established to increase the party's control over the activities of state and public institutions.

Recent efforts through the Soviet and East European region have been directed also at improving the qualifications of party cadres, enabling them to exercise more effective leadership in administrative and participatory institutions. A Soviet commentator remarks that "as socialist society develops, changes occur in the activity of leading personnel, and the demands made on them increase. This determines the need for further improvement in leaders' style of work."[52] Present requirements necessitate better competence on the part of officials in both administrative/technical and political areas. The education and training of party officials have thus been subject to a dual emphasis, aimed at developing their practical abilities and ideological responsibilities.[53] In the first place, promotion to leadership positions is increasingly dependent on the candidate's specialized qualifications, on the basis of which he/she can cope with the impact of the scientific and technical revolution on society. The danger is that the focus on expertise can lead to a neglect of the political program of the communist party. To offset the technocratic tendency, greater attention is given to Marxist-Leninist education at all levels of the political hierarchy. The party's vanguard political role is therefore closely tied to the infusion of ideological education for party officials, mass activists, and rank-and-file members who are subject to more sophisticated doctrine and tighter requirements for individual and group study.[54] The culmination of these efforts has resulted in a higher proportion of political personnel with ideological schooling throughout the party and state bureaucracies. Political commitment as well as professional competence are the marks of leadership in developed socialism. To assert that both attributes are present in the party membership and among cadres, several of the communist parties initiated in the 1970s an exchange of party cards.[55] These occasions served to evaluate the records of each party member in order to purge those lacking the necessary qualifications and mobilize the rest for increased political initiative.

The political evolution of communist societies over the past decade, coinciding with the introduction of a developed socialist state, has been characterized by the implementation of extended forms of socialist democracy and the accentuation of the leading role of the party. Citizens of the Soviet and East European countries have been provided with better opportunities to fulfill participatory political roles, whether by increased mass adherence to party membership or the assumption of local political positions. Simultaneously those institutions, such as people's councils and public associations, which are the repository of mass involvement have gradually expanded their areas of local jurisdiction. The focus of the intensification of democratic socialism has therefore been directed at the grass root level, where the benefits of political participation are most relevant to the lives of the people. The opportunity to improve their environment and living conditions may indeed provide the incentive for attracting citizens into appropriate forms of political behavior. The regimes' need to contain mass involvement in policy and retain governmental control over local issues, however, also necessitates the congruent expansion of the political authority's capacities. This goal was successfully reached by the communist regimes through the expansion of the leading role of the party in the period of developed socialism. Provisions for greater responsibilities of party organs within state and public organizations, as well as the upgrading of the quality of party members and officials in terms of professional qualifications, ideological commitment and political activism, served to guarantee the commanding role of the party vanguard in the face of democratic innovations. The simultaneous promulgation of the ideas of the leading role of the party and the expansion of socialist democracy has been resolved in the political sphere in favor of the party's leadership of society and its institutions.

MANAGEMENT OF THE WORKPLACE

A most important feature of developed socialism is the participation of workers in the decision making and implementation aspects of economic management. Leaders and scholars in all the Soviet and East European states have proclaimed the participatory role of labor in the workplace as the primary criterion in the development of socialist democracy in the contemporary era. The factory is viewed as the most important sphere of people's life and work, in which the interests and attitudes of blue-collar labor can be shaped through provisions for workers' involvement in the affairs of the enterprise. The goal of the political authorities is to use workplace participation as a means to stimulate efficiency in production and socialize workers in support of socialist ideals. The hope is that workers' involvement in policy will increase worker identification with production tasks and spur greater work efforts, as well as foster collective and socialistic human relations which will reinforce social integration and political support for the state.[56]

The communist governments have advanced the claim that workers' interests are channelled through the direct participation of labor in economic policy-making. The workers' rights to influence decisions on the socioeconomic development of the enterprises is said to exist in the system of collective management, in which manual laborers can voice their preferences alongside economic managers and political cadres.[57] Hungary, Romania, and Poland are at the forefront of proclaiming the working class' ability to exercise influence through participation in meetings of enterprise governance. The leaders of the other communist countries are more cautious, although they too advocate increasing workers' involvement in management in the form of the established production conferences. All the Soviet and East European regimes claim that existing enterprise institutions and procedures enable workers to fulfill genuine participant roles and exercise considerable authority.

The evidence on workers' participation in factory organizations reveals that although attendance at meetings is high, their involvement in both preparation for discussion and policy deliberations is significantly lower. Soviet data shows that participation by workers in various plant meetings was overwhelming (98%, Table 7.4), and similar trends are evident in case studies of Romanian laborers.[58] These findings are not surprising for they refer to attendance only, and since in the Soviet enterprise meetings are held once a month and require at least 50% of the membership to be present. Soviet scholars acknowledge that not all workers participate actively at these gatherings, but claim that manual laborers influence decisions

TABLE 7.4. Participation in Factory Meetings by Workers

	Soviet Union	
	Yes	No
% of Workers Attending Meetings	98.0	2.0
% of Workers Working in Committees	57.0	43.0
	Romania	
% of Workers Making Proposals	35.6	64.4
	Poland	
	Blue-Collar	White-Collar
# of Participants in Discussion	54	194

Sources: Adapted from V.I. Ussenin et al., "Soviet Workers and Automation of the Production Process," in Jan Furslin, Adam Sarapata and Arthur Whitehill, eds., Automation and Industrial Workers (Pergamon Press, 1979); Dan Nelson, "Workers in a Workers State: Participatory Dynamics in Developed Socialism" (mimeo, 1979); and Roman Stefanowski, "Workers' Councils 1956-1977," Radio Free Europe RAD BR/ 160 (9 August 1977).

through their votes.[59] Nonetheless, the impact of workers' opinions on the content of policy is bound to be low in such circumstances. This view is supported by evidence regarding industrial labor's involvement in the more critical work of the committees of several factory organizations. Fifty-seven percent of the workers were active in the latter institutions, whose tasks range from the preparation of policy discussions to the implementation of decisions. Even though a majority of laborers took part in such work, their influence on policy is likely much less than that of the white-collar employees who dominate these committees (Table 7.4). Indeed a Romanian study of production meetings shows that the majority of workers (64%) do not make proposals on work-related issues; while a Polish survey of 30 workers' self-government conferences in the mining industry reveals that only 54 out of 248 participants in the policy deliberations were manual toilers! It is clear from these data that the presence of economic administrators and technical specialists at gatherings of enterprise management organizations is an inhibiting factor in the exercise of the democratic rights of workers and greatly reduces their influence in factory affairs.

Not surprisingly, the workers' evaluation of the effectiveness of workplace participation and the impact of activism on labor's socioeconomic environment is generally genative. Workers' involvement in enterprise governance is therefore largely formal, since manual employees are well aware that factory conferences only have a marginal impact on employment conditions and benefits. The Romanian study measured the sense of efficacy of these workers who took an active part in discussion by making proposals, and found that about 60% thought that their suggestions had an impact on decisions while the remaining 40% did not believe that their intervention had a positive consequence.[60] Furthermore, those workers who commented on policy deliberations at meetings numbered only 35% of those attending. It is most likely that the 65% who remained silent did not think that suggestions would be effective, meaning that only 20% of the enterprise industrial employees saw their intervention in policy through proposals as effective. Similar conclusions emerge from surveys in the other East European states. For example, the majority of Hungarian workers at an automobile factory felt that it was impossible to criticize personnel above the position of foreman (Table 7.5). Since many of the discussions of enterprise issues involve opinion differences between management and manual labor, there is no doubt that the negative perceptions on criticism hamper the workers' advocacy of preferred programs. Similarly, the vast majority of Hungarian industrial employees did not look to the trade-unions for help with problems on a variety of work-related issues, preferring instead to turn to their immediate supervisors. Clearly, the institutions of workers' representation are seen by blue-collar

TABLE 7.5. Workers' Opinions on Factory Relationships in Hungary

Persons Affected	% of Workers Who Felt that Criticism	
	Was Possible	Was Not Possible
Workers	85	15
Foremen	61	39
Plant engineers	36	62
Plant leaders	35	64
Factory unit leaders	25	74

Matters	% of Workers Relying for Help on	
	Immediate Supervisors	Trade-Unions
Wages and norms	75	1
Work problems	87	-
Professional education	76	2
Improvement of work conditions	75	15
Personal problems	80	2
Health and social questions	74	20

Sources: Lagos Hethy, "Plant Democracy and the Interests of the Workers in Participation," Joint Publications Research Service, June 1979; and Csaba Mako and L. Hety, "Worker Participation and the Socialist Enterprise: A Hungarian Case Study," in Cary L. Cooper and Enid Mumford, eds., The Quality of Working Life in Western and Eastern Europe (Greenwood Press, 1979).

employees as inadequate agencies for the advocacy of their interests, resulting in their belief that workplace socialist democracy is ineffective for the channeling of workers' aspirations.

At the same time there is considerable evidence that those workers who view their involvement in economic management as efficacious find their jobs and environment much more satisfying than those employees whose evaluation of workplace participation is negative. A study of the relationship between workers' participation on several policy questions and attitudes towards work demonstrated that the more intense the workers' involvement in issue deliberations, the greater was their satisfaction with performed occupations. In addition, employees who felt "their own boss" derived more satisfaction from their labor activities, and tended to work with more concentration and in better moods (Table 7.6). Clearly, participation inputs that are perceived as effective lead the workers to perform better on the job and derive greater satisfaction from the work tasks. The consequence is bound to be an improved productivity contributing to economic growth. This was the case with a Czech factory's experiment in extensive participation which resulted in a rapid increase in production.[61] At the same time, the workers' more positive assessments of their work environment are likely to be manifested in greater social stability. Without doubt, then, workers' involvement in the management of the workplace can be of considerable economic and social benefit to the political authorities. In particular, it can alleviate some of the major problems faced by the communist states in the contemporary period.

The problem is that while the positive effects of mass participation in workplace governance are recognized in the descriptions of Soviet and East European socialist democracy, in actual practice the participation opportunities remain inadequate. The levels of labor's involvement in management are considerably low, consisting primarily in workers' attendance at factory meetings. The reason for this is the continuing dominance of the enterprise by white-collar employees and politically reliable activists, a condition in keeping with the leading role of the party principle. It appears that the communist leaders are unwilling to provide more open channels for manual labor's inputs into policy deliberations, in fear that such activities will have undesirable political consequences. For that reason, the democratic aspects of factory management are subject to limitations providing for control by more trusted political elements.

The leadership function of party organizations and cadres is therefore recognized as an essential practice in the system of worker participation in the communist states. The party's right to political control over various areas of plant life is viewed as indisputable, for it guarantees the proper development of economic and social forces.[62] To assure the direct exercise of this role, for example, the communist party secretary of Romanian enterprises is automatically the chairman of the working people's council. The guidance of workers by the party is in fact assured in the Soviet and East European factories by the dominance of membership in workplace institutions by political activists and white-collar managerial groups. In several USSR plants, workers were systematically

TABLE 7.6. Soviet Workers' Attitudes Towards Work (%)

Attitude toward job	Do you feel you are your own boss in your collective? yes	no
I always get satisfaction from work	71.7	28.3
Frequently	43.8	56.2
I more often do not get satisfaction	22.1	77.9
I am constantly dissatisfied with work	20.7	79.3
Job is interesting; I like it	57.0	43.0
Job is no better and no worse than any other	33.3	66.7
Job is not interesting; I do not like it	20.0	80.0
I always work calmly and with concentration	65.9	30.1
I am in a positive and busy mood	43.5	30.1
I experience annoyance on the job	23.2	76.8
I am always nervous	22.2	77.8

Source: N.I. Alekseev, "The Interrelationship of Social Factors Determining Work Attitudes," International Journal of Sociology, VIII (4), Winter 1978-1979.

underrepresented in enterprise committees. The coefficients of representation for the laborers were below .86 in all cases, while administrative and technical personnel consistently show coefficients of overrepresentation above 1.2 (Table 7.7). Most notably, even those organizations which are geared towards the involvement of workers in economic management still do not give advantage to that strata. The same evidence pertains to the pre-1980 Polish workers' councils where the majority of members were white-collar employees, and the dominance of the latter extended even further on the presidiums of the councils (with a 65% to 80% membership).[63] Since administrative and technical employees are much more likely to be members of the communist party than manual toilers,[64] the overrepresentation of the former in enterprise organization also translates into the domination of party activists over factory policy. This is again evident from the data in Table 7.7, which shows that the extent of representation of CPSU members far exceeds those with no political affiliation: the respective coefficients are 2.9 and .70! In terms of the contributions made by participants to enterprise assemblies, members of the Romanian Communist Party were consistently far more involved than their counterparts who did not belong to the party. The difference was especially marked in the all-important activity of preparing for assembly sessions. Obvious differences in the scope of participation are present, and party members appear to be able not only to dominate the discussion but also to direct its course by better preparation.[65]

The leading role of the party in Soviet and East European enterprises is assured by the policy of providing the party organizations with supervisory rights over plant participatory institutions, and by the practice of political activists dominating the membership and controlling the discussion of workers' conferences. No wonder that in these circumstances the mainstream of blue-collar laborers do not take part in management conferences beyond attendance at the meetings, with only a small minority attempting to gain more influence by participating in discussions and offering suggestions. The prevalence of party cadres and white-collar employees in factory assemblies and committees is perceived as assuring the policy outcomes, culminating in the workers' belief that their interference in discussions will be ineffective. The potential for increasing workers' involvement in economic management is limited as long as the present conditions persist. In order to attract more interest in the participatory mechanisms at the workplace on the part of manual employees, the authorities need to move beyond symbolic participation and provide more genuine opportunities for the expression of workers' interests. This requires the devolution of the party controls in the factory, a step which the communist regimes are unwilling to initiate for fear of unleashing greater workers' demands. The leadership role of the party is unquestionable in the factory as in society, and for that reason workplace participation does not appear to be a useful vehicle for the increased satisfaction of industrial labor with their work and life conditions.

TABLE 7.7. Representation Coefficients by Political Affiliation and Occupation in Soviet Factories

Organization	CPSU	Komosmol	No Affiliation	Workers	Engineer-Tech. Personnel	Employees
Party Committees	NA	NA	NA	.62	2.40	1.22
Factory Committees	1.73	.64	.94	.86	1.22	2.09
Komsomol Committee	1.6	4.02	NA	.86	1.24	2.13
Standing Production Conferences	2.90	.37	.76	.70	2.07	1.28
People's Control Committee	2.95	.57	.69	.77	1.79	1.28

Source: Adapted from V.I. Mukhachev and V.S. Borovik, Robochii klass i upravelenie proizudstvom (Politicheskoi Literatury, 1975) in Charles E. Ziegler, "Political Participation in the USSR: The Workers' Role in the Developed Socialist State," Paper presented at the Midwest Slavic Conference, Cincinnati, May 1980.

CONCLUSION

Changes in the political system of developed socialism reflect the theoretical concerns with socialist democracy and the leading role of the party. New participatory modes were introduced in the 1970s in the Soviet and East European states, and citizens had greater opportunities to become involved in political activities. Participation by the people increased through workers' recruitment into party memberships, the extension of political roles for the masses in state and public organizations, and in a more limited way through provisions for workers' activity in enterprise management. In all these cases, the development of mass participation channels was circumscribed by the continuing emphasis on the primacy of party institutions in directing the socioeconomic and political progress of socialist societies. The intensification of socialist democracy was contained by the expanding functions of party organizations and the increasing responsibilities of party activists and cadres. While presenting Soviet and East European citizens with an extended possibility to become involved in policy formulation and implementation, the communist regimes sought to mobilize popular participation in directions favored by the party. As a consequence, participation by the masses remained largely under the guidance of the party. The tension evident in the simultaneous advocacy of the growth of socialist democracy and the leading role of the party was clearly resolved in favor of the continuing command functions of the ruling communist parties. Participation opportunities in developed socialism were provided within well-defined limits, assuring the primacy of the "leading role of the party" principle.

Mass participation, nonetheless, attained an increasingly visible role in the political system of mature socialism. The propagation of citizen involvement in local neighborhood and workplace institutions facilitated the integration of the individual with society. The communist governments concern with social harmony and political legitimacy at a time of rapid transformations in Soviet and East European states brought about an intensification of participatory opportunities. The conception of socialist democracy, however, differs considerably from Western principles of participation.[66] Pluralism recognizes the existence of conflicts in society, based on differences over fundamental values. To safeguard their interests, citizens must organize into groups which engage in conflictual politics in order to influence the adoption of policies reflective of their preferences. The pluralist concept of political participation, then, assumes permanent conflict and bargaining among organized interests to define societal programs. In contrast, the theory of socialist democracy presumes the existence of a common value for all of society: the construction of communism. In this context, political participation rests on strong consensual interests and is meant to facilitate the attainment of collective goals. Institutions of mass participation are designed to facilitate the better integration of the fundamental values and not to provide the mechanisms for the advocacy of conflicting interests. The socialist model of participation is therefore collectivist, integrative and unitary.

This does not mean that there are no diverse interests in socialist society. On the contrary, the theory of developed socialism recognizes the proliferation of interests in the modern socialist state. The differentiation, however, is not caused by fundamental class divergences and conflicts are considered to be non-antagonistic. The essential unity of society, theorists argue, is dominant in mature socialism. Precisely because of this basic harmony, channels for the expression of different interests may be safely expanded. The tasks of participatory procedures are not to advance the interests of separate groups but rather to promote the closer identification of individuals with the common values and objectives of society. The role of the communist party organizations is to facilitate group and societal integration by assuring adherence to the program of socialist construction. The party remains the "best" interpretor of the common purpose, and therefore acts to direct all social forces in the pursuit of socioeconomic and political progress. For that reason, the leading role of the party and its expansion is essential as the advanced socialist society gives rise to an increasing differentiation of interests. The growth in the party's functions is necessary to cope with this development and assure that participation continues to express the basic harmony of developed socialism.

NOTES

1. For general works on developed socialism, see G.E. Glazerman, ed., Razvitoe sotsilisticheskoe obschestvo (Moscow: Mysl, 1975); E. Chekharin, The Soviet Political System under Developed Socialism (Moscow: Progress, 1977); P.A. Rodionov, ed., Partiia v period razvitogo sotsialisticheskogo obsvchestva (Moscow: Politicheskoi Literatury, 1977); V.S. Shevtsov, Gosudarstvo razvitogo sotsializma (Moscow: Politicheskoi Literatury, 1978); Adam Lopatka and Zbyslaw Rykowski, eds., Formy panstwa socjalistycznego (Wroclaw: Ossolinskich, 1977); "The present-day problems of socialist democracy and its perspectives," World Marxist Review (WMR), 18: 2 (February 1975), pp. 41-83, and 18: 3 (March 1975), pp. 100-126; and "Political system of developed socialism," WMR, 22:6 (June 1979), pp. 31-40.

2. For discussion of these issues, see Alfred B. Evans, Jr., "Developed Socialism in Soviet Ideology," Soviet Studies, 29: 3 (July 1977); Donald R. Kelley, "Developments in Ideology," in Soviet Politics in the Brezhnev Era, ed. Donald R. Kelley (New York: Praeger, 1980); and Robbin Laird and Erik Hoffmann, "The Soviet Concept of Developed Socialism," Paper presented at the Annual Meeting of the American Association for the Advancement of Slavic Studies, New Haven, Conn., 1979.

3. Robbin F. Laird, "'Developed' Socialist Society and the Dialectics of Development and Legitimation in the Soviet Union," Soviet Union 4: 1 (1977), pp. 134-141.

4. See the essays in H. Gordon Skilling and Franklyn Griffiths, eds., Interest Groups in Soviet Politics (Princeton: Princeton University Press, 1971); and Jerry F. Hough, "The Soviet System:

Petrification or Pluralism," *Problems of Communism* 21: 2 (March-April 1972).

5. For example, Zbigniew Brzezinski, "The Soviet Political System: Transformation or Degeneration?," *Problems of Communism* 15: 1 (January-February 1966).

6. For descriptions of socialist democracy, see the comments at the theoretical conferences "The present-day problems of socialist democracy," and "The political system of developed socialism," *op. cit*.

7. Alexander Lilov, "An objective law of building the new society," *WMR* 18: 2 (February 1975), p. 42.

8. Edward Gierek, *Trybuna Ludu*, 8 April 1977.

9. Sylwester Zawadski, "Demokracja a Formy Panstwa Sojalistycznego," in *Formy Panstwa Sojalistycznego*, *op. cit*., pp. 175-190.

10. Thad P. Alton et al., *Economic Growth in Eastern Europe* (New York: L.W. International Financial Research, 1978), p. 16.

11. Constantin Dascalescu, "Worker participation in running society," *WMR* 21: 11 (November 1978), p. 52.

12. Csaba Mako and L. Hethy, "Worker participation and the socialist enterprise: a Hungarian case study," in *The quality of working life in Western and Eastern Europe*, eds., Cary L. Cooper and Enid Mumford (Westport, Conn.: Greenwood, 1979).

13. See, for example, R. Kalecka, "Stan Samorzadu Robotniczego," *Trybuna Ludu*, 24 May 1978; Helmut Koziolek, comments at the conference on "Economics and politics under developed socialism," *WMR* 20: 3 (March 1977); Pal Romany, "Searching for new solutions," *WMR* 18: 2 (February 1975), pp. 81-82; and Todor Zhivkov, "Developed socialism: the immediate task," *WMR* 19: 6 (June 1976), pp. 20-21.

14. Ilie Radulescu, comments at the conference on "Economics and politics," *op. cit*., p. 54.

15. Girgin Girginov, comments at the conference on "Political system of developed socialism," *op. cit*., p. 32. For similar views see comments by Georgi Shakhnazarov, Sylwester Zawadzki and Pal Romany in "The working-class party -- the guarantor of socialist democracy," *WMR* 18: 3 (March 1975), pp. 100-102.

16. Laird and Hoffmann, *op. cit*., pp. 21-26.

17. Lilov, *op. cit*., p. 45. See also V.G. Afanasyev, *The Scientific and Technical Revolution -- Its Impact on Management and Education*. (Moscow: Progress, 1975).

18. Paul M. Cocks, "Administrative Rationality, Political Change, and the Role of the Party," in *Soviet Society and the Communist Party*, ed. Karl W. Ryavec (Amherst: University of Massachusetts, 1978), p. 51.

19. Zawadzki, *op. cit*., p. 102.

20. Shakhnazarov, *op. cit*., p. 101. See also Romany, *op. cit*., p. 102; and Mikulas Beno, "Guiding the building of a developed socialist society," *WMR* 22: 5 (May 1979), pp. 68-73.

21. For a discussion of the Soviet constitution, see Robert Sharlet, "Constitutional Implementation and the Juridicization of the Soviet System," in *Soviet Politics in the Brezhnev Era*, *op. cit*.

22. Boris Spassov, *Socialist Democracy in the People's Republic of Bulgaria* (Sofia: Sofia Press, 1977), p. 25.

23. Adam Bromke, A New Juncture in Poland," *Problems of Com-*

munism 25: 5 (September-October 1976), pp. 12-13.

24. Jerry F. Hough, "Political Participation in the Soviet Union," Soviet Studies 28: 1 (January 1976); T.H. Rigby, "Hough on Political Participation in the Soviet Union," Soviet Studies 18: 2 (April 1976); and D. Richard Little, "Mass Political Participation in the U.S. and the U.S.S.R.," Comparative Political Studies 13: 4 (January 1976).

25. Darrell P. Hammer, "The Dilemma of Party Growth," Problems of Communism 20: 4 (July-August 1971). For analyses of party membership trends, see T.H. Rigby, "Soviet Communist Party Membership under Brezhnev," Soviet Studies 28: 3 (July 1976); Aryeh L. Unger, "Soviet Communist Party Membership under Brezhnev: A Comment," Soviet Studies 29: 2 (April 1977); Jan B. de Weydenthal, "Party Development in Contemporary Poland," East European Quarterly 11: 3 (Fall 1977); and Mary Ellen Fischer, "The Romanian Communist Party and Its Central Committee: Patterns of Growth and Change," Southeastern Europe 6: 1 (1979).

26. For a discussion of this concept, see Kelley, op. cit., p. 195; and Fischer, op. cit., p. 16. See also Todor Zhivkov, Rabotcheskoe Delo, 7 April 1978.

27. Hough, op. cit., pp. 15-17.

28. Jerry F. Hough, "Party 'Saturation' in the Soviet Union," in The Dynamics of Soviet Politics, eds. Paul Cocks, Robert V. Daniels, and Nancy Whittier Herr (Cambridge, Mass.: Harvard University Press, 1976).

29. L.I. Brezhnev, Report to the 25th CPSU Congress, Pravda, 25 February 1976.

30. Edward Gierek, Trybuna Ludu, 15 Arpil 1977; Miklos Ovari, "A new stage in building developed socialism," WMR 18: 8 (August 1975), p. 25; Barbu Zaharescu, "A new stage in the development of socialist Rumania," WMR 21: 3 (March 1978), pp. 54-60; and Zhikov, op. cit., pp. 20-21.

31. "KPSS v tzifrah," Partinaia Zhizn 21 (November 1977); "Portret Partii," Zycie Partii 2 (February 1980); Fischer, op. cit., pp. 9-10; Beno, op. cit., p. 16; and Bennett Kovrig, "Hungary," in Yearbook on International Communist Affairs 1979, ed. Fredrick Staar (Stanford, Cal.: Hoover Institution Press).

32. de Weydenthal, op. cit., p. 346.

33. Unger, op. cit., pp. 310-13.

34. Rigby, op. cit., and de Weydenthal, op. cit.

35. Rigby, op. cit., p. 335.

36. Dascalescu, op. cit., p. 59; Sandor Jakab, "The traditional and the new in cadre policy," WMR 18: 7 (July 1975); and D.M. Kukin, "Personnel Work of the Communist Party of the Soviet Union at its Present Stage," Soviet Law and Government 17: 2 (Fall, 1978).

37. Kelley, op. cit., pp. 196-97.

38. Mary Ellen Fischer, "Participatory Reforms and Political Development in Romania," in Political Development in Eastern Europe, eds. Jan F. Triska and Paul M. Cocks (New York: Praeger, 1977), pp. 230-33; and Jan de Weydenthal, "Poland," in Yearbook on International Communist Affairs 1979, op. cit.

39. Theodore H. Friedgut, Political Participation in the USSR (Princeton: Princeton University Press, 1979), pp. 167-68; Krzysztof

Jasiewicz, Role Spoleczne Radnych Wojewodzkich Rad Narodowych (Wroclaw: Ossolinskich, 1979), pp. 52, 112; and Radio Free Europe Research, Bulgaria SR/5 "People's Councils Elections," 2 April 1979.

40. Friedgut, op. cit., pp. 159-162.

41. Dascalescu, op. cit., p. 52; Romany, op. cit., pp. 80-81; and Barbara Zawadzka, "Efektywnosc dzialania rad narodowych," Nowe Drogi 3 (March 1980), pp. 160-168.

42. Thomas A. Baylis, "Socialist Democracy in the Workplace: The Orthodox and Self-Management Models," in Authoritarian Politics in Communist Europe, ed. Andrew Janos (Berkeley: Institute of International Studies, 1976), pp. 142-43; Mako and Hethy, op. cit., pp. 310-315; and Wladyslaw Ratinski, Partia i zwianzki zawodowe w Polsce Ludowej (Warsaw: Kziazka i Wiedza, 1977), pp. 360-389.

43. Michal Waligorski, "Samorzad mieszkancow miast," in Rady Narodowe i Terenowe Organy Administracji po Reformach, ed., Zbigniew Leonski (Warsaw: PWN, 1976); Radio Free Europe Research, Bulgaria SR/6 "New Territorial Division Taking Shape," 28 March 1978; Radio Free Europe Research, Bulgaria SR/9 "Details on Reorganization of Agro-Industrial Complexes Released," 22 May 1978; Lenart, op. cit., p. 9; Friedgut, op. cit., pp. 235-66.

44. George Blazynski, Flashpoint Poland (New York: Pergamon, 1979), pp. 57-60, 310-311; and Radio Free Europe Research, Romania SR/10 "New Ways of Handling Citizens' Complaints," 25 April 1978.

45. Lenart, op. cit., p. 10.

46. Friedgut, op. cit., pp. 302-314; Jerry F. Hough and Merle Fainsod, How the Soviet Union is Governed (Cambridge, Mass.: Harvard University Press, 1979), pp. 492-517; and Dan Nelson, "Dilemmas of Local Politics in Communist States," Journal of Politics 41: (February 1979), pp. 42-43.

47. Friedgut, op. cit., p. 52.

48. Mako and Hethy, op. cit., p. 313.

49. Jack Bielasiak, "Recruitment Policy, Elite Integration and Political Stability in People's Poland," in Policy and Politics in Gierek's Poland, eds., Maurice Simon and Roger Kanet (Boulder, Colo.: Westview, 1980).

50. Cocks, op. cit., pp. 52-53; T.H. Rigby, "The Soviet Communist Party and the Scientific and Technical Revolution," in Political and Administrative Aspects of the Scientific and Technical Revolution in the USSR, eds. T.H. Rigby and R.F. Miller (Canberra: Australian National University, 1976), pp. 39-40; and Lenart, op. cit., p. 14.

51. Friedgut, op. cit., pp. 38-39; V.A. Iatskov, "Improving the Style of Work of Leaders of Work Forces is One of the Principal Emphases in the Activity of Party Committees," Soviet Law and Government 15: 1 (Summer 1976); and Radio Free Europe Research, Romania SR/9 "The RCP's Cadre Policy," 17 April 1978.

52. Iatskov, op. cit., p. 37.

53. Kukin, op. cit., p. 30; Jakab, op. cit., p. 35; and George Cioranescu, "Law on Education and Instruction: 'Red or Expert'?," Radio Free Europe Research BR/30, 6 February 1979.

54. Rigby, "The Soviet Communist Party and the Scientific and Technical Revolution," op. cit., p. 25.

55. Rigby, "Soviet Communist Party Membership under Brezhnev,"

op. cit., pp. 321-33; Radio Free Europe Research, Bulgaria SR/2 "Exchange of Party Cards Imminent" 27 January 1978; Radio Free Europe Research, Hungary BR/150 "CC Plenum" 3 November 1975; and Radio Free Europe Research, Romania SR/7 "Party and Government Changes" 9 April 1979.

56. Edmund Wnuk-Lipinski, "Job Satisfaction and the quality of working life: the Polish experience," International Labour Review 115: 1 (January-February 1977), pp. 59-61; Mako and Hethy, op. cit., pp. 300-302; Zoltan Fusko and Ivan Perlaki, "Increasing the socio-economic effectiveness of socialist work groups and organizations," in The quality of working life in Western and Eastern Europe, op. cit., pp. 282-84; and A.V. Tikhonov, "The Influence of a worker's on-the-job independence on his attitude toward work," International Journal of Sociology 8: 4 (Winter 1978-79), pp. 123-24.

57. L. Hethy and C. Mako, "Workers' direct participation in decisions in Hungarian factories," International Labour Review 116: 1 (July-August 1977); Dan Nelson, "Workers in a Workers' State: Participatory Dynamics in Developed Socialism," mimeo, 1979; Roman Stefanowski, "Workers' Councils 1956-1977," Radio Free Europe Research BR/160, 9 August 1977; Murray Yanowitch, "Introduction," International Journal of Sociology 8: 4 (Winter 1978-79); and "Production councils foster worker role in management," Pravda (Bratislava) in Joint Publication Research Service, February 1980.

58. Nelson, "Workers in a Workers' State," op. cit., p. 9.

59. Vladislav Ussenin et al., "Soviet Workers and Automation of the Production Process," in Automation and Industrial Workers, eds. Jan Forslin, Adam Sarapata and Arthur M. Whitehill (Oxford: Pergamon Press, 1979), p. 164.

60. Nelson, "Workers in a Workers' State," op. cit.; Ussenin et al., op. cit., p. 165; and Radio Free Europe Research, Poland SR/28 "A Discussion about Labor-Management Relations," 8 December 1978.

61. Fusko and Perlaki, op. cit., p. 293.

62. Kalecka, op. cit.; "Production councils foster worker role in management," op. cit., p. 23; and Dascalescu, op. cit., pp. 55-56.

63. Ozdowski and Alexander, op. cit., pp. 568-69; and Stefanowski, op. cit., p. 17.

64. O.I. Shkaratan, "Social groups in the working class of a developed socialist society," International Journal of Sociology 3: 1-2 (Spring-Summer 1973), p. 83.

65. Nelson, "Workers in a Workers' State," op. cit., p. 8.

66. For a discussion of these issues, see Thomas A. Baylis, "Participation without Conflict: Socialist Democracy in the German Democratic Republic," East Central Europe 3: 1 (1976), pp. 40-42; and Laird, op. cit., pp. 144-49.

8
Developed Socialism and Consumption Policies in the Soviet Bloc: An Empirical Evaluation

Cal Clark and John M. Echols III

The preceding essays demonstrate that the theoretical or ideological concept of "developed socialism" possesses significant implications for practical politics in the Soviet Union and Eastern Europe. Yet, they also indicate that it is far from a complete and coherent theoretical structure from which policy blueprints may be directly deduced by denizens of the proletariat's vanguard. Most communist theoreticians conclude that developed socialism describes societies that have reached a high level of industrial and technological development with complex and differentiated economic structures. Class differences have vanished by the stage of developed socialism although it is recognized that social differentiation in complex, advanced communist economies creates different (albiet "nonantagonistic") social and political interests. The policies most relevant for such societies are more controversial, however. Centralization and the scientific direction of society are advocated by some, while institutional decentralization and expanded popular participation are seen by others as vital to the further progress of socialist society. Developed socialism, hence, has both "orthodox" and "reformist" implications; and political factions and groups in the various bloc nations have appealed to the ones most consonant with their own interests.

Still, there is almost universal agreement on one aspect of developed socialism. This is that it connotes a substantial rise in the standard of living and a commitment by the regime to protect the citizens' level of material consumption. There is also unrefutable evidence that a "consumer revolution" did hit the Soviet Union and Eastern Europe during the late 1960s and early 1970s. Support for this conclusion can be found in a wide variety of sources, from mounds of arcane statistics to impressionistic travelogue statements. Thus, at least in temporal coincidence, there is evidently a link between the communist consumer revolution and the pronouncement of the concept of developed socialism. The form of this relationship is still questionable, though, since several possibilities exist. First, developed socialism might be a cause for rising consumerism if the construction of the theory caused changes in consumption policies and brought practice into line with theory. Second the causal connection may run in the other direction if the new consumerism were just one facet of industrial development to which the label of "developed socialism" was applied in retrospect. Third, the relationship could be wholly spurious if consumption policies resulted from idiosyncratic factors in different communist countries that are unrelated to the theory of developed socialism.

Time sequence can be used to provide a partial test of these three competing hypotheses about the relationship between developed socialism and rising consumption. The concept of developed socialism was first promulgated by Leonid Brezhenv in 1967, but it did not become common parlance in the Soviet Union and especially in Eastern Europe until the 1970s. According to Brezhnev, the Soviet Union reached the stage of developed socialism in the early 1960s, while evidently none of the fraternal East European nations have yet crossed this great divide.

If the first hypothesis that changes in consumption policies were stimulated by the theory of developed socialism is true, the major thrust of the consumer revolution should originate after the late 1960s and should start in the USSR and then spread to the other members of the socialist commonwealth. The second hypothesis presumes that rising consumption accompanied the industrialization of these societies and forms a central aspect of the socio-economic transformation which Brezhnev later dubbed developed socialism. This implies that the rise in the standard of living should significantly predate Brezhnev's revelation about the new stage through which socialist societies must pass, should occur throughout the bloc probably without direct evidence of Soviet leadership, and should be highly correlated with a country's level of industrialization and affluence. The third hypothesis that the relationship between developed socialism and communist consumer policies is spurious implies that changes in Soviet bloc standards of living should be sporadic and occur at different times in the various nations in response to idiosyncratic political and economic factors. In contrast to the first two hypotheses which predict fairly similar policies toward consumption and social welfare throughout the bloc, the third implies that substantial differences might exist among these countries. In addition, the first and third hypotheses presume that sharp jumps will occur in the standard of living at one time or another following major reorientations in government policy, while the second hypothesis suggests that changes should be more gradual and continuous with no regime directed radical shifts.

This essay, hence, will examine evidence about the phases of Soviet bloc policies toward popular consumption and social welfare in an attempt to test these three competing hypotheses. Their relative validity, in turn, should be quite suggestive about the role of the theory of developed socialism in communist politics. There are several distinct dimensions of the standard of living in the European communist countries which are relevant for assessing developed socialism's impact upon the new "consumer societies" in these nations. Personal income is a central indicator of the standard of living, but especially in the Soviet bloc where shortages of consumer goods are chronic, actual consumption may differ significantly from the potential for consumption provided by disposable income. In the command economies of the Soviet bloc, unlike capitalist societies, income and consumption can be directly controlled by the government through the setting of wages and prices and through planning the production level of consumer goods. Income and consumption, therefore, can be considered direct indicators of government policy in these states. The regime is, of course, responsible for social or communal consumption that is specifically funded by the State. Socialist ideology would suggest that this so-called "social wage" should be especially important in communist countries. The following three sections, then, review analyses of these different facets of the standard of living--real income, consumption, and social wage benefits--for the Soviet Union and her East European allies in Comecon and the Warsaw Pact. The conclusion then asks what these findings mean for the concept of developed socialism.

As a methodological digression, two principal types of data are presented in this essay--the primary "raw statistics" reported by the bloc nations themselves and "reconstructions" or "estimations" derived by Western economists and political scientists. The first suffer from gaps, inconsistencies over time and among countries, divergencies from normal Western definitions and operationalizations, and other well known and much discussed problems, while the latter often rest on important untestable assumptions. Most of the statistics and tables below, therefore, probably merit lengthy (and usually inconclusive) methodological discussions which are clearly inappropriate for this type of essay. The data to be presented, then, should be considered approximations--the "best estimates" that we can make at present.[1]

INCOME GROWTH IN THE SOVIET BLOC

The acquisition of income to purchase various goods and services is the first step in consumption. Income itself can be a complex concept in that it is possible to distinguish among several types of income accruing to individuals. Narrowest is money income which includes earnings and monetary transfers from the state, such as pensions and social security benefits. Second is personal income which includes money income plus nonmonetary income such as in-kind payments from collective farms and the consumption of privately grown agricultural products. Finally, total incomes equals personal income plus the consumption of social services, such as education and health care.[2] While most indicators focus on money income, they do not account for the changes in money income which might be offset by changes in the other components--for which, unfortunately, few systematic estimates exist.

Communist parties claim to be the best (and only) representative of the working class or proletariat, and once in power, they should be expected to pay special heed to raising living standards. However, this has not been the case. In the Soviet Union, Stalin's forced-draft industrialization policies required the suppression of consumption from the late 1920s on;[3] and these policies were imposed on Eastern Europe following World War II. In the early 1950s, hence, the Soviet bloc was marked by an extremely low standard of living compared to the Western industrial democracies. The next three decades, in contrast, have seen a "consumer revolution" in the Soviet bloc. Since rising incomes were necessary to provide the wherewithal to finance increased consumption, this section begins the description of the consumer revolution by looking at how real income, i.e., income changes corrected for changing price levels, grew in the Soviet Union and Eastern Europe.

Table 8.1 presents Denton's sophisticated reconstruction of the growth of real disposable income in the USSR between 1950 and 1977 with McAuley's estimates of the growth of real total income for 1960-1974 included for comparative purposes. The data in this table clearly indicate that rises in Soviet incomes are only weakly correlated at best with Brezhnev's enunciation of the doctrine of developed socialism. The period of greatest growth was 1950-1955, while the 1970s, the decade when the doctrine of developed socialism came to the fore, witnessed the slowest rise.

The greatest jump in postwar real income in the Soviet Union occurred during 1950-1955, although the 9.9 percent average may be somewhat higher than the actual gains made by Soviet consumers.[4] Political considerations evidently explain this jump as Stalin's heirs tried to win support through economic concessions to the populace. Real income grew by approximately five percent a year during the Khrushchev decade of 1955-1965, indicating a steady increase in the standard of living as part of Khrushchev's program of "goulash communism." The growth rate then jumped from 4.7 percent for 1960-1965 to 6.7 percent for 1965-1970.

This might suggest either that the Brezhnev succession was accompanied by another attempt by a new Soviet regime to curry popular favor or that the doctrine of developed socialism stimulated much more favorable consumption policies. A closer look, however, negates both these hypotheses. The increase in real incomes did not occur evenly over this period but was primarily the result of a large jump in 1968 when the minimum wage was raised from forty to forty-five rubles per month to sixty rubles per month. Since this was more than three years after Nikita S. Khrushchev was retired, the time lag seems too long to interpret this change in income policy as a succession gambit. Likewise, several reasons can be adduced for dismissing the linkage between developed socialism and the 1968 jump in Soviet incomes. First, the timing does not seem right. The jump occurred before the theory of developed socialism was really fleshed out; and the 1970s, supposedly the era of developed socialism in the USSR, had by far the slowest rate of growth in real income since 1950. Second, a significant portion of this growth in incomes after 1965 probably resulted, according to McAuley, from the loss of central control over the way in which local enterprises implemented wage policies.[5] Therefore, this upward stimulus clearly cannot be attributed to regime policy preferences. Third, the much lower rise in total real income, as opposed to money income, between 1960-1965 and 1965-1970 suggests that money supply overstates the actual income rise (presumably because the increase in money incomes was given an upward bias by

TABLE 8.1
Growth of Real Per Capital Disposable Income in the Soviet Union

	1950-55	1955-60	1960-65	1965-70	1970-75	1975-77
Real disposable income p.c.	9.9%	5.1%	4.7%	6.7%	3.5%	2.7%
Real total income per capita			4.5%	4.9%	3.1%[a]	

Sources: M. Elizabeth Denton. "Soviet Consumer Policy: Trends and Prospects," in Joint Economic Committee, _Soviet Economy in a Time of Change_. Washington, D.C.: U.S. Government Printing Office, 1979. p. 775, for real disposable income per capita; and Alastair McAuley. _Economic Welfare in the Soviet Union: Poverty, Living Standards, and Inequality_. Madison, Wis.: University of Wisconsin Press, 1979. p. 46, for real total income per capita.

[a]1970-1974

the continuing monetization of the collective farm sector). Thus, this period may not represent such a major change in income policy after all.

Data on Eastern Europe are generally less systematic. Tables 8.2 and 8.3 contain figures that can only give a rough comparison to the Soviet series discussed above. Table 8.2 describes the growth in real wages, i.e., wage levels adjusted for inflation, for 1960-1975 for the Soviet bloc countries. This differs from money income in that it does not include some of the components of money income nor people working outside the state sector, e.g., collective farmers. Generally, wages seem to rise more slowly than overall real income because of the faster rise in social than personal consumption in most of these countries and because of the increasing monetization of the agricultural sector that was occurring in the bloc. Table 8.3 presents the data from several sources on the

TABLE 8.2
Annual Growth Rate in Real Wages Per Capita of State Employees

	1960-1965	1965-1970	1970-1975
Bulgaria	1.1%	5.1%	2.6%
Czechoslovakia	0.5%	3.5%	2.9%
Hungary	1.4%	3.4%	3.2%
Poland	0.5%	1.2%	7.0%
Romania	4.9%	2.4%	2.9%
Soviet Union[a]	1.6%	5.0%	3.6%

Source: Sovet Ekonomicheskoi Vzaimopomoshchi, Statisticheskii Ezhegodnik Stran-chelnov SEV, 1976. Moskva: SEV Sekretariat, 1976. pp. 7 & 48.

[a]Per worker.

growth of real income in various East European countries (real wages for Poland during 1949-1970). These series are almost certainly not strictly comparable to one another, but they do show when changes in East European incomes policy were implemented.

The data for Poland and Czechoslovakia show a replication of the Soviet pattern at the beginning of this period. Both had stagnating or even declining real incomes until the death of Stalin, followed by a major leap at the time of the 1953-1955 "New Course" of political and economic relaxation, which confirms the conclusion that Soviet policies were still imposed throughout Eastern Europe up to the mid-1950s.[6] National diversity emerged soon thereafter. Both Poland and Czechoslovakia had growth rates near the Soviet one for 1955-1960 reported in Table 8.1, but their temporal sequence differed significantly. The Czech growth rate over these

TABLE 8.3
Annual Growth Rate in Real Income Per Capita

	1948-53	1953-55	1955-60	1960-65	1965-70	1970-75
Czechoslovakia	- .7%[a]	7.0%	4.9%	1.3%	3.9%	
East Germany[b]				2.6%	4.6%	
Hungary[c]				3.4%	7.2%	4.6%[d]
Poland[e]	-3.3%[f]	12.1%	5.8%	1.6%	2.0%	11.5%′
Romania	7.4%[g]		3.5%	6.6%	4.6%	7.8%

Sources: Zbigniew M. Fallenbuchl. "The Polish Economy in the 1970s," in Joint Economic Committee, East European Economies Post-Helsinki. Washington, D.C.: U.S. Government Printing Office, 1977. p. 831, for Poland 1970-75; Marvin R. Jackson. "Industrialization, Trade and Mobilization in Romania's Drive for Economic Independence," in Joint Economic Committee, East European Economies Post-Helsinki. Washington, D.C.: U.S. Government Printing Office, 1977. p. 935, for Romania; Bogdan Mieczkowski. Personal and Social Consumption in Eastern Europe: Poland, Czechoslovakia, Hungary, and East Germany. New York; Praeger Publishers, 1975. pp. 110, 128, & 144 for Poland 1949-70; p. 212, for Czechoslovakia; p. 238, for Hungary, 1960-70; and p. 271, for East Germany; and Richard Portes. "Hungary: Economic Performance, Policy, and Prospects," in Joint Economic Committee, East European Economies Post-Helsinki. Washington, D.C.: U.S. Government Printing Office, 1977. p. 805, for Hungary 1970-75.

a For blue collar workers.

b. Per worker.

c The 1970-75 figures come from a different source than the earlier series, but for overlapping years the two series are fairly similar.

d 1971-1975

e For 1948 to 1970, these are rates of growth in real wages only, while the 1970-75 figures are for real income. This change from one category to another explains some, but not most, of the huge jump here.

f 1949-1953

g 1950-1955

five years was fairly even while there was a major discontinuity in Poland's. The Gomulka regime that came to power in 1956 in the wake of the "Polish October" initially was seen as the most liberal in Eastern Europe (excepting maverick Yugoslavia), but by the beginning of the 1960s it had become much more orthodox in policy.[7] This change of heart (or soul) is clearly reflected in the income data. Real wages per capita grew by 10.4 percent annually between 1955 and 1957, but the growth rate then plummeted to 2.3 percent a year for the last three years of the decade.

The more complete data on the post-1960 trends demonstrate that diversity has been the rule over the last couple of decades. The growth of real wages in Poland remained minuscule throughout the 1960s under Gomulka's increasingly conservative rule and undoubtedly contributed to the popular frustration that exploded in the riots of 1970 which followed the annoucement of a sharp rise in consumer prices and a revision of wage norms. Gomulka fell among this explosion of discontent, and the succeeding Gierek regime quickly moved to revitalize economic growth and raise the standard of living based on a substantial increase in Western imports. This resulted in spectacular economic growth and rising real incomes for the first half of the 1970s, but skyrocketing oil prices and hard currency debt again put the Poles in an economic squeeze in the late 1970s, as riots again broke out in 1976 to protest a major price increase.[8] Romania, as well, clearly deviated from the Soviet pattern after 1960, although her rapid rise in real income during 1950-1955, followed by a significant deceleration over the next five years, was similar to the USSR and most of the other bloc countries. The growth rate of Romanian real income per capita almost doubled during 1960-1965 as opposed to the previous five year span; and it then fell greatly during 1965-1970 when it was rising elsewhere in the bloc. The annual growth rate of real incomes jumped back up in 1970-1975 from 4.8 percent to 7.6 percent, just as it was beginning to decline in most of the other countries. In addition, the much higher increase in real incomes, as opposed to real wages, led Jackson to conclude that there must have been a very large increase in Romania's "social consumption."[9] The Romanians, hence, were clearly marching to the beat of a different drummer.

Czechoslovakia and Hungary resemble the Soviet pattern displayed in Table 8.1 in the aggregate statistics; yet, a closer look shows that they seemed to be doing their own thing as well. Hungary replicates the Soviet five year trends of moderate growth during 1960-1965, a jump in 1965-1970, and a subsequent decline during 1970-1975, as does Czechoslovakia with the exception of its very low growth rate during 1960-1965. Hungary's growth spurt in 1965-1970 differed from the Soviet Union's, though, in that it was evenly spaced rather than concentrated in 1968. Thus, rising incomes in Hungary predated the big jump in the USSR and were presumably part of the general liberalizing trend under Janos Kadar that resulted in the market-oriented New Economic Mechanism (NEM) a few years later. Also, the drop in the growth rate in real incomes in 1970-1975 was significantly less in Hungary than in the Soviet Union. Czechoslovakia more nearly matches the Soviet temporal sequence with a big jump in real income occurring in 1968-1969. However, since this was obviously associated with the Prague Spring, it is rather hard to impute Soviet influence here. This leaves only Bulgaria and East Germany, the countries generally considered to be the most loyal (or subservient) to the USSR. Some analysts have argued that their policies toward raising the popular standard of living have been part of a larger bloc-wide and especially Soviet trend.[10] Even if this were true, however, it represents a far cry from a unitary bloc-wide movement under Soviet tutelage.

The passing of the grand and glorious Stalin, then, brought an end, or at least a modification, to his idea of exploiting the consumer in order to produce maximum economic growth. Very substantial increases in real incomes occurred in all the bloc countries during the two decades after his demise; and in many there were special spurts between 1965 and 1970 when the doctrine of developed socialism was first proclaimed. Despite this correlation of timing, however, the major Soviet jump in real incomes in the late 1960s does not appear directly tied to Brezhnev's new ideological vision. Changes in the income policies of the East European states were generally derived from internal political and economic factors, rather than the Soviet leadership in implementing the theoretically inspired components of developed socialism.

THE CONSUMPTION REVOLUTION

Rising incomes in these countries led to a massive upsurge in consumption that was only slightly tarnished by the continuing low quality of many consumer goods and by the large gap that still existed between Eastern and Western consumption. The description of Soviet consumption during the post-war period by Schroeder and Severin serves as a good summary for the entire bloc:

> Meeting in the Kremlin in early 1976 for the 25th Party Congress, the leadership of the Soviet Communist Party could look back with both pride and frustration on the fruits of its policies affecting the welfare of the population over the preceding quarter century. The period (1950-1975) was one of relative peace and quiet, witnessing none of the upheavals of the preceding 25 years--the advent of central planning, the collectivization of agriculture, the political purges, World War II with its catastrophic loss of life, property, and production in the economy. Even with the restored output by 1950, the population had benefitted little from the advent of socialism. Per capita consumption was not much above the level of 1928 or 1913, and the goods and services provided were primitive and inferior in mix and quality, even for a semi-developed country. The subsequent quarter century has brought great progress, particularly in quantitative terms. By 1975, the level of living of the Soviet people was more than double that of 1950 and had gained significantly relative to industrialized countries of the West. Qualitative gains were much less spectacular....Despite such rapid progress, per

> capita consumption in the U.S.S.R. is still only about one-third of that in the U.S. and well behind that of Eastern Europe. The disparities are even greater when allowance is made for the inferior quality and limited assortment of Soviet goods and services.[11]

Rising consumption has also stimulated what might be called the consumer mentality and higher expectations about what constitutes the "good life:"

> But almost everywhere I traveled later it was apparent that while American bourgeois materialism might be officially censured, the American middle-class way of life embodied the aspirations of a growing number of Russians, especially in the cities. People wanted their own apartments, more stylish clothes, more swinging music, a television set and other appliances, and for those lucky enough, a private car...What is new and revolutionary in the Soviet Seventies is that Russian consumers are becoming fussier shoppers. The country folk may still buy practically anything, but urbanites are more discriminating and fashion-conscious. They may have more cash in their pockets than ever before, but they are less willing to part with it.[12]

A quantitative picture of rising consumption patterns is presented in Table 8.4. The time series for all these countries except Bulgaria include two sources, but a check on the overlaps between the series suggests that they are fairly comparable. As would be expected, changes in consumption generally parallel the income data. Table 8.4 implies several additional conclusions as well, however.

Overall, a substantial jump in consumption in the late 1960's followed by a significant decline in the latter 1970s is clearly evident throughout the bloc. This point is also reinforced by the data on real incomes discussed in the previous section. Another similarity among most of the nations is that consumption grew at significantly slower rates than real income. The explanation for this disparity in growth rates, most analysts agree, is that these communist regimes have not been willing and/or able to provide the quantity and quality of consumer goods sufficient to meet the demand created by rising incomes. As a result, savings have risen substantially because of this "repressed consumer demand."[13] While the governments may view this as helping maintain a high rate of investment, such a phenomenon is obviously not consistent with a developed socialist society that provides a high standard of living to its people.

Poland during the 1960s forms an exception to this generalization about the comparative growth rates of real income and consumption since consumption growth rates are about double the minuscule gains in real income. Such gains in consumption, however, were certainly not enough to meet the demands of the population, as the riots of December 1970 showed. Thus, Mieczkowski's conclusion seems well warranted: "The 1960s, therefore, can be classified as

TABLE 8.4
Annual Growth Rates of Per Capita Personal Consumption

	1950–55	1955–60	1960–65	1965–70	1970–75	1976	1977	1978
Bulgaria			3.9%	3.4%	3.3%	3.7%	0.6%	2.4%
Czechoslovakia	– 0.0%	2.8%	0.7%	2.2%	2.0%	1.4%	1.7%	2.6%
East Germany	12.6%	5.6%	1.4%	2.3%	4.1%	3.6%	0.8%	2.2%
Hungary	2.8%	4.4%	1.6%	3.4%	2.9%	1.0%	4.1%	2.4%
Poland	1.7%	3.8%	2.2%	3.1%	4.6%	5.2%	2.5%	0.2%
Soviet Union	5.9%	4.6%	2.7%	5.1%	3.4%	1.9%	2.4%	2.2%

Sources: Thad P. Alton, Elizabeth M. Bass, Gregor Lazarcik, and Wassyl Znayenko. "Personal Consumption in Eastern Europe, Selected Years, 1960–1978." Occasional Paper's of the Research Project on National Income in East Central Europe, OP–57. New York: L.W. International Financial Research, Inc., 1979, p. 17, for Eastern Europe 1960–1978; M. Elizabeth Denton. "Soviet Consumer Policy: Trends and Prospects," in Joint Economic Committee, Soviet Economy in a Time of Change. Washington, D.C.: U.S. Government Printing Office, 1979. p. 768, for Soviet Union 1976–1978; Bogden Mieczkowski. Personal and Social Consumption in Eastern Europe: Poland, Czechoslovakia, Hungary, and East Germany. New York: Praeger Publishers, 1975. p. 290, for Eastern Europe 1950–1960; and Gertrude E. Schroeder and Barbara S. Severin, "Soviet Consumption and Income Policies in Perspective." in Joint Economic Committee, Soviet Economy in a New Perspective. Washington, D.C.: U.S. Government Printing Office, 1976. p. 622, for Soviet Union 1950–1975.

a period of unsatisfactory progress in the area of consumption, even in terms of official statistics."[14]

In contrast to these similarities within the bloc, the disparities that emerged among the individual countries in terms of their incomes policy were generally reflected in the consumption data in Table 8.4. Several more idiosyncracies also appeared here. East Germany was the one country whose consumption grew throughout 1950-1955 and not just during the New Course subperiod. It also had the highest rate of growth in the bloc during 1955-1960 which then plummeted to the next to the lowest during the next five-year period. This distinctive pattern has been explained by the regime's need to conciliate the population during the 1950s before the erection of the Berlin Wall since, unlike elsewhere in the bloc, dissatisfaction with living conditions could produce significant outmigration. The construction of the Wall, though, vitiated this need and allowed the imposition of less liberal policies.[15] In addition, postwar consumption levels had rebounded far less in East Germany than in the other bloc countries by 1950;[16] so that the high growth rate of consumption during the 1950s can be at least partially attributed to postwar reconstruction. Bulgaria also appears different from most of the other members of the Socialist Commonwealth in that the highest growth rates in consumption occurred during 1960-1965 and then declined slightly over the next decade (note the similarity to the pattern of real income growth in Romania). Thus, the only two countries, which the incomes data suggested might be following the Soviet lead, manifest distinct patterns of consumption growth.

Comparing growth patterns between 1965-1970 and 1970-1975 also points toward another divergence within the bloc. Crawford and Haberstroh suggest that the trauma of the Polish riots pushed the succeeding round of bloc Five-Year Plans into a greater emphasis on the consumer sector.[17] Yet, this effect was clearly limited. The rates of consumption growth continued to increase in the first half of the 1970's, only in East Germany, in addition to Poland. Since East Germany seems to be one of the lowest ranking bloc governments in terms of popular support. The regime would be expected to be particularly sensitive to the "trauma" of socialist workers in open revolt.

The idea that developed socialism contained policy prescriptions for increasing the popular standard of living is another theory which would have wrongly predicted increasing rates of growth in most of these countries in the early 1970s. According to this hypothesis, the full articulation of the concept of developed socialism in the USSR and its spread to the ideological lexicons of most of Eastern Europe in the 1970s should have resulted in increased emphasis on consumer satisfaction, beginning in the Soviet Union and spreading to the other countries. In point of fact, however, growth rates in consumption fell in at least half of the bloc during 1970-1975, and by the late 1970s the growth rate of consumption had universally declined. Moreover, if the Soviet Union were a leader, it led with a declining emphasis on the consumer sector since consumption growth rates fell earliest and farthest in the Soviet Union.

The hypothesis that the Soviet Union should be the leader in a bloc movement into developed socialism's land of milk and honey and consumer paradise really takes a beating when one considers the absolute level of consumption as well as its growth rate over time. The most stringent requirement for Soviet leadership would be that the USSR have the highest standard of living which would seem commensurate with its status as the only nation to have reached the exalted stage of developed socialism thus far. However, as David Paul's essay in this volume concludes, the Soviet Union is clearly not the bloc leader in level of consumption. This might result from the fact that the USSR is not the most economically developed country in the bloc, as measured by such standards as income per capita. Since consumption levels are very highly correlated with income per capita, the lower level of Soviet consumption might be explained by normal developmental differences. Thus, a second, less stringent criterion for Soviet leadership would be that the consumption level in the USSR be the highest in the bloc relative to its GNP per capita.

Table 8.5 provides the data for testing both these criteria. GNP per capita as an indicator of development level is reported in column one. Column two is the overall rank in terms of consumption levels assigned to these countries by Keith Bush for the late 1970s:

> Most observers would place the GDR first in any aggregate comparison of consumption in Eastern Europe (followed by Czechoslovakia, Poland, Hungary, Bulgaria, the USSR, and Romania, more or less in that order).[18]

Column three is Edwin Snell's estimates of their consumption levels of a scale where 100 equals the level of consumption in East Germany. Table 8.6 then compares the consumption of food products and consumer durables to provide empirical justification for these rankings. These data definitely refute any idea of Soviet leadership toward a consumer nirvana. The rankings on consumption and GNP per capita are almost exactly the same for all the countries except the USSR whose level of consumption is well below, not above, her ranking on GNP per capita. Thus, the Soviet Union is quite evidently a straggler, not a leader, in the realm of consumption.

Table 8.6 shows that significant dietary differences exist among these countries with the more developed states having high consumption of meat and eggs, while the less developed make up for this with a higher consumption of bread and grain products. The differences between the high and low consumption states in the bloc are even greater in the acquisition of consumer durables. One interesting aspect of the consumer durable data is that although the Soviet Union is near the bottom of the bloc in terms of the ownership of telephones, passenger cars, refrigerators, and vacuum cleaners, its relative ranking is much higher on radios and televisions, which suggests that Soviet propaganda goals may have stimulated the development of consumer durables involved in the mass media.

As indicated by the Schroeder-Severin quote at the beginning of this section, the level of Soviet consumption lags well behind that of the Western industrial countries. Even East Germany, which leads

TABLE 8.5
Bloc Rankings on Consumption and Development Level

	GNP per capita, 1975	Bush Ranking on Consumption	Snell Rating of Consumption Level
Bulgaria	$2,648	5	65-75
Czechoslovakia	$3,824	2	80-90
East Germany	$4,166	1	100
Hungary	$2,638	4	70-80
Poland	$2,643	3	75-85
Romania	$2,419	7	40-50
Soviet Union	$3,401	6	

Sources: Keith Bush. "Indicators of Living Standards in the USSR and Eastern Europe," in Comecon: Progress and Prospects. Brussels: NATO Directorate of Economic Affairs, 1977. pp. 201-202, for GNP per capita and Bush rankings; and Edwin M. Snell. "East European Economies between the Soviets and the Capitalists," in Joint Economic Committee, East European Economies Post-Helsinki. Washington, D.C.: U.S. Government Printing Office, 1977. p. 27, for Snell rankings.

the bloc in consumption, fluctuated between 60 and 70 percent of West German consumption during the 1950s and 1960s, according to the calculations of Harper and Snell, underlining the substantial East-West gap that remains.[19] Such aggregate data comparisions, furthermore, significantly understate the differences between East and West for several reasons. First, the quality of many consumer goods in the bloc, especially in the Soviet Union, is abysmally low.[20] Second, the mix of consumption in the Soviet bloc is generally considered inferior in that food products constitute a much higher proportion of consumers' expenditures than in the West; and although this proportion has been declining over time throughout the bloc, it still generally exceeded 40 percent in these countries during the early 1970s.[21]

The fact that food composes such a high proportion of Soviet and East European consumption means that the agricultural policies of these countries are exceedingly important for the consumer sector. It is generally believed in the West (but at least not publicly in the East) that the system of collectivized agriculture which exists in all these states except Poland has led to substantial problems and inefficiencies in agricultural production. It is in the field of agricultural policy (and probably only in this area), however, that a leading role toward helping the consumer may be ascribed to the USSR in general and to the Brezhnev regime in particular. Despite Khrushchev's reputation for being a friend and protector of agriculture, the Brezhnev regime introduced major changes benefitting agriculture (although some of them were very

TABLE 8.6
Comparative East European Consumption

	Bulgaria	Czech.	E. Germany	Hungary	Poland	Romania	USSR
Annual Consumption of Foods p.c., 1975							
Bread and grain products (kgs)	157	107	94	118	120	--	141
Meat and meat products (kgs)	61	82[a]	78[a]		78	35	57
Fish and fish products (kgs)	6	6	9	71[b]	7	--	17
Eggs (number)	146	295	268	270	209	210	215
Milk and milk products (kgs)	198	212[c]	--	125[c]	432	--	315
Potatoes (kgs)	23	98	142	65	173	--	120
Vegetables (kgs)	127	78	97	165[d]	94	110	87
Sugar and sugar products (kgs)	33	39	38	40	43	--	41
Possession of Consumer Durables							
Televisions (per 10000 pop) 1975	1726	2483	3100	2261	1893	1267	2159
Radios (per 10000 pop) 1975	1596	2184	3660	2369	2380	1455	2340
Telephones (per 10000 pop) 1975	890	1762	1523	991	754	404	663
Passenger cars (per 100 hshlds) 1973	7	21	21	12	5	4	4
Refrigerators (per 100 hshlds) 1973	36	66	75	53	42	--	41
Vacuum cleaners (per 100 hshlds) 1973	18	60	25	40	41	--	12

Source: Keith Bush, "Indicators of Living Standards in the USSR and Eastern Europe," in Comecon: Progress and Prospects. Brussels: NATO Directorate of Economic Affairs, 1977. pp. 208-209.

a Excluding Lard.
b Including fish and fish products, excluding lard.
c Excluding butter.
d. Including fruit.

probably on the drawing board before Khrushchev was sent packing to his dacha): (1) a large increase in agricultural incomes, especially in wage security and pension rights, (2) massive increases in investments in agriculture, (3) increased subsidy of food consumption by keeping retail food prices stable despite substantial increases in production costs, and (4) a strong commitment to maintaining levels of food consumption even during years of crop failure. While not all these policy changes were introduced throughout Eastern Europe, the other bloc nations did manifest increased concern with agriculture, long the undernourished step-child of communist economies. Most followed the Soviet lead in promoting the "industrialization" of agriculture through capital inputs, farm consolidations, and management innovation.[22] As a result, as shown in Table 8.7, food consumption jumped greatly throughout the bloc after 1960 and, unlike the overall level of consumption, did not generally suffer a decline in the 1970s. Thus, the regime of Leonid Brezhnev, the discoverer of developed socialism, did implement new policies promoting higher standards of living and seemed to be exercising some positive leadership in the bloc in this direction in the field of agriculture. Whether these policies devolved from the theory of developed socialism is still debatable because the genesis of some of these policies clearly predated the 1967 unveiling of developed socialism.

Thus far, this essay has described in isolation the tremendous growth in consumption in the Soviet bloc after the death of Stalin. Tables 8.8 and 8.9 give a broader perspective on the relative emphasis placed on consumption within the total economy during the 1960s and 1970s. Table 8.8 presents the share in total capital investment going to industry, agriculture, and the "nonproductive sphere" (i.e., consumer products), and Table 8.9 contains the ratio between the growth rates of consumer and producer goods. These data may somewhat understate the emphasis accorded to consumption since some consumer durables are counted among the outputs of heavy industry,[23] but these tables do give at least a rough approximation of how the consumer sector fares in the Soviet bloc.

The investment data demonstrate that after 1960 the consumer revolution was achieved without a massive reorientation of the bloc economies. Only Hungary among these seven countries recorded a significant increase in the proportion of capital investment in the nonproductive sphere. Most of the increase came between 1970 and 1975, presumably because the market mechanisms of the NEM created a more consumer conscious economy. The Soviet Union, in addition, had the only significant increase in the percentage of agricultural investment with increases of three to four percentages occurring in 1960-1965 and 1970-1975. These figures support the previous qualifications about the connection between Brezhnev's theory of developed socialism and possible Soviet leadership in developing a more consumer oriented agricultural policy. Half the increase in investment occurred during Khrushchev's era of "hare-brained" schemes, and none of the other bloc members followed the Soviet lead in changing investment priorities.

The data in Table 8.9 present a somewhat more favorable picture for the consumer. The output of consumer goods has grown

TABLE 8.7
Growth Rates For Per Capita Food Outputs

	Meat			Vegetables			Milk and Milk Products		
	1960-65	1965-70	1970-75	1960-65	1965-70	1970-75	1960-65	1965-70	1970-75
Bulgaria	25.7%	1.4%	38.7%	- 7.4%	4.4%	7.6%	8.7%	17.5%	23.0%
Czechoslovakia	8.6%	16.5%	14.0%	21.6%	- 0.4%	2.2%	4.0%	8.9%	8.2%
East Germany	6.7%	12.6%	17.7%	5.1%	32.9%	13.9%	--	--	--
Hungary	8.4%	11.6%	18.1%	- 8.8%	7.2%	2.0%	-14.9%	13.4%	13.6%
Poland	12.2%	9.3%	28.1%	--	--	--	0.1%	12.5%	4.6%
Soviet Union	2.5%	17.1%	18.8%	2.9%	13.9%	6.1%	4.6%	22.3%	2.5%

Source: Sovet Ekonomicheskoi Vzaimopomoshchi. Statisticheskii Ezhegodnik Stran-chelnov SEV, 1976. Moskva: SEV Sekretariat, 1976. pp. 52-53.

TABLE 8.8
Shares of Capital Investment in the National Economy

	NonProductive Sphere	Industry	Agric.	NonProductive Sphere	Industry	Agric.
	Bulgaria			Czechoslovakia		
1960	26.4%	34.1%	29.7%	27.0%	40.2%	16.8%
1965	23.0%	44.7%	19.7%	25.1%	42.9%	13.9%
1970	23.8%	45.2%	15.7%	29.6%	38.5%	10.7%
1975	24.3%	39.9%	14.6%	28.5%	36.5%	12.3%
	East Germany			Hungary		
1960	21.6%	49.7%	12.0%	28.2%	39.1%	14.1%
1965	15.1%	55.1%	13.5%	29.6%	37.5%	14.5%
1970	16.4%	52.0%	13.3%	30.5%	33.1%	19.0%
1975	18.0%	50.5%	12.7%	34.5%	32.7%	13.8%
	Poland			Romania		
1960	33.4%	37.6%	12.6%	24.2%	42.3%	19.6%
1965	26.3%	39.8%	16.4%	17.4%	47.0%	18.5%
1970	25.3%	39.0%	16.3%	16.7%	47.2%	16.4%
1975	19.7%	45.2%	13.5%	16.2%	49.1%	13.5%
	Soviet Union					
1960	34.8%	36.1%	13.1%			
1965	30.4%	37.0%	16.8%			
1970	30.3%	35.6%	17.7%			
1975	26.3%	35.6%	20.8%			

Source: Sovet Ekonomicheskoi Vzaimopomoshchi. Statisticheskii Ezhegodnik Stran-chelnov SEV, 1976. Moskva: SEV Sekretariat, 1976. pp. 139 & 143.

TABLE 8.9
Ratio of Growth Rates of Consumer to Producer Goods For Gross Industrial Production

	1960-1965	1965-1970	1970-1975
Bulgaria	.61	.79	.71
Czechoslovakia	.73	.88	.88
East Germany	.75	.60	.65
Hungary	1.11	1.06	1.05
Poland	.62	.68	.77
Romania	.61	.68	.77
Soviet Union	.62	.96	.80

Source: Sovet Ekonomicheskoi Vzaimopomoshchi. Statisticheskii Ezhegodnik Stran-chelnov SEV, 1976. Moscow: SEV Sekretariat, 1976. pp. 21-28.

faster than producer goods in only one country--Hungary, which again displays a relatively pro-consumer profile. Still, the trends elsewhere in the bloc show a narrowing of this gap since the ratio rose appreciably in five of the other six states (East Germany excepted). However, it is important to point out that the growth rate in producer goods remained higher throughout this decade and a half in all these nations except Hungary; only the ratio denoting the relative disadvantage of consumer goods declined.

In sum, there has been a massive upsurge in consumption throughout the Soviet bloc over the last twenty-five years. Yet, paradoxically, the relative emphasis placed on the consumer sector has stagnated or even declined since 1960. The trend data simply mask the low level to which consumption had fallen in these countries. Recent growth has still not come at substantial expense to other sectors of the economy. Declining economic growth rates in the bloc from the early 1970's onward,[24] thus, put increasing pressure on the policy of expanding consumption. The slowdown in growth was compounded by increasing foreign trade problems as well. A high proportion of the growth of both consumer and producer goods for most of these nations has come through increased imports which brought, in turn, growing trade imbalances. As a result, mounting hard currency debts to the West have put a decided damper on the further stimulation of growth through imports.[25] Major sacrifices elsewhere would be necessary, therefore, if consumption were to continue its substantial rise, but the regimes that rule the Soviet bloc have shown few signs thus far of being willing to make such sacrifices.[26] The 1965-1975 consumer boom, then, may have reached a plateau. This component of developed socialism may only have had a ten-year run with a new emerging of a secular reduction in consumption growth, concurrent with sharply increased variations in individual country trends.

COMMUNAL CONSUMPTION

State services provide a significant component of the quality of life afforded to the citizenry of any industrialized nation, but they naturally would be expected to be especially important in communist countries. This section, then, considers the development of social consumption in the Soviet bloc. It includes a detailed description of Soviet communal and welfare expenditures, a discussion of the relative rates of growth of personal and social consumption throughout the bloc, a review of budgetary patterns in these countries, and a brief evaluation of the adequacy of social services.

Soviet state contributions to income and consumption, which might be called the Soviet welfare system, have two components. The first is transfer payments to individuals which the recipients can then use for their own personal consumption. Second, there are free or subsidized government services which constitute communal or social consumption. Table 8.10 presents McAuley's piecing together of these data for the Soviet Union between 1950 and 1974. Nominal (i.e., current year), rather than real, expenditure data are used because it is impossible to estimate how changing price levels would affect the value of social services, but Denton's index of retail prices is included to give an idea of the changing purchasing power of the transfer payments.

The huge increase in Soviet expenditures to finance the "welfare state" is readily apparent from these data, especially since the retail price index grew only marginally between 1950 and 1974. Over these two and a half decades, there has been an appreciable change in the emphasis of these expenditures with transfer payments becoming more important and social consumption, per se, less important as the growth of pensions accounted for most of this change. The three major components of social consumption are education, health care, and housing subsidies. Education has been the largest category of social consumption with about double the spending for health care in most of these six years; and housing subsidies rank a distant third, varying between one-ninth and one-fifth of educational expenditures. Absolute expenditures for all three areas grew substantially throughout the 1950-1974 period, but in terms of the relative share of welfare spending only housing subsidies, the least important category, increased.

Despite the huge growth in expenditures for social consumption over the last few decades, social services still only constitute a minor share of most Soviet citizens consumption. According to McAuley's calculations, the social consumption expenditures (education, health, housing, and social security) were 12.8 percent of real income (which, note, does not exactly equal total consumption) in 1960, 14.0 percent in 1965, and 13.9 percent in 1970.[27] Data from several East European countries show that social consumption usually equals between 10 percent and 20 percent of total consumption.[28] Thus, whatever the philosophical implications of Marxism-Leninism, personal spending and consumption still remain the central

TABLE 8.10
Soviet Welfare Expenditures

	1950	1955	1960	1965	1970	1974
Total Expds. (bil. rubles)	13.0	16.4	27.3	41.9	63.9	83.0
Percent of Welfare Expds						
Cash Transfers	44.6%	43.9%	49.4%	48.0%	51.2%	51.9%
Holiday pay	13.1%	14.0%	11.7%	12.2%	14.2%	14.0%
Pensions	18.5%		26.0%	25.3%	25.4%	26.6%
Allowances	9.2%	26.8%[a]	9.5%	8.4%	9.6%	8.8%
Stipends	3.8%	3.0%	2.2%	2.2%	2.0%	2.5%
Social Consumption	55.4%	56.1%	50.6%	52.0%	48.8%	48.1%
Education	33.8%	31.7%	26.7%	29.4%	27.1%	26.8%
Health care	16.9%	18.9%	18.3%	16.5%	15.5%	14.5%
Social security	0.8%	1.2%	1.1%	0.7%	0.8%	1.1%
Housing subsidy	3.8%	4.3%	4.4%	5.5%	5.5%	5.8%
Expds per cap (rubles/yr)	72.8	84.4	128.5	182.5	264.4	330.8
Retail Price Index	100.1	87.1	88.2	96.0	100.0	107.6

Sources: M. Elizabeth Denton, "Soviet Consumer Policy: Trends and Prospects, in Joint Economic Committee, Soviet Economy in a Time of Change. Washington, D.C.: U.S. Government Printing Office, 1979. p. 766, for retail price index; and Alastair McAuley. Economic Welfare in the Soviet Union: Poverty, Living Standards, and Inequality. Madison, Wis.: University of Wisconsin Press, 1979. p. 262, for welfare expenditures.

a Pensions and allowances combined.

ingredients in the standard of living of these communist states.

In the Soviet Union, moreover, personal consumption has grown much faster than social consumption since 1950. Table 8.11 shows that communal (social) consumption outstripped household (personal) consumption only at the end of Khrushchev's regime. The early Brezhnev years, when consumption increased at the greatest rate since 1955, had the highest ratio of personal to social consumption growth rates in the table. In the Soviet Union, then, communal consumption has paid part of the cost of the increased growth in personal consumption as the regime evidently decided to increase individual well-being in a more direct manner. Eastern Europe, however, has yet to replicate the Soviet pattern in this regard. The available data on the relative status of social and personal consumption in Eastern Europe are too disparate--some are in constant prices while some are in current prices, some are growth indices while some are percentages of total consumption in a given year, some are tied to GNP while some are calculated in terms of Net Material Product (the communist concept of GNP)--to be combined in a meaningful table. Still, they all tell the same story--that from the 1950s to the mid-1970s social consumption inevitably grew faster than personal consumption throughout Eastern Europe.[29] Here again, the Soviet Union is obviously not leading the rest of the bloc toward any common consumption policy.

TABLE 8.11
Soviet Annual Growth Rates of Personal and Social Consumption

	1950-55	1955-60	1960-65	1965-70	1970-75
Household	6.1%	4.8%	2.5%	5.4%	3.4%
Communal	4.8%	3.0%	3.8%	3.3%	3.1%
Ratio Hshld/Com	1.27	1.60	.66	1.64	1.10

Source: Gertrude E. Schroeder and Barbare S. Severin. "Soviet Consumption and Income Policies in Perspective," in Joint Economic Committee, Soviet Economy in a New Perspective. Washington, D.C.: U.S. Government Printing Office, 1976. p. 622.

Since the components of the social wage are directly determined by state budgets, they should be very sensitive to changes in regime policy. While no budgetary analysis exhaustive enough to test the relationship between the theory of developed socialism and budgetary changes in the Soviet bloc exists, the study of the impact of regime change on communist budgets by Valerie Bunce provides some interesting data. Bunce found that regime changes tended to produce larger shifts in budgetary policy among the seven Soviet bloc countries than among a sample of eight capitalist nations (Austria, Canada,

Great Britain, India, Japan, Sweden, United States, and West Germany).[30] These findings further led her to argue:

> The major conclusion of this study is that first secretaries seem to pursue similar economic policy priorities at similar points in their administrations in what seems to be a response to the succession process. These priority shifts involve a tendency to pump up public consumption in the period immediately following succession, and then a tendency to move toward less popular policies, once the succession crisis has been resolved.[31]

If the concept of developed socialism did bring changed policy perspectives, one might hypothesize that regime changes after the mid-1960s should almost universally bring marked budgetary changes of the type outlined by Bunce, while those before then would be less likely to do so.

Bunce used two types of statistical tests to evaluate the impact of regime change. She first assessed the immediate policy change, if any, by using the budgetary behavior of the previous regime (the total budget; budgetary outlays for health, education, and welfare; total capital investment; and capital investment in all industry, heavy industry, light industry, agriculture, and construction) to predict the spending levels for the first year of the new regime. These predictions were then compared with actual spending to see whether the initial budgets of the new regimes were significantly different from past spending patterns. Her second test compared the long-term spending patterns of successive administrations in terms of the slopes over time of data series on the percentage of budget and capital investment going to the various categories enumerated above. Table 8.12 presents a rough summary of Bunce's findings by categorizing the policy changes associated with the new regimes as "substantial" if there were significant changes in most of the short-term and long-term categories, as "partial" if one or the other type of effect were significant, and as "minor" if most of the areas showed no significant change in either the short-term or the long-term.

The results in Table 8.12 give only muted support at best to the hypothesis that regime changes after the mid-1960s should more universally produce substantial policy impacts than earlier shifts in power. In aggregate terms, the hypothesis clearly fails because the pre- and post-1965 periods are very similar in the impact of regime change--three substantials and two partials for the latter as compared to three substantials, two partials, and one minor for the former. Another tack seems more promising, however, at least at first glance. Bunce herself emphasizes that regime changes in some countries produce more substantial policy impacts than in others. Most prominent among these is the Soviet Union where all three successions brought substantial budgetary changes. If the Gomulka and Gierek accessions are seen as very special cases where widescale rioting forced a change in political leadership and presumably provided a very strong impetus for policy changes to shore up the new regime, the USSR stands out as the country where regime changes have the biggest policy impact. If Stalin could create Stalinism and Khrushchev hare-brained schemes, therefore, the Brezhnev succession could well have led to another set of substantial policy innovations which the master chose to call developed socialism.

The fact that the Brezhnev regime brought substantial policy innovation might appear especially telling in that the propounder of the theory of developed socialism also raised budgetary outlays substantially in an attempt to help raise living standards and popular welfare. However, there is significant evidence that the impetus for the policy changes described by Bunce predated Brezhnev's assumption of power. McAuley, for instance, dated changed Soviet priorities toward incomes and welfare policy to the mid 1950s;[32] and Bahry's budgetary analysis showed that significant changes in spending patterns had emerged by 1964--a year when the state budget remained subject to the whims of Nikita Khrushchev.[33] Here again, hence, an initial correlation of temporal setting, which is consistent with developed socialism's having a direct policy impact, seems less compelling under closer examination.

TABLE 8.12
Policy Impact of Regime Successions

Regime	Country	Impact
Zhivkov	Bulgaria	Minor
Novotny	Czechoslovakia	Partial (long-term)
Husak	Czechoslovakia	Partial (short-term)
Honecker	East Germany	Partial (short-term)
Kadar	Hungary	Partial (long-term)
Gomulka	Poland	Substantial
Gierek	Poland	Substantial
Ceausescu	Romania	Substantial
Stalin	Soviet Union	Substantial
Khrushchev	Soviet Union	Substantial
Brezhnev	Soviet Union	Substantial

Source: Valerie Bunce. "Elite Succession, Petrification, and Policy Innovation in Communist Systems: An Empirical Assessment," Comparative Political Studies 9(April 1976): 19, 22 & 24.

As with personal consumption, the aggregate data showing a spectacular growth in social consumption throughout the bloc do not necessarily mean that the Soviet bloc has been transformed into the land of milk and honey for the consumer. Progress seems clearest in the field of education where a revolution has occurred in most of these countries under communist rule transforming largely peasant societies into literate, well-educated populations over the past few decades (Czechoslovakia and East Germany are exceptions here). Frederic Pryor, for example, compared the seven bloc countries with a matched sample of market economies (the United States, West Germany, Austria, Ireland, Italy, Greece, and Yugoslavia) and found no significant difference between the two samples in terms of several indicators of educational systems and achievement.[34] Aggregate data on health inputs and outputs, such as physicians and hospital beds per capita and infant mortality rates, also show that the bloc countries have made considerable progress and are fairly similar to comparably Western nations.[35] However, especially for the Soviet Union, questions can certainly be raised about the quality of health care available in the bloc.[36] Still, the conclusion of Schroeder and Severin about the USSR seems fair for the rest of the bloc as well:

> Although the quality of both personnel and facilities may be poor by Western standards, the U.S.S.R. has developed a generally adequate public health system available to everyone without direct charge.[37]

Housing, however, provides a major area where the quality of bloc consumption is clearly inferior. Comparative data show, for example, that the Soviet bloc nations rank below almost all Western countries on households per housing units as all seven average more than one household per housing unit.[38] Thus, Byrne concluded that "communist governments have been prone to postpone satisfaction of housing needs, giving housing fairly low priority among consumer goods and services."[39] The place of the Soviet Union in the bloc in regard to housing again appears to be a lagger rather than a leader. In 1970, for instance, the USSR ranked well behind all other bloc countries except Bulgaria in households per housing units, although the more detailed data on housing conditions in Table 8.13 suggest that she should not rank quite so low in the provision of housing. Moreover, the housing sector in the Soviet Union has undergone a decline in emphasis since 1965, in contrast to the rest of Eastern Europe. The Soviet push in housing peaked in 1959 at 2.7 million new units and has not returned to that figure since.[40] In Eastern Europe, conversely, housing was very depressed until 1965 and, with the exception of Romania, has taken off since then as the data on the rates of growth in Table 8.13 demonstrate. Construction levels have reached the point where Czechoslovakia and Hungary (and perhaps East Germany as well, though its data include other types of units) are building more housing units per capita than the Soviet Union. Thus, if the present trends continue, the USSR will fall even farther behind many of its East European counterparts in the amount of living space and units available to its population.[41] The USSR comes out better as a protector of the consumer, though, in the degree to which housing is subsidized:

> The Soviet authorities are proud to claim that house rentals in the Soviet Union are the lowest in the world. In the late sixties such rents only accounted for 2-3% of the average urban

TABLE 8.13
Indicators of Housing Conditions

	Households per 100 Housing Units 1970	Percent Housing State Financed 1975	Per Capita Floor Space 1967 (sq ft)	Percent Housing Equipped 1966				Annual Growth Rate in Number of Apartments Built Per Capita		
				Piped Water	Bath or Shower	Toilet	Electricity	1960-65	1965-70	1970-75
Bulgaria	125[a]	56.1%	--	--	--	--	--	-2.5%	-0.4%	4.4%
Czechoslovakia	110	45.3%	60.8	52.3%	36.8%	35.7%	97.4%	-0.3%	8.5%	5.5%
East Germany	106[b]	39.3%	--	--	--	--	--	-2.9%	2.2%	17.5%
Hungary	107	38.2%	62.2	25.4%	22.0%	24.8%	75.1%	-1.5%	8.9%	4.3%
Poland	113[a]	33.3%	51.0	39.0%	13.9%[c]	18.9%[c]	92.0%	2.5%	2.1%	6.0%
Romania	107	51.8%	--	--	--	--	--	-5.3%	-4.4%	- 0.2%
Soviet Union	123	74.4%	44.5	52.0%[d]	--	--	88.0%	-4.0%	-1.2%	- 1.1%

Sources: Terence E. Byrne. "Levels of Consumption in Eastern Europe," in Joint Economic Committee, Economic Development in Countries of Eastern Europe. Washington, D.C.: U.S. Government Printing Office, 1970. pp. 311-312, for per capita floor space and percentage of housing equipped with various utilities; Henry Morton, "The Soviet Quest for Better Housing--An Impossible Dream?" in Joint Economic Committee, Soviet Economy in a Time of Change. Washington, D.C.: U.S. Government Printing Office, 1979. pp. 797 & 803, for households per housing units and percent of housing financed by the state; and Sovet Ekonomicheskoi Vzaimopomoshchi, Statisticheskii Ezhegodnik Stran-chelnov, SEV, 1976. Moskva: SEV Sekretariat, 1976. p. 171, for growth rates in apartment building.

a 1965.
b 1971.
c 1960.
d urban housing 1959.

TABLE 8.14
Public Expenditures as a Percentage of Factor Price GNP

	Education		Health		Welfare	
	1956	1962	1956	1962	1956	1962
Command Economies						
Bulgaria	5.1%	3.6%	3.4%	2.4%	5.5%	6.2%
Czechoslovakia	3.8%	4.0%	4.2%	3.6%	11.9%	13.7%
East Germany	3.8%	4.3%	--	--	10.7%	13.1%
Hungary	2.7%	2.6%	2.6%	2.6%	5.6%	5.4%
Poland	2.9%	3.1%	2.6%	3.4%	6.5%	6.6%
Romania	3.4%	3.7%	2.7%	2.9%	3.8%	5.6%
Soviet Union	4.4%	3.8%	3.0%	2.5%	6.4%	8.1%
Average	3.8%	3.6%	3.1%	2.9%	7.2%	8.4%
Market Economies						
Austria	2.5%	2.6%	2.8%	3.2%	15.6%	17.8%
Greece	1.5%	1.6%	1.1%	1.2%	5.9%	8.1%
Ireland	2.5%	2.7%	3.6%	3.4%	9.5%	7.6%
Italy	3.0%	4.0%	3.3%	3.9%	10.7%	11.7%
United States	2.4%	3.0%	0.9%	1.2%	4.8%	6.7%
West Germany	2.2%	2.4%	2.7%	3.2%	13.5%	15.0%
Yugoslavia	2.1%	4.0%	3.1%	4.1%	7.4%	7.7%
Average	2.3%	2.9%	2.5%	2.9%	9.6%	10.7%

Source: Frederic L. Pryor. *Public Expenditures in Communist and Capitalist Nations*. Homewood, Ill.: Richard D. Irwin, 1969. pp. 145, 168 & 213.

> family budget (4-5% if the cost of communal services is included). Rental income covers approximately one-third of the cost of maintaining and operating the existing housing stock.[42]

Over the past decade or so, in contrast, housing subsidies in the rest of Eastern Europe have been substantially reduced.[43] Table 8.13 indicates that a much higher proportion of new housing is financed by the state in the USSR than elsewhere in the bloc, although this may be one of the reasons for the faster growth rate of new housing in her client states.

One might also suppose that communist countries, motivated by the norms of developed socialism, should spend more on social services than their capitalist competitors. Frederic Pryor's data, presented in Table 8.14, do not support this hypothesis. The Soviet bloc nations spent a higher proportion of their GNP for education and health and a lower proportion for welfare. Only the education differences are statistically significant, however, and the two sets of countries were becoming more similar in all three spending areas. In addition, the Soviet Union is obviously not the bloc leader in the proportion of GNP devoted to these services as the more affluent Czechoslovakia and East Germany have the highest ratios among the bloc members. Unfortunately, Pryor's data series does not extend into the post-1965 period. Still, at the dawn of developed socialism, the hypothesis that socialist countries should spend more than capitalist ones for basic social services is clearly unconfirmed.

This section, then, has reviewed data about social consumption in the Soviet bloc. As in the previous sections about real income and consumption, rapid growth in social consumption is evident throughout the bloc, but its linkage to developed socialism appears tenuous at best. In terms of budgetary allocations, the Brezhnev regime did bring significant innovation and change, but much of this was foreshadowed by the previous administration. Comparison of communist and capitalist spending patterns, furthermore, failed to find intersystemic differences. Most particularly, the Soviet Union did not exercise the leading role which might have been imputed to her as the first implementor of developed socialism. The post-1965 period of developed socialism was marked by higher growth rates of personal than social consumption in the USSR, just the opposite of what occurred in Eastern Europe. In addition, Soviet spending for social services clearly trailed Czechoslovakia and East Germany, and her poor position in the area of housing is especially striking.

DEVELOPED SOCIALISM AND THE CONSUMER REVOLUTION: CONNECTION OR COINCIDENCE?

This essay has sought to decipher the relationship between the theory of developed socialism and the consumer revolution that occurred in the Soviet bloc in the two decades after Stalin's death. There are three possible forms that this relationship could take. First, consumer policy could have been explicitly changed to bring it into line with the philosophical dictates of the new theory, i.e., developed socialism caused the consumer revolution. Second, the causal direction might be reversed if rapidly rising consumption were simply part of the economic transformation of these societies which Brezhnev labeled the path to developed socialism. Third, the relationship might be spurious if consumer policies resulted from idiosyncratic factors in the different bloc states that were unrelated to the concept of developed socialism.

In terms of overall trends, the third theory is supported because it is the only one that correctly predicted that the growth of consumption would be discontinuous over time with interspersed spurts and lags and would be dissimilar among the various bloc natons. The first presumed discontinuous temporal growth with developed socialism's promoting a major jump. It also pictured a similar movement throughout the entire bloc under Soviet leadership. The second hypothesized that the growth of consumption should be primarily tied to economic, not political, influences. Thus it should not be too discontinuous and should vary among nations, if at all, in conjunction with a country's development level. Several of the more specific results also support the third theory. First, changes in the East European states were clearly the result of various internal political and economic factors that had little or no connection with Brezhnev's ideological visions. Second, the substantial impact, which Bunce found regime change to have on budgetary policy, also indicates that idiosyncratic political style is an important determinant of policy outcomes in the Soviet bloc.

In contrast, most of the data presented here are inconsistent with either causal hypothesis about the linkage between developed socialism and the consumer revolution. Regarding the first hypothesis that the new theory influenced consumption policy, the jump in consumption that occurred in most of the bloc during 1965-1970 suggests that Brezhnev's initial pronouncements about developed socialism could have stimulated changed priorities favoring the consumer sector. The timing of this growth spurt seems too early for it to have been the result of the new theory, however, since the concept of developed socialism did not become particularly prominent, even in the USSR, until the early 1970's. Furthermore, the growth rate of consumption declined throughout the bloc after the early 1970's just as the theory of developed socialism was coming into vogue. In addition to the question of timing, Soviet leadership of the bloc implied by the first hypothesis is clearly refuted. The previously noted diversity among these states means that there was no unitary bloc-wide movement, whether led by the Soviet Union or not. In fact, the Soviet Union was definitely a lagger, rather than a leader, in the bloc's consumer revolution. Moreover, if developed socialism did have a causal impact on consumer policy, Brezhnev's policies should have been markedly different from Khrushchev's. Yet, Brezhnev's new "proconsumer" policies appear at least partially rooted in the previous regime, even in the field of agricultural policy which presents the best example of major Brezhnev policy initiatives favorable to the consumer. Finally, cross-systemic comparisons disconfirm the hypothesis that communist countries, especially in the era of developed socialism, should put more emphasis on popular welfare than nations still falling prey to capitalist exploitation. The continuing East-West gap in the quantitiy, and especially the quality, of consumption is clearly inconsistent with the professed goals of developed socialism; and Pryor's budgetary analysis shows little difference in budgetary allocations for social services between command and market economies.

The second theory that the consumer revolution was simply a concomitant of economic growth fares only a little better. The discontinuity of growth in consumption and the significant impact of changes in political leaders obviously do not conform to the basic economic determinism of this theory. The idea that consumption should be related to development level receives partial support. On the one hand, a cross-sectional comparison finds level of consumption to be closely correlated with development level (except for the Soviet Union's lagging position on consumption), but on the other hand, the longitudinal data show that the jump in real income and consumption during the 1960s began in Bulgaria and Romania, two of the least developed bloc states. Finally, this second hypothesis is consistent with the investment data which show that few significant reorientations occurred after 1960 in the relative emphasis placed on the consumer sector. This indicates that a large share of the growth in consumption (although not necessarily its specific phasing) can be explained by the bloc's general economic growth and, conversely, that the economic slowdown of the 1970s has put increasing constraints on consumption policy.

The individual data and hypothesis testing, therefore, generally favor the third hypothesis of a spurious temporal coincidence between the theory of developed socialism and the rising fortunes of Soviet bloc consumers. Before discarding developed socialism with respect to its relationship with the popular standard or living, a broader linkage between developed socialism and the consumer revolution can be suggested. It posits some degree of reciprocal causal influence moving in each direction. Thus, even if a significant relationship is presumed, it is difficult to say whether the desire to advance into "developed socialism" is the engine of these trends in consumption or is, rather, an ex post facto effort to provide an evocative lable and justification. The problem of labeling can be illustrated by a recent American case. Lyndon Johnson did not awake one morning with a revelation about the need for a "Great Society." Rather, programs and policy ends came first, some having an impact and some not; and the label was gradually attached as the era evolved. Policies, demands, justifications, and labels were intertwined. Some significant programmatic changes, under a general theme, did take place, and the Great Society label summarized the theme and provided some additional impetus for change.

It is plausible to suggest that the same process has operated in the case of developed socialism. Concern with raising the standard of living appeared before the label, at varying times and to varying degrees across the bloc. A host of factors undoubtedly spurred this concern--pressures or at least potential pressures from the masses; a desire on the part of leaders,especially new leaders, to generate support and consolidate power; a concern over the remarkably low standard of living and the length of the "era of sacrifice" in those societies; a desire to balance the cancellation or reduction of economic and political reforms with other ameliorative measures; and the felt need in "progressive" societies to evolve into a different socio-economic order. It is, of course, the last concern that is most closely linked to the creation of the concept of developed socialism. Thus, it is possible to suggest some relationship between the changes in standard of living and the concept of developed socialism said to underlie them. Yet that relationship, though not simply tangential, is hardly determinative. About all that can be said with confidence is that some changes in consumption have taken place; and these changes do reflect some of the considerations underlying the evolution toward a "developed socialist" society.

The analogy between Johnson's Great Society and Brezhnev's Developed Socialism also suggests that the post-Brezhnev communist world may face some significant strains in the realm of the standard of living. The Great Society certainly did not solve all of America's social and economic problems; and the Viet Nam War compounded a deteriorating economic situation to put a definite crimp in the American style of life. The same thing seems to be happening in the Soviet bloc. Economic growth rates have declined since the mid-1970's; and a worsening energy situation certainly does not lighten the load. Also, foreign affairs may increase these economic pressures as crumbling East-West detente in the wake of Afghanistan could quite conceivably impose heavier burdens of defense expenditures and could make vital imports from the West much more costly and harder to obtain. As a result, growth rates in real income and consumption have already trailed off significantly.

With the evident revolution of rising consumer expectations among the bloc populations, stagnation or deterioration of the standard of living could well create substantial political problems as evidenced by the Polish worker riots of 1970, 1976, and 1980-1981 which brought down the Gomulka and Gierek regimes, the labor strife in Romania's Jiu Valley in 1977, and the reported worker unrest in several major Soviet cities in 1980. Jane Shapiro captures this potential political dilemma for these states (as well as the lagging position of the USSR in catering to the consumer):

> Although Soviet leaders are unlikely to adopt the prevalent Eastern European pattern of implementing policies that provide for greater quantitites of consumer goods and services in an effort to acquire and retain a measure of popular support, they will need to attend more adequately to consumer demand in a more coherent and less piecemeal fashion than they have thus far. Rising popular expectations provide them with no viable alternative.[44]

The implicit premises of developed socialism about the standard of living, therefore, may well create problems similar to the ones that Daniel Nelson's essay pointed out about participation in that citizens want more than these regimes want to deliver, given their evident reluctance to make significant sacrifices in other sectors to promote consumption. In short, post-Brezhnev governments throughout the bloc will probably face increasing popular pressure to produce more for the producers.

NOTES

1. The cited sources generally contain methodological discussions of the various statistical series presented here. For general treatments of some of the conceptual, methodological, and statistical issues concerning data from the Soviet bloc see Philip Hanson, The Consumer in the Soviet Economy (Evanston, Ill.: Northwestern University Press, 1968), especially Chapter 2; Alastair McAuley, Economic Welfare in the Soviet Union: Poverty, Living Standards, and Inequality (Madison, Wis.: University of Wisconsin Press, 1979), especially Chapter 1; and Bogdan Mieczkowski, Personal and Social Consumption in Eastern Europe: Poland, Czechoslovakia, Hungary, and East Germany (New York: Praeger Publishers, 1975), especially Part 1 concerning income and consumption data. Frederic L. Pryor, Public Expenditures in Communist and Capitalist Nations (Homewood, Ill.: Richard D. Irwin, 1968) especially Chapter 2 and Appendix A; and Donna Bahry, "Measuring Communist Priorities: Budgets, Investments, and the Problem of Equivalence," Comparative Political Studies, 13(October 1980), provide a methodological treament of the budgetary data.

2. McAuley, op. cit., pp. 8-13.

3. Hanson, op. cit., Chapter 3 describes changes in Soviet consumption between the beginning of the twentieth century and the mid-1960s.

4. Based on the data in Gertrude in Schroeder and Barbara S. Severin, "Soviet Consumption and Income Policies in Perspective," in Joint Economic Committee, Soviet Economy in a New Perspective (Washington, D.C.: U.S. Government Printing Office, 1976), p. 631. about half of this increase in real income was caused by rising incomes, while the other half resulted from a major cut in the price of consumer goods. McAuley, op. cit., p. 244 questions the availability of many of these lower priced goods; so that, in his opinion, indices of real income "overstate the gains accruing during this period."

5. McAuley, op. cit., pp. 249-251.

6. Zbigniew K. Brzezinski, The Soviet Bloc: Unity and Conflict (Cambridge: Harvard University Press, 1971), Chapter 8 provides a good overview of the New Course period.

7. For a discussion of Gomulka's Poland see Adam Bromke, Poland's Politics: Idealism vs Realism (Cambridge: Harvard University Press, 1967).

8. Zbignew M. Fallenbuchl, "The Polish Economy in the 1970's," in Joint Economic Committee, East European Economies Post-Helsinki (Washington, D.C.: U.S. Government Printing Office, 1977), pp. 816-864. Roger E. Kanet and Maurice D. Simon, eds., Policy and Politics in Gierek's Poland (Boulder, Colo.: Westview Press, 1979) provide a broader discussion of the political evolution of the Gierek regime.

9. Marvin R. Jackson, "Industrialization, Trade, and Mobilization in Romania's Drive for Economic Independence," in Joint Economic Committee, East European Economies Post-Helsinki, p. 899.

10. Mark Allen, "The Bulgarian Economy," in Joint Economic Committee, East European Economies Post-Helsinki, p. 686; and Michael Keren, "The Return of the Ancien Regime: The GDR in the 1970's," in Joint Economic Committee, East European Economies Post-Helsinki, pp. 751-752.

11. Schroeder and Severin, op. cit., pp. 621-622.

12. Hedrick Smith, The Russians (New York: The New York Times Books Company, 1979) pp. 55 & 61.

13. Keith Bush, "Indicators of Living Standards in the USSR and Eastern Europe," in Comecon: Progress and Prospects (Brussels: NATO Directorate of Economic Affairs, 1977), pp. 206 & 209; and M. Elizabeth Denton, "Soviet Consumer Policy: Trends and Prospects," in Joint Economic Committee, Soviet Economy in a Time of Change (Washington, D.C.: U.S. Government Printing Office, 1979) pp. 765-766.

14. Mieczkowski, op. cit., p. 145.

15. Ibid., pp. 264-270.

16. According to the calculations of Ibid., p. 290, the 1950 level of per capita consumption as compared to 1937 or 1938 = 100 was 111.4 for Czechoslovakia, 76.8 for Poland, 75.2 for Hungary, and 58.5 for East Germany.

17. J.T. Crawford and John Haberstroh, "Survey of Economic Policy Issues in Eastern Europe: Technology, Trade, and the Consumer," in Joint Economic Committee, Reorientation and Commercial Relations of the Economies of Eastern Europe (Washington, D.C.: U.S. Government Printing Office, 1974), p. 46.

18. Bush. op. cit., pp. 201-202.

19. Edwin Snell and Marilyn Harper, "Postwar Economic Growth in East Germany: A Comparison with West Germany," in Joint Economic Committee, Economic Developments in Countries of Eastern Europe (Washington, D.C.: U.S. Government Printing Office, 1970), p. 589. For other comparisons of bloc and Western consumption, see Mieczkowski, op. cit., Chapter 10; and Imogene Edwards, Margaret Hughes, and James Noren, "U.S. and U.S.S.R.: Comparisons in GNP," in Joint Economic Committee, Soviet Economy in a Time of Change, pp. 379-380.

20. Schroeder and Severin, op. cit., pp. 632-635; and Jane P. Shapiro, "Soviet Consumer Policy in the 1970's: Plan and Performance," in Donald R. Kelley, ed., Soviet Politics in the Brezhnev Era (New York: Praeger Publishers, 1980), pp. 111-122.

21. Hanson, op. cit., pp. 55-56 for the USSR; and Mieczkowski, op. cit., pp. 210 & 238 for Czechoslovakia and Hungary. Mieczkowski, op. cit., pp. 210, 238 & 266 showed that this percentage declined significantly over time in Eastern Europe; and Schroeder and Severin, op. cit., p. 622 found the same thing for the USSR.

22. A good comparative treatment of bloc agricultural policies is provided by Ronald A. Francisco, Betty A. Laird, and Roy D. Laird, eds., Agricultural Policies in the USSR and Eastern Europe (Boulder, Colo.: Westview Press, 1980). Shapiro, op. cit., pp. 111-115 describes the impact of agricultural policy on consumption in the Soviet Union.

23. James A. Buss, "Consumer Good Production by the Heavy Industrial Sector in Several East European Nations," Social Science Quarterly 57(December 1976): 680-696; and Shapiro, op. cit., p. 108.

24. Thad P. Alton, "Comparative Structure and Growth of Economic Activity in Eastern Europe," in Joint Economic Committee, East European Economies Post-Helsinki, p. 235; and Herbert Block, "Soviet Economic Performance in a Global Context," in Joint Economic Committee, Soviet Economy in a Time of Change, pp. 127-135.

25. Joan Parpart Zoeter, "Eastern Europe: The Growing Hard Currency Debt," in Joint Economic Committee, East European Economies Post-Helsinki, pp. 1350-1368.

26. Schroeder and Severin, op. cit., pp. 638-641; and Denton, op. cit., pp. 776-784 provide a good discussion of the policy options and constraints facing the USSR regarding the consumer sector.

27. McAuley, op. cit., p. 328.

28. Mieczkowski, op. cit., pp. 207, 234 & 250.

29. Ibid., pp. 147, 207, 234 & 250; Alton, op. cit., p. 234; and Jackson, op. cit., p. 899.

30. Valerie Bunce, "Elite Succession, Petrification, and Policy Innovation in Communist Systems: An Empirical Assessment," Comparative Political Studies 9(April 1976): 3-42.

31. Valerie Jane Bunce, "The Succession Connection: Political Cycles and Political Change in the Soviet Union and Eastern Europe," American Political Science Review 74(December 1980): 966-977.

32. McAuley, op. cit., Chapter 12.

33. Bahry, op. cit.

34. Pryor, op. cit., pp. 190-198.

35. Ibid., pp. 157-161; and Bush, op. cit., p. 210.

36. For example, see the impressions of Smith, op. cit., pp. 71-75.

37. Schroeder and Severin, op. cit., p. 626.

38. Henry Morton, "The Soviet Quest for Better Housing--An Impossible Dream?" in Joint Economic Committee, Soviet Economy in a Time of Change, p. 797.

39. Terence E. Byrne, "Levels of Consumption in Eastern Europe," in Joint Economic Committee, Economic Developments in Countries of Eastern Europe, p. 307.

40. Morton, op. cit., p. 792.

41. Ibid., pp. 791-792; and Byrne, op. cit., pp. 307-308 & 311-312.

42. McAuley, op. cit., pp. 288-289.

43. Morton, op. cit., pp. 802-804.

44. Shapiro, op. cit., p. 125.

Index

Activism, 138
Aczel, G., 48
Administrative law, 11
Administrative reform, 11
Administrative science, 13
Afanasev, V., 10, 126
Affluence, 22
Affluent society, 31
Afghanistan, 45
Agricultural employment, 68
Agriculture, 10, 23, 26, 42, 157, 168, 170, 172
Alekseev, N., 145
Aleksic, R., 85
Alienation, 111
Allen, M., 163
Almond, G., 22
Alton, T.P., 66, 124, 165, 173
Anarcho-liberalism, 85, 86, 90, 91, 92
Anarchy, 84
Andelman, D., 46
Article 58, 9
Articulate conflicts, 104
Aspaturian, V., 73
Automation, 23, 26
Automobiles, 41

Badina, O, 70
Bahry, D., 157
Balanced growth, 10
Balint, J., 44
Barry, D., 11
Barry, J., 33
Baylis, T., 137, 146
Belgrade, 83
Bell, D., 22, 27
Beno, M., 127
Berlin wall, 166
Bielaskiak, J., 139
Bilic, J., 91
Biszku, B., 49
Blazevic, J., 83
Blazynski, G., 138
Bliakhman, L.S., 11, 15
Block, H., 173
Borsanyi, G., 39
Bosnia, 90
Breslauer, G., 17
Brezhnev, L., 5, 7, 9, 10, 11, 12, 13, 15, 16, 17, 24, 37, 75, 80, 133, 156, 158, 163, 168, 170, 183, 185
Bromke, A., 129, 162
Brown, A., 52
Brzezinski, Z., 31, 32, 122, 160
Bucharest, 62, 72
Bulgaria, 126, 137, 160, 163, 165, 166, 168, 169, 171-173, 178-181
Bunce, V., 75, 176-178, 183
Bureaucracy, 9, 28
Bureaucratic-technocratism, 85, 86, 89
Bureaucratism, 102
Bush, K., 164, 167, 168, 169
Buss, J., 170
Byrne, T., 180

Campeanu, P., 69, 70
Capital formation, 26
Capital investment, 172
Capitalism, 7, 29, 30, 31, 102, 104

Catholic Church, 109, 113
Ceausescu, N., 63, 64, 69, 72, 74
Censorship, 112
Central Asia, 45
Central command approach, 101, 102
Centralism, 121
Centralization, 155
Charter 77, 46
Charvat, F., 44
Chekharin, E., 8, 121
Chernikov, G., 29
Chernogolovkin, N., 8
Cioranescu, G., 140
Citizen access, 136
Citizen participation, 104, 112
Civil liberties, 32
Civil rights, 106
Class, 27, 44, 104, 121, 135
Club of Rome, 23
CMEA, 63, 65
Cocks, P., 10, 11, 65, 126, 139
Cohen, L., 85
Cold war, 23
Coleman, J., 22
Collective decision-making, 108-109
Collective farmers, 44
COM, 73
COMECOM, 157
Communication, 24
Communism, 24, 26, 27
Communist party, 8, 14, 15, 28, 61, 105, 106, 121-153
Competition, 9
Compromise, 106
Conflict, 10, 22, 46, 61-62, 70, 89, 91, 92, 93, 94, 104, 105
Conservative, 6
Constitution, 8, 9, 83, 128, 129
Consumer goods, 6, 10, 26, 40, 104
Consumerism, 124
Consumer revolution, 158
Consumption, 42
Consumption policies, 155-188
Convergence, 21-36
Cooperation, 26
Council of Ministers, 108
Counterculture, 23
CPC, 37, 48
CPSU, 24, 52, 61, 80, 133, 163
Cranford, J.T., 166
Croatia, 91
Cserhati, J., 47
Culture, 31, 45
Czechoslovakia, 37-59, 65, 80, 131, 160, 161, 162, 163, 168, 169, 171-173, 178-181

Dahrendorf, R., 25
Damian, L. 70
Dascalescu, C., 125, 136
Debt, 173
Decentralism, 50, 52, 84, 92
Decentralization, 12, 103, 112
Decentralize, 81
Delegate system, 88, 90
Demenchonok, E., 29
Demichev, P., 39
Democracy, 32, 107, 123
Democratic centralism, 139
Demoralization, 103
Denton, M., 158-159, 164, 165, 175
Deutscher, I., 22
Developing Socialism, 63
Development, 3
deWeydenthal, J., 101, 129, 137
Dissent, 46, 108
Distribution of wealth, 25
Diversity, 84
Division of labor, 23
Djilas, M., 82
Dobrescu, E., 70
Doctors, 42
Doder, D., 51
Dolanc, S., 91
Dordevic, J., 82
Dudinskii, I., 37
Due process, 107
Duverger, M., 22

Eastern Europe, 79, 80, 81
East Germany, 38, 72, 125, 161, 163, 165, 166, 168, 169, 171-173, 178-181
Echols, J., 75
Economic growth, 85, 94, 124
Economic planning, 102
Education, 24, 25, 27, 43, 44, 104, 140, 174, 179
Edwards, I., 168
Egalitarianism, 104
Egorov, A., 14
Electoral process, 107
Electrical energy, 68

Elite, 24, 27, 122, 130
Elitist liberalism, 18
Engels, F., 28
Environment, 30
Equality, 25, 44, 45, 86, 107
Evans, A., 3, 25, 44

Fainsod, M., 138
Fallenbuckl, Z., 161, 162
Federalization, 45
Fedoseev, P., 25
Feher, F., 47
Firuta, A., 69
Fischer, M., 129, 137
Fleron, F., 25
Food, 171
Food consumption, 40, 167
Foods, 169
Foreign policy, 26
Francisco, R., 170
Freedom, 86, 106
Friedgut, T., 137, 138
Fusko, Z., 141

Galbraith, J., 22, 29
Gary, Indiana, 30
Gaspar, S., 50
Gatovskii, L., 11
Gdansk Agreements, 112
Gellner, F., 44
Georgia, 45
Germans, 45
Gierek, E., 99, 111, 112, 122, 133, 162, 177, 185
Girginov, G., 126
Gitelman, Z., 65
Glezerman, G., 8, 12, 121
Gomulka, W., 99, 177, 185, 162
Gray, J., 52
Great Society, 184-185
Griffiths, F., 122
Gross National Product, 40, 66
Growth, 4, 11, 173
Grupp, F., 45
Gvishiani, D., 15, 30

Haberstroh, J., 166
Hahn, J., 27
Hammer, D., 129
Hanson, P., 155
Harper, M., 168
Health, 104, 175
Heavy industry, 10, 26
Hegedus, A., 47
Heller, A., 47
Hethy, L., 125, 141
Higher education, 67
High technology, 26
Hoffman, E., 25, 122, 126
Homogeneity, 27
Hooliganism, 70
Hospital beds, 43, 67
Hospitals, 42
Hough, J., 12, 33, 122, 129, 132, 138
Housing, 179-181
HSWP, 37, 48
Hungary, 37-59, 65, 73, 80, 143, 160, 161, 162, 163, 165, 168, 169, 170, 171-173, 178-181
Huntington, S., 31, 32
Husak, G., 50, 52

Income, 157, 158, 163, 174
Income inequality, 104
Incrementalism, 79
Industrial culture, 24
Industrial development, 22, 109
Industrial employment, 68
Industrialization, 104
Industrial production, 173
Industrial society, 21, 28, 29, 31
Industry, 172
Inequalities, 71
Inequality, 24
Infant mortality, 67
Inflation, 54
Innovation, 93, 99
Institute of Philosophy and Sociology, 103
Institutionalization, 81
Integration, 27, 122
Intellectuals, 43, 111
Intelligentsia, 15, 27, 112
Interest groups, 108
Investment, 94
Iran, 45

Jackson, M., 69, 74, 161, 162
Jakab, S., 136
Janos, A., 137
Jaruzelski, W., 99, 113
Jasiewicz, K., 137
Jiu Valley, 62, 73
Job dissatisfaction, 70
Johnson, C., 21, 22

Jones, E., 45
Jones, T., 44
Jowitt, K., 48

Kadar, J., 47, 49, 51, 53, 162
Kalecka, R., 125
Kaminski, A., 102
Kanet, R., 139, 162
Kania, S., 111
Kardelj, E., 83, 86, 87, 88, 89, 90, 91, 92, 93
Kasianenko, V., 12, 15
Kassof, A., 13
Katushev, K., 37
Kelley, D., 4, 5, 9, 11, 25, 26, 27, 75, 122, 130, 136, 168
Keren, M., 163
Kerr, C., 22, 23
Khrushchev, N., 3, 4, 7, 10, 11, 24, 158, 168, 170, 176, 183
Komsomol, 147
Konrad, G., 47
KOR, 74
Kornhauser, W., 84
Kosolapov, R., 42, 10
Kosygin, A., 6
Kovalev, A., 6
Kovrig, B., 133
Krauze, T., 72
Kukin, D., 136
Kuzminov, I., 11

Labor, 25, 141, 144
Labor, manual, 27
Labor outlook, 72
Labor productivity, 26
Laird, B., 170
Laird, R., 25, 122, 126, 170
Lane, D., 23, 84
Lascus, V., 70
Latskov, V., 139
League of Communists, 81, 83, 85, 86, 87, 88, 89, 91, 93
Legitimacy, 54, 124, 125, 132
Lenart, J., 45, 50, 138
Lenin, 28
Leonski, Z., 137
Lesnyi, V., 8
Lewis, A., 22
Liberalism, 22, 89
Life expectancy, 67
Lilov, A., 123
Literacy, 24
Little, D., 33, 129
Local government, 138
Lopataka, A., 121

Machonin, P., 44
Mako, C., 125, 141
Mamali, C., 70
Manpower shortage, 26
Marjanovic, J., 85
Markus, M., 44
Martial law, 99, 113
Marxism, 3, 13, 28, 53
Marxist-Leninism, 47, 89, 63, 107, 174
Mass society, 84
Matrix organization, 14
Matthews, M., 71
Medical doctors, 43
McAuley, A., 157, 158-159, 174, 175
Meritocracy, 104
Meyer, A., 21, 22, 33
Middle class, 24
Mieczkowski, B., 161, 164, 165
Mihu, A., 70
Military, 41
Military Council for National Salavation, 113
Minorities, 45
Miric, J., 84
Mobility, 136
Mordzhinskii, E., 10
Morton, H., 180
Muddling through, 11
Multilateral development, 62, 64
Multiple candidacies, 137
Muslims, 45

<u>Nase Teme</u>, 91
Nationalism, 18, 27, 39, 45, 82
Naylor, K., 84
Nazi Germany, 31
Neighborhood assemblies, 84
Nelson, D., 25, 61, 69, 73, 138, 141, 185
NEM, 49, 137, 162
Nemes, D., 50
Nomenklatura, 8
Novosibirsk, 30
<u>Nowe Drogi</u>, 100

Occupational mobility, 23
OOUR, 85

Optimism, 22
Orthodox, 111
Orthodoxy, 53
OUR, 85
Ovari, M., 46, 133

Pareto-optimal, 85
Parliament, 50, 124
Participation, 12, 24, 33, 39, 84
121-153
Partiinost, 139
Party membership, 129-132
Pasic, N., 83
Paul, D., 44, 167
Pavic, Z., 84
Pavicevic, R., 84
Pax sovietica, 28
PCR, 62, 63, 65, 70, 73, 74
Peace, 22, Peasantry, 43, 104
Pechenev, V., 27
People's councils, 100
Pensions, 170
Peric, I., 91
Perlaki, I., 141
Petrescu, I., 73
Pezlar, L., 45
Pivtsaikin, G., 15
Planning, 10, 11, 24
Pluralism, 32, 46, 69, 88, 92,
94, 102, 105, 106, 109, 112,
113, 122
Poland, 62, 80, 99-115, 125, 129,
137, 160, 161, 162, 164, 165,
166, 168, 169, 171-173
Policy tradeoffs, 87
Polish Academy of Sciences, 103
Political change, 21, 28
Political communication, 103
Political institutions, 107
Political participation, 85
Polityka, 100, 103, 108
Pollution, 30
Population growth, 23, 26
Portes, R., 161
Post industrial society, 22, 27
Pozgay, I., 44
Pragmatism, 54
Preda, M., 70
Price manipulation, 101
Prices, 54
Private ownership, 42
Private sector, 42
Privileged access, 72
Productivity, 11, 23, 39, 70, 124
Proletariat, 25, 28, 43, 44, 132
133, 157
Prosperity, 55
Protests, 101
Pryor, F., 157, 181, 182
Purge, 135
PUWP, 62, 99, 100, 108, 113, 147

Radio production, 68
Radulescu, I., 126
Rakowska-Harmstone, T., 45
Rakowski, M., 103, 108
Rankovic, A., 82
Ratkovic, R., 86
Ratynski, W., 103, 137
Rausser, V., 63
Referenda, 107
Reform, 5, 6, 10, 12, 13, 100,
104, 105
Refrigerators, 68, 167
Reich, C., 23
Religion, 47
Remnek, R., 27
Renewal, 111, 112, 113
Representation, 106
Resistance, 90
Revisionism, 103
Rigby, T., 33, 135, 129, 139
Roads, 42, 68
Rodionov, P., 121
Romania, 61-78, 80, 125, 137, 144,
160, 161, 162, 165, 168, 169,
172-173, 178-181
Romany, P., 50, 125
Rostow, W., 22, 29
Roszak, T., 23
Roubal, K., 39
Rural areas, 70
Rush, M., 7
Russite fundamentalism, 18
Rykowski, Z., 121

Sblizhenie, 25
Schools, 42
Schopflin, G., 52
Schroeder, G., 41, 164, 165, 173,
176
Schattsneider, E., 84
Science, 22, 27, 30, 126
Scientific cultural revolution,
21
Scientific management, 11

Scientific and technological revolution, 10, 12, 25, 26, 28, 30, 48, 52, 99, 100, 101, 121, 125, 126
Secularization, 24
Sejm, 105, 107, 108
Self-management, 82, 85, 108, 113
Semenov, I., 29
Separtism, 18
Serbia, 90
Seroka, J., 84, 91, 94
Severin, B., 164, 165, 167, 173, 176
Shakhnazarov, G., 126
Sharlet, R., 8, 128
Shevtsov, V., 14, 121
Shkaratan, O., 11, 15, 146
Sik, O., 49
Sikorskii, V., 13
Simon, M., 25, 139, 162
Sirbu, M., 70
Skilling, G., 46, 122
Slomczynski, K., 104, 71
Smith, H., 164
Snell, E., 167, 168
Social change, 127
Social composition, party, 132-136
Social consciousness, 100
Social control, 110
Social development, 104
Social differentiation, 122
Social disorder, 102
Social fragmentation, 81
Social justice, 100
Social management, 15
Social structure, 109
Social Structure Section, 103
Social services, 174
Social wage, 177
Socialist Alliance, 91
Socialist democracy, 25, 50, 52, 69, 106, 107, 123, 129, 139,
Socialist ethos, 104
Socialist Self-managed pluralist democracy, 79, 80, 81, 84, 87, 88, 93, 94
Societal change, 23
Socio-political organizations, 124
Solidarity, 51, 76, 113
Sorokin, P., 22
Soviet bloc, 155-188
Soviet leadership, 61
Soviet Union, 3-20, 21-36, 42, 48, 79, 80, 100, 105, 160, 162, 165, 166, 167, 168, 169, 171-181
Spassov, B., 128
Stability, 3, 87, 89, 93
Stalin, J., 9, 22, 26, 28, 47, 81, 129, 157, 163, 170, 182
Stalinization, 24
Standard of living, 15, 40, 155, 156, 163, 170, 184, 185
Stefanowski, R., 141
Stepanian, T., 10
Strikes, 102, 111, 112
Structural collisions of interests, 104
Structural differentiation, 23
Subjective factors, 101, 103
Succession, 9, 11, 16
Suslov, M., 25, 26
Svestka, O., 46
Szczepanski, J., 100, 109, 110, 111
Szelenyi, I., 47

Technocratic-elitism, 102
Technocratism, 103
Technocrats, 18
Technology, 21, 22, 23, 24, 25, 27, 101
Television, 40, 70, 167
Television Production, 68
Third World, 64
Tigby, T., 139
Tikhomirov, I., 6, 12, 28, 141
Tismaneau, L., 64
Tito, J., 80, 81, 82, 92, 93, 94
Tito Initiative, 93
Toma, P., 50
Tomasek, F., 47
Tomic, S., 84
Totalitarianism, 31
Trade deficits, 54
Trade imbalance, 65
Trade unions, 50, 51, 92, 102, 105, 107, 112, 137, 138
Triska, J., 65
Trust in cadres, 4
Tyszka, A., 104, 105

Ukraine, 45
Ulc, O., 42, 44, 50

Underground publications, 111
Unemployment, 30
Unger, A., 129
Urban decay, 30
Urbanization, 24
Urban population, 67
Urban-rural inequality, 100
Ussenin, V., 142
USSR, 37, 38, 40, 122, 137, 145, 147, 156

Varga, G., 49
Varkonyi, P., 51
Veljic, A., 83
Vida, I., 70
Vishnevskii, A., 28
Volgyes, I., 44, 50

Wages, 71, 160
Waligorski, M., 137
Warsaw Pact, 63, 64, 157
Weinberg, I., 31
Welfare, 175
Welsh, W., 69
Wesolowski, W., 100, 102-103, 104
Wesson, R., 75
White collar workers, 104
Wiatr, J., 100, 105-106, 107
Widerszpil, S., 39, 100, 103, 108
Wnuk-Lipinski, E., 141
Wolfe, B., 31
Women, role, 23, 27
Workers, 133, 135
Worker-party relations, 62
Working class, 27, 100
Workers' councils, 50, 84, 125, 103, 107
Workplace democracy, 103
World War II, 81, 158

Youth groups, 137
Yugoslavia, 50, 73, 79-97, 162, 181

Zaharescu, B., 39, 133
Zaharia, R., 64
Zawadzki, S., 100, 102, 104, 106-107, 108
Zhivkov, T., 125, 130
Ziegler, C., 147
Zoeter, J., 163

Contributors

Jack Bielasiak is an associate professor of political science at the Russian-East European Institute at Indiana University. He has written extensively on East European elites, workers' participation in communist states, and on the political crisis in Poland.

Cal Clark is associate professor of political science at the University of Wyoming. He has contributed extensively to professional journals on the subjects of Soviet Bloc relations and comparative public policy, and he is co-author of Comparative Patterns of Foreign Policy and Trade.

John M. Echols III was assistant professor of political science at the University of Illinois, Chicago Circle. He had published extensively in communist budgetary analyses and comparative public policy.

Jeffrey W. Hahn is an associate professor of political science at Villanova University, specializing in Soviet and East European affairs. His work has appeared in Youth and Society, Problems of Communism, Polity, The Experimental Study of Politics, the Journal of Youth and Adolescence, as well as other edited collections.

Donald R. Kelley is associate professor and chairman of the Department of Political Science at the University of Arkansas, Fayetteville. He is the author of numerous works on domestic Soviet politics.

Daniel N. Nelson is an associate professor of political science at the University of Kentucky. He is the author of Democratic Centralism in Romania, editor of Romania in the 1980s (Westview) and Communist Legislatures in Comparative Perspective, and contributor to various professional journals and edited volumes on communist politics.

David W. Paul is a scholar of Soviet and East European politics, history, and culture. In addition to numerous articles and reviews, he has written Czechslovakia: Profile of a Socialist Republic at the Crossroads of Europe (Westview) and The Cultural Limits of Revolutionary Politics: Change and Continuity in Socialist Czechoslovakia and edited a book on East European film that is soon to be published.

Jim Seroka is an associate professor of political science in the Master of Public Affairs program at Southern Illinois University, Carbondale. He has published extensively on Yugoslav political issues as well as in public policy and administration.

Maurice D. Simon, associate professor of political science at the University of North Carolina, Greensboro, has conducted research in Poland on numerous occasions since 1966. Dr. Simon has recently published articles on Polish politics and society in *Problems of Communism*, *Legislative Studies Quarterly* and the *International Journal of Political Education*, and is co-editor of *Background to Crisis: Policy and Politics in Gierek's Poland* (Westview).

Other Titles of Interest from Westview Press

National Communism, Peter Zwick

Communist Armies in Politics: Their Origins and Development, edited by Jonathan R. Adelman

**The Impasse of European Communism*, Carl Boggs

Terror and Communist Politics: The Role of the Secret Police in Communist States, edited by Jonathan R. Adelman

Background to Crisis: Policy and Politics in Gierek's Poland, edited by Maurice D. Simon and Roger E. Kanet

Hungary: A Nation of Contradictions, Ivan Volgyes

Romania: A Developing Socialist State, Lawrence S. Graham

Czechoslovakia: Profile of a Socialist Republic at the Crossroads of Europe, David W. Paul

Romania in the 1980's, edited by Daniel N. Nelson

**The Domestic Context of Soviet Foreign Policy*, edited by Seweryn Bialer

**Eastern Europe in the 1980's*, edited by Stephen Fischer-Galati

Perspectives for Change in Communist Societies, edited by Teresa Rakowska-Harmstone

Yugoslavia After Tito: Scenarios and Implications, Gavriel D. Ra'anan

Innovation in Communist Systems, edited by Andrew Gyorgy and James A. Kuhlman

Law and Economic Development in the Soviet Union, edited by Peter B. Maggs, Gordon B. Smith, and George Ginsburgs

*Available in hardcover and paperback